MEMOIRS OF A GURKHA WIFE DURING LOCKDOWN

LILA SELING MABO

authorHOUSE

AuthorHouse™ UK
1663 Liberty Drive
Bloomington, IN 47403 USA
www.authorhouse.co.uk
Phone: UK TFN: 0800 0148641 (Toll Free inside the UK)
UK Local: (02) 0369 56322 (+44 20 3695 6322 from outside the UK)

© 2022 Lila Seling Mabo. All rights reserved.

No part of this book may be reproduced, stored in a retrieval system, or transmitted by any means without the written permission of the author.

Published by AuthorHouse 23/02/2022

ISBN: 978-1-6655-9291-8 (sc)
ISBN: 978-1-6655-9293-2 (hc)
ISBN: 978-1-6655-9292-5 (e)

Print information available on the last page.

Any people depicted in stock imagery provided by Getty Images are models, and such images are being used for illustrative purposes only.
Certain stock imagery © Getty Images.

This book is printed on acid-free paper.

Because of the dynamic nature of the Internet, any web addresses or links contained in this book may have changed since publication and may no longer be valid. The views expressed in this work are solely those of the author and do not necessarily reflect the views of the publisher, and the publisher hereby disclaims any responsibility for them.

Introduction

I was born in Oyam-6 (Yangwarak-3), Panchthar, Nepal, Himalayas and near the iconic Mount Everest. I lived with my father, Mr Bhim Kumar Seling, former head teacher, chair of the school government body and author and my mother, Ram Maya Seling, former president of the Women's Association at Oyam. I am the oldest of seven children.

I was the first woman to pass the school leaving certificate (SLC) obtained from Gupteshowar High Secondary School Oyam-Panchthar, where my father used to be the head teacher. I qualified as a teacher and became head teacher of Dharma Bhakta Primary Oyam Bhanjyang Pachthar Nepal. I studied in Mahendra Multiple Campus Ilam and in Pachthar Campus for a bachelor's degree.

I moved to the UK in 2000 due to my husband Shree Mab's career in the British Army (part of the Gurkhas). I have travelled all over the world with him. Our family started to grow as my children were born, one in Brunei, (a girl, Siliya Mabo) and the other two (a girl Silija Mabo and boy Phurup Mabo) in the UK.

When I arrived in the UK, I had to start from scratch. I couldn't use any of my education, my qualifications, or my own language. My husband used to leave me regularly on my own with small children and no one to communicate with or any family support. It was very hard. At the time, those were the worst days of my life. Although I had to face many obstacles being an army (Gurkha) wife, I was determined to work hard to carry on my studies and volunteering whilst looking after the children and the house.

When I wasn't studying, I wrote poems and songs in Nepali, Limbu language (my own tribe), and English. These were published by Lahureni Pida in Nepal. Along with my writing, I am a social activist. I received first position in a poem presentation competition in Brunei and second position in a poem citation online in the Nepali language.

I have continued my education and gained an MSc in criminology (corporate crime and corporate responsibility) as well as a BSc (Hons) in psychology and criminology gaining an Academic Endeavour Award. I received both qualifications from the University of Surrey and all whilst working as a dental nurse. I used to stand as a candidate councillor in the local election. I am always interested in the welfare of others and take a great interest in my community projects and improving people's health and well-being. I enjoy social challenges of this kind.

I have received many awards for volunteering and establishing Nepali Limbu communities, including KYC women's community/thamengdingma UK and KYC Rushmoor Branch UK, as well as being a pattern member of KYCUK. I'm senior vice president of NEFIN UK. I'm also board trustee of Rushmoor Healthy Living UK.

What follows is a diary of my experience living through the Covid-19 pandemic at a time when I was also studying for a master's degree, working part-time, participating in important organisations, and raising three children. I have noted certain facts in my diary entries, including news stories of the time and the constantly rising death toll. But I've also included details on how my family and community made it through the lockdown disruptions and fear, one day at a time.

March 2020

🖉 Tuesday, 17 March 2020
Time of coronavirus pandemic, but before lockdown in the UK

I woke up at 7.30 a.m., yawning because of a late bedtime the previous night. I had gone to bed late because I had to submit an assignment and the deadline is today. I also had to attend class.

In a big rush, I uploaded my assignment, then drove to the university because my class was going to start at 1 p.m. I'm always concerned about car parking problems at university, especially during rush hour, when I get in a panic. Luckily, I found a space today and then went to class. We are only three students and attend online for both lectures (Crime and Offending, and Law and Society).

The class ended at 6 p.m., and I decided to stay in the library for my next assignment, because it was also due next week. I sat down and searched materials from SurreyLearn and started typing for a long time. I was focusing only on my assignment, and I didn't realise it was 11.23 p.m.—nearly midnight.

I contacted my elder daughter, who is at Portsmouth University for undergraduate study. She reminded me that I would be affected by corona quickly because of my weak immune system. I have a problem my thyroid.

I went to check the university shop, but it was closed. I realised I was concentrating too much on my assignment rather than my health. I decided to stay longer in the library on that day because it was so quiet. I stayed a long time in the library, but my thoughts were on my children and that I wasn't able to cook dinner and feed them on time because of my assignments.

Finally, I drove back home. I heard on the 12 a.m. BBC News on the way to Farnham that the UK government was announcing billions of pounds of support for corona pandemic issues. The news was saying it was the worst pandemic in 100 years.

I arrived home 12.20 a.m., had dinner, and washed and cleaned up the kitchen. All the children had already gone to bed. My husband was on night duty, so I had to clean and do all the housework, as I'm a mum and a wife. I went to bed at 13.30 a.m.

✎ Wednesday, 18 March 2020
Time of coronavirus pandemic, but before lockdown in the UK

I was trying to focus on my assignment for the Crime and Offending topic due the following Monday, but I have to go to work over the weekend, so only today did I have a chance to type my essay as well as cook food for the family, clean, and hoover the house. None of the children are taking responsibility yet as I do.

I attended an online lecture at 1 p.m. from home.

✎ Sunday, 22 March 2020
Last day before lockdown

I woke up at the same time as usual, although I went to bed late last night. I went to work at the Sandhurst Royal Military Academy army camp. I have been working with this company for seventeen years. I used to work as a waitress full-time for five years, then I changed my career and worked once a week, only on Sunday. All staff are working a normal week, and the majority of staff/waitresses are Gurkha ladies (Nepali).

I'm a full-time post-graduate student this year. However, all schools and universities are totally locked down, and all class courses and lectures are accessed online.

We gave food service to all army officers, but everyone looked very sad, and no one was talking. They just took the food and sat down at a distance from one another. They ate lunch (brunch) very quickly and left, but in bronze week, they do not have breakfast, they have only lunch. It opens from 10 a.m. to 1 p.m., so they come at that time. They don't come at the same time as for a a normal lunch.

The staff members have informed me that seven soldiers have coronavirus. Some are in hospital, and some are isolated in their room. Therefore, some soldiers would take food for their friend who is in quarantine. The government and the BBC have alerted us that social distancing is very important, but it's not possible to obey the rules 100 per cent.

All us staff have been talking about the lack of masks and gloves. Everything is running out, and it has been very difficult to find a pair of disposable gloves. We were informed that we had to wipe the table all the time when the officers had finished eating. I was nervous to wipe near the officers, but I had no choice due to my job.

We all continued to work until the shift was finished. All the ladies and I talked about Mother's Day and felt sorry that we were not able to visit our mothers. I was concerned about my parents, who were in Hong Kong on holiday with my youngest sister. I was feeling hungry and starving, but I decided not to eat any food from my workplace due to the coronavirus.

One of the staff members made a cup of tea, and there was some small black stuff in it. My friend complained about it. I made a joke about the tea and how quickly corona grows, just like gnats. Everyone was scared and ran away so fast.

I went to Tesco shopping centre at 1 p.m. Tesco is organising free food for NHS workers, doctors, and nurses, so there were a few cars in front of Tesco and the rest of the car park was empty. Some mothers were arguing with their children due to the lack of choice of kids' stuff. All the shop shelves were empty, so I just watched from outside and went home.

My children were preparing special food for Mum. They were celebrating Mother's Day. The two girls are teenagers. My son is the youngest at just 12 years. My husband joked, "Take a picture of Mum, she may get corona."

I did not say a word. I just stayed calm. Tears dropped from my eyes, but I wiped them away as quickly as possible. I could not stop thinking about coronavirus. I felt if I really did die with coronavirus this year, I would be terribly missed by my children and family on next year's Mother's Day. I was really emotional, but I did not show it to them.

It is Mothering Sunday in the UK, but I could not smile as usual on Mother's Day due to the global pandemic (Covid-19). I went jogging and walking with family in Long Valley Field. It is between Church Crookham, Aldershot, and Farnham.

All the family decided to go out for a walk, and we spent an hour and twenty minutes out. We met lots people, but social distancing was on everyone's mind. We tried to keep away from people. If we saw small groups of people, we changed direction. It seemed to me that we had lost trust in each other. Nobody wanted to talk face to face or stand close. We walked through muddy swamps and bushes and then back home.

Pictures of my dear mother Ram Maya Seling uploaded on mothers's day

I tried to contact my mother on Facebook. As I mentioned earlier, she is on holiday in Hong Kong. Time there is very different, so I was not able to wish her a happy Mother's Day verbally. I did not have a chance to call her due to rushing out for duty in the morning. I felt regret about not being able to talk to her. I just quickly uploaded two images of Mum and wished her a happy Mother's Day 2020 and said we will celebrate next year.

I decided to make dinner for the family because my eldest daughter had prepared the Mother's Day special lunch in the morning. Everyone is at home due to the pandemic. It is 11.15 p.m., and we all have online classes tomorrow. I have decided to go to bed now.

Thank you, diary, for giving me today's memory of the global coronavirus pandemic. I mean, how corona has created panic and human distrust and not being able to celebrate Mother's Day either. Many bunches of flowers have been ruined at every shop, and many mums are in quarantine and hospital. Some mums have already left the world, even though they have little babies or grown-up children. Many people are separated from their family, home, and relatives.

✎ Monday, 23 March 2020
First day of lockdown

> ➢ ***In the news***: 47 people died in a single day today because of Covid-19.

As we all know, it is a very emotional time. We are in lockdown. This is the first day of online teaching and lecturing for all school, college, and university students owing to Covid-19. I cleaned the house, kitchen, toilet, bathroom, wiped all walls, windows, and mopped the floor to maintain hygiene for the family. All the children are sleeping in their rooms, but I did not realise until 10.30 a.m.

After completing all the housework and making breakfast for the kids, I sat down to work on my assignment. The actually deadline was the next day, 24 March, but I wanted to complete and upload it the day before. That makes it easy to focus on the next day's online lecture. In addition, I have to start looking for reading materials for the next topic assignment tomorrow.

There are four students in this home who have to access online classes and study. We have three laptops and one iPad. I'm a postgraduate student in my second semester. My eldest daughter is an undergraduate second-year student. My youngest daughter is in her second year in sixth-form college. My youngest child, my son, is in secondary school in year 8. My first priority is for the children's healthcare and education. Therefore, I offered everyone a chance to have a laptop to go online and study, although I had an assignment deadline.

I let everyone to have the first go while I was preparing food for lunch. I invited them to the dining table to have lunch together, but my husband went on duty at his barracks. I sat down at the computer for a few hours to complete my assignment, then uploaded it. I felt relief for a few hours, because at least I'd got something done.

I received a message from friends at the university and found that a few students are in quarantine and some are in hospital. I offered to help the international students while they are in quarantine, but they said there is good teamwork at the university accommodation. I asked a stupid question: "Why did you guys not go back to your home or country in this situation? You need family support." They told me that they did not want to affect their relatives, friends, and families. Mostly, they could not fly home during the lockdown.

Time flies so fast. I can't imagine that it is time now to make dinner. I'm starting to do my usual chores. I have got to make everything ready before my husband comes home from duty. Then we can have dinner as a family together, according to my family norms and value.

I started to do yoga for 15 minutes, but my husband came home, and it was time to have dinner. Today, we decided to delay dinner due to the UK Prime Minister Boris Johnson coming on the news at 8.30 p.m. about the lockdown.

Forty-seven people died in a single day today because of Covid-19. This is the second week of deaths reported in the UK. The result was similar to the number of deaths in Italy fourteen days before. The prime minister announced very important and wide-ranging measures. Everyone should stay home except to get food and medication. He promised that the government of the UK would give support for everything.

After watching this news, all the family felt scared and worried, as if we are going to lose each other soon. It was such an emotional and complex situation at this time because of this very selfish pandemic.

Tuesday, 24 March 2020
Second day of lockdown

> ***In the news***: The war in Iraq began on 24 March 2003, exactly seventeen years ago today.

[Note: This entry was published in Everestimes.net to highlight not only what today is to me but to show others what I was doing with my time in lockdown.]

I woke up earlier than normal and finished cleaning the house. I sat down to do my homework before signing in to my online class lecture. I had an assignment due and two lectures today. Therefore, I had to wake up early. I had to set up two alarms, one for home work and one for preparing lunch for the children.

Today is the second day of lockdown in the UK due to the global pandemic (Covid-19). An average of 14,000 people have died, and many people are in quarantine and in emergency wards in hospitals. The 24th of March will always be an important historic and frightening day for me, because it was the first bombardment in Iraq in 2003, exactly 17 years ago today.

This historic event has a lot of significance for me, because my husband, Shree Prasad Mabo, who was in the British Army, was deployed to Iraq from his regiment (the Royal Irish Regiment) under command of OBE Colonel Tim Collins at Howe Barrack Canterbury Kent UK.

Back in 2003, I had awakened to the news that a missile had been dropped in Iraq, and six British soldiers had died due to this. From the news report, I was constantly checking to see if my husband's name was listed as one of the men who had tragically died. We'd had no contact with my husband for two weeks since he had left the barracks, and it was an agonising time waiting to find out if he was OK. I didn't know if he was injured or lying in a hospital bed. The families of the six people who died did have some comfort knowing their individuals' fate.

Shree Mabo preparing for War in Iraq

Shree Mabo is now the third generation to have been involved in the British Army as part of the Gurkha regiment. Mabo's father, the late Sgt Purna Bahadur Mabo, fought as part of the Second World War, and his grandfather, the late Sgt Kanbir Mabo (7th Gurkha Rifle), fought in the First World War, and unfortunately died in action. To this day, we do not know where his body is buried or located. He is still classed as missing in action.

The lack of information surrounding the late Sgt Kanbir Mabo, his death and location, affected the family greatly. His wife Pabimaya Ijam-Mabo, who was pregnant with Purna Bahadur Mabo, spent the rest of her life waiting for her husband to return home, which is something that never happened. They never really knew the circumstances surrounding his death, which became a financial strain upon the family. Due to the late Sgt Kanbir Mabo(seventh Gurkha Rifle) being classed as missing in action, he hasn't been accredited with the same recognition as his fellow troops who came home. As a family, we are continuing to find out more information regarding this all the time.

Late Sgt. Purna Bahadur Mabo (ex.7GR) who fought in the Second World War

Due to the family history, I believed (for some reason) that my husband would have the same fate as his father and grandfather before him. We Gurkha wives have a 200-year history with the British Army—how much we have suffered after our husbands died or became injured. We are built, as wives of soldiers, to understand that we have to spend time alone waiting for our husbands to return. But we did not, and still do not, get the support from the British Army that we should.

Over 1 million Gurkhas were enlisted, and over 150,00 Gurkhas have died for Britain, including during the First and Second World Wars and modern wars such as Iraq Iran and Afghanistan. Yet nothing is said about the Gurkha wives who were back home, needing emotional and financial support. They were forgotten after their husbands, brothers, and grandfathers had done their duty. They were left without any consideration. You get time to mourn for the loss of a family pet, but we have no time or support to mourn the loss of these important men in our lives.

Shree Mabo was in the Iraq War on the 24/3/2003

Our husbands fought for the British Empire, for Queen and country, which is the same as the soldiers from India, Burma, West Indies, and Africa, amongst many more next to many Gurkhas soldiers. Yet, to this day, the Gurkhas are one of the only regiments that does not have the same rights or financial support as the rest of the British Army.

I did not know then that my husband was being deployed that morning. My children and I didn't have a chance to say goodbye. We were incredibly lucky that we were able to talk to him on his return. But this is something that I didn't know then.

Gurkha soldiers are very loyal to their families as well as their residential army career, but their army career comes first. When I married my husband, I had to wait for seven years to join him. We had to keep our family separated for all this time. I had to be on my own after we got married, which is very strange, frustrating, and emotional. I had to wait for my monthly letter from him to know where he was and if he was OK. We had no phones and no social media—not like now. For nearly three years, we only communicated by letters. I didn't hear his voice; I only had his letters to hold on to.

I don't know how I survived those days. Some relationships now need to have constant communication. People will end up divorcing if one doesn't respond back to messages and phone calls within the hour. I had to survive for three years without hearing my husband's voice. This was the role of a Gurkha wife.

Back then, in those days, I was suffering from war stress. I was alone with two little girls who were 1 year and 3 years old in the UK. I was constantly thinking and crying about the welfare of my husband in the Iraq war. My husband was not allowed to contact his wife and family until two weeks after he left home.

I used to watch the news all the time, seeing if his name would come up on a list of dead soldiers, although I was not able to understand English properly at that time. I hadn't been educated in the UK then but only my homeland, Nepal.

I used to cry all the way home from work due to worrying about my two young daughters. I constantly kept thinking that if my husband died in the war, I not only would have lost my husband but they would have lost their father. This is what always made me so upset.

A relative's friend who I used to go to work with would alternate work and childcare with me. For example, I used to work the morning shift while she looked after my girls, and she used to do the late shift while I took care of her two daughters.

Back then, I could not speak English clearly. I was not familiar with UK law and culture. I also felt very, very homesick. There was a big gang problem, and I couldn't communicate the problems I was having to the police. I had no way of reporting this crime, and I had to keep quiet, keep my head down, and get on with it, I didn't want to cause a problem due to the length of my visa. I wanted to stay in the UK close to my husband's barracks whilst my visa was valid, and I didn't want anyone reporting me to the authorities and sending me back early.

This fear with my visa continued until we were granted settlement rights, which wouldn't happen until many years later. There were not many Nepali families, relatives, and communities established back then, not like there are now. Therefore, I felt alone and constantly bullied by these gangs.

The gangs used to throw eggs at my windows and bang loudly on the door. Sometimes they got inside the house and threatened us. The four children (my two daughters and my friend's two daughters) were so scared they hung around me like a mother hen with her chicks. I was very scared to report it to the police, and the gangs took advantages of my lack of English.

Gurkha soldiers were discriminated against for a long time, and it was brought to the media spotlight by Joanna Lumley in 2004. One of the main issues was that Gurkha soldiers who fought for the British Army were not allowed to come back to the UK after retiring from the army. The soldiers had to have achieve staff sergeant rank in order to have their wives and families living with them for the second family tour.

Therefore, I had to stay outside the barracks, and only my husband was allowed to stay in the barrack accommodation. The junior army ranks could keep their wife with them for only one tour (three years). My husband had junior rank, so I was not allowed to stay with him in the barracks.

I was renting far from the camp. He was in Kent, and the children and I were in Black Water, Camberley, Surrey. I was allowed to stay in the UK until my visa expired. Due to visa laws, I really felt like I was a victim of discrimination by the UK Ministry of Defence. I had to leave when my visa expired, with my small children. But, under UK law, my 12-month-old daughter could stay, due to her being born in Britain and having a British passport. Myself and my other daughter had to go back to Nepal.

The stupidity of this at the time—that a small baby could stay in Britain with no parents, but as her mother, I couldn't stay with her due to not having a visa or a British passport. A lot has changed in twenty years, but at the time we knew no better.

My plan was to stay for the duration of my visa in the UK. Because I was on leave from my job as a teacher in Nepal. I had something to return to—a job that would provide for my family whilst my husband was away at war.

Today, my eldest daughter and I went out for forty minutes jogging, and she expressed her feeling of the first day of lockdown thus: "Mummy, I already feel that I'm in prison, and human life will be generally very badly affected by Covid-19.

We walked away from people when we could see a few people with dogs and some people running away from us. We were all following social distancing and also worrying and slightly distrusting our fellow human beings. We both felt so sad from watching the BBC News and seeing that eighty-seven people had died of coronavirus within the past twenty-four hours. We also lost one great member of the Labour Party from my area.

My mum kept telling me about her mum (my grandma) who buried two children in a day owing to a bad pandemic similar to the Covid outbreak, and many people died through lack of food and water. I cannot guess exactly how many years ago this was—roughly seventy-three.

My grandfather, the late Phaudasing Seling was an ex British Army gurkha (7th Gurkha Rifles) joining at the age of 14.

It was a pandemic time and he went to help and support his uncle's family during this time of pandemic flue. He went with his friends without letting family know they would have been fearful of him catching the virus. My grandmother, the late Bal Kumari Lingden Seling went after him with a group of people to try and stop him but they couldn't find him so he got away and later joined the army.

My grandmother used to worry so much about him during the time of the First World War. He served for a few years and came back home. Unfortunately, his friend and next-door neighbour did not come home with him because he died during a bombardment and my poor grandpa saw his friend's legs flying over the bonfire of war. He bought home the death certificate and information to his family. My grandpa also suffered, losing his young daughter my aunty to illness before he came back home.

My grandpa was excellent at map reading and helped his comrade to find their way through swamps and difficult terrain. My dad would not have been born if he had died at that time. Once he came home many Limbu people gathered and requested him to stay home because he was the limbu headman (subba). In those days he had to rule over certain groups of Limbu people, their lands, society, laws and regulations, work which is done today by mayors and councillor. All his family and friends were afraid to send him back to the Army due to the war, so consequently he resigned and did not get any pension although he had worked and fought hard for the British colonies for approximately 10 years. Unfortunately, he died at the early age of 49. If he had been alive, he would have come to join the Gurkha Lives Matter Protest in London. My father Bhimkumar Seling told me all about my grandfather's life and his achievements.

I reminded my daughter about her great grandparents lives on the way back home from jogging. After that, she made a Korean-style dinner for the family, which meant I was off in the kitchen that evening. She laid dinner out on the table when her dad came home from work, and we enjoyed the different taste for dinner and watched television too. All the members of the family were concentrating on hand sanitiser, alcohol wipes, and hand-washing more than loving and caring for each other.

I was thinking of myself while having dinner; for instance, if I catch coronavirus, and how much I would miss all these people. I'm more prone to being affected by this disease because I'm a thyroxine patient. Finally, it was 11.30 at night, so decided to go to bed.

This photo shows an empty car park by a big supermarket on Mothering Sunday weekend. It should be packed, but there was nobody here, and there was no food on the shelves because of everyone panic-buying due to the lockdown.

Wednesday, 25 March 2020
Third day of lockdown

> ***In the news***: Prince Charles tested positive for coronavirus.

The weather was bright and sunny outside, with a few screaming noises of children playing on this early morning. I tried to wake up late, about 8 a.m., and contact families in Nepal about Covid-19. The whole world is speechless.

My relatives in Nepal were also in lockdown in the house at KTM. The good news was that there were not many cases yet. We wished each other safety and talked to Hong Kong. Mummy looked so pale, and she could not sleep the whole night. She imagined that she could die in HK. Life is riskier for Mum and Dad—they are 72 and 74 years old. The whole family is worried about our parents who are stuck in Hong Kong.

Again, I have finished the house cleaning. It took about an hour and half, and then I had a glass of water. My main target for the day was to complete my ethics form for my proposal. It has been pending for the last two weeks because of two other assignment deadlines. It took nearly two hours to complete and check all the numbers, words, and lines.

After completing the whole thing, I emailed my dissertation supervisor all these ethics forms to check and comment on. I needed a short break and planned to cook lunch and make popcorn and fry chiura (beaten rice) for the children. I began to prepare lunch when I was on this short break and invited the kids to have food at the dining table.

The BBC News announced that Prince Charles had tested positive for coronavirus, and also that top British diplomat Steven Dick, deputy ambassador to Hungary, had died today at 37 from coronavirus. It made me feel so sad to hear. It is very uncertain what will happen in life tomorrow. In Italy, 683 people died out 7,503 cases today. This panic is creating emotional trauma, violence, abuse, and crime throughout the world.

My eldest daughter Siliya ordered pizza for dinner. For that reason, I did not have to cook dinner this evening. I have warned the children to wash their hands and use sanitiser and spray, and I left a bucket of Dettol soap with water outside the door for my husband. When he comes home from work, he has to clean his shoes and leave his army uniform outside the house.

When I had five minutes, I ordered extra masks, gloves, alcohol spray, and disinfecting wipes online. I used to hate using PPE at home. Why?

Because I used to use a box of gloves and a box of masks every day at work for my job of dental nursing.

✏️ Thursday, 26 March 2020
Fourth day of lockdown

The time was early morning, bright and chilly, and my mind was on TV all the time because I was thinking too much about coronavirus and feeling emotional at all the time. I went out into the back garden for an hour of yoga and prepared lunch for the children. I did not realise that I had forgotten to brush my teeth and shower until 1:00 p.m. I did not feel thirsty either, because my concentration was only on lockdown and the complaints of people who had lost their jobs and were starving and hungry. I was thinking mainly about how unpredictable and unsustainable human life and the human condition was around the world today.

I made sure to provide my family with food and the basic necessities for a healthy life—a toothbrush and shower facilities. What more can one do? I cleaned the kitchen toilet and mopped the floor, then sprayed alcohol disinfectant on all surfaces.

I began to study a journal article about the London riot of 2011—reading materials for a new assignment. The time was set on the alarm clock for one hour fifteen minutes of reading. Meanwhile, my son was on the computer for his online study and homework, because I wanted to give him first priority for his work, and he did feel more comfortable on the computer.

I contacted my husband's niece in Nepal to see how her studies were going. She is studying for a post-graduate degree in Kathmandu, and she was saying that she could not access any study when trapped at home. I mentioned to her that all the children and I were able to access our courses from home although we are in lockdown, which is a very good use of time during this difficult situation.

Next, I contacted my sister. She was also complaining about the children upsetting her because there was no way to access online. They had to stick with books, but children are bored quickly.

I went back to my studies. First, I looked at the Crime and Offending essay question and the reading materials. Second, I focused on the Criminal Justice System module essay question and reading articles and books. I did not realise it was 7 p.m. I was thinking of clapping hands for the NHS to show appreciation for tirelessly battling the coronavirus pandemic but forgot to make dinner, so my eldest daughter cooked dinner. We watched the clapping hands show while we were having dinner.

The whole family felt so sad due to the loss of a hundred people every single day in the UK. The people dying in Italy and Spain are making the whole world very worried, as they are losing massive numbers of people from coronavirus. We all felt so extremely emotional and speechless for a few minutes. The pandemic is not only creating a great deal of stress, it is also creating starvation, hunger, fighting, and gangs, especially among the working class. Marginalised people are suffering so much with this situation.

Friday, 27 March 2020
Fifth day of lockdown

I woke up late morning. It is bright and chilly outside. Children are playing and shouting, and the birds are singing and making chi-chi-like sounds. I went out for a breath of fresh air while my husband made breakfast for the family. I had breakfast and prepared for my online class, the Corporate Crime module, which started at 1 p.m.

The teachers asked everyone how they were getting on in the current situation. Only a few students attended class today. All the students gave an update about lockdown in their countries. A Swiss friend talked about a very bad experience when she was trapped in her country from the beginning of March. A friend from America was worried about her country, which was highly affected by coronavirus, and people from the UK were experiencing extra stress and panic because Prime Minister Boris Johnson has also tested positive for Covid-19. The global pandemic is killing many people day by day, and therefore, I found it hard to focus on the lecture for the first lesson.

We did the seminar exercise and lecture slides, and the teacher wished everyone safety and good health and promised to get back to normal classes after the Easter break. After that, I attended the Criminal Justice System class from 2 to 4 p.m. Very few students participated in that class today too, and the lecture changed to a group discussion. Coincidentally, that lecturer was from Italy, which has also been badly affected by the virus. Everyone was feeling depressed and negative about the future of our life.

I had a dissertation class for only one hour, but I could not concentrate properly. My husband and I went out jogging for about an hour. I had ordered a box of masks and hand sanitiser a long time before, but it had still not arrived, and I was upset. However, my eldest daughter had made a pair of masks with a needle and thread, which looked nice and useful.

It was 6.30 p.m., and cold and dark. Although we met a few people, we were careful to social distance—just as if we were enemies! Whenever we saw a group of people coming along, we twisted out of their way as if they were tigers or lions who were going to attack us. Our jogging came to an end, because I had attended three lessons that day, and I was tired. I kept telling the family to use disinfectant spray and sanitiser cream before going back into the house.

My eldest daughter made dinner, and we ate together at the same table. We discussed having separate spaces for food and water. I cannot imagine how people all over the world can cope with this global serious and terrible global pandemic.

Saturday, 28 March 2020
Sixth day of lockdown

Oyam, Nepal (my birthplace) and the school where I studied up to the age of 16 (the yellow building in the foreground)

It is the weekend, sunny and bright outside in the early morning, 7.30 a.m. I was rushing to have a shower and worship, then go out for food shopping. Before that, I contacted my parents, who are in Hong Kong for a short tour. Mum looked so worried because we are all apart around the world but not allowed to meet each other. We are at risk because of our age, and I could not sleep the whole night hoping my family will be safe wherever they are.

I planned to go food shopping early to avoid standing in a long queue. My husband and I had breakfast as soon as possible and went to ASDA in Farnborough. Many people were already queueing, so we were near the end of SMYTHS store to stay in the queue It took ages to do the shopping and get back home.

This waiting in the queue took me back to my childhood days, when we used to go early to get water (*okharbote-kuwa*) from a small pond before we had a proper water system. Many people had to use water from that pond. It was slowly running water that collected in a small pond. So that there was a regular supply, people made a small cave or pond to reserve the water.

People from the whole village relied on that water for their survival, so many used to come early to queue to get a gallon or drum of water. It was far away from home, so we had to carry the water pot on our back until we got home. There was no regular drinking supply at that time the way we have now.

The general public complained many times to the government. Then, thirty-two years ago, we had the UNICEF project to supply enough running drinking water twenty-four hours a day. Before that time, we had suffered a lack of drinking water, and people had to go miles and miles away to get water.

The current situation really brought back memories of Koteshowar Mahadeshthan Marga KTM, my home, where I used to stand in a long queue for water. When the water tanker came, I had to grab a bucket and make a run for the queue. If I tell this story to future generations, they won't believe me, because it has changed so much for the better now, but I have real experience of those days.

The news report says that 280 died from coronavirus today. It made the whole family find the situation around the world terrifying and painful.

My House 'Koteshowar' in KTM (Kathmandu) near the airport. The house I was reminded of when in Farnborough UK at the supermarket, because of the planes flying over.

Back home, the children helped us to pack food into the fridge and store. I sat down for a few minutes to check the BBC News, then found that the death rate had doubled to 181 within two days in the UK and within three days in Italy. This result made me panic, thinking *Will I be among those numbers sometime?* I was thinking of the many possible outcomes of this pandemic and lockdown. It will be damaging to society and the economy. It will also be linked to mental health problems and suicides because of isolation and loneliness, and heart problems due to a lack of activity. It will also increase unemployment and reduce living standards.

Sunday, 29 March 2020
Seventh day of lockdown

The world is so silent and speechless. Everyone has lost hope of survival due to Covid-19, but my focus must still be on my essay and assessment, although life is so uncertain. I contacted my parents, who were still stuck in lockdown in Hong Kong. My mum especially was worrying so much that she might not be able to go back to her homeland of Nepal.

My son sat down for his online schoolwork while I studied a journal article on the London riots 2011 as part of an essay question, "Shopping for free, looting, consumerism and the 2011 Riots". Back in 2011, I was studying A level, and a teacher from the Farnborough College of Technology brought a newspaper on the riots to a class discussion in sociology. People were scared to go to London, and the panic created by this riot resulted in a real dilemma for all those living in and out of London. The article was worthwhile and knowledgeable as regards the history of riots in the UK. It took me more than two hours to complete the reading.

I read the online BBC News that there had been 260 deaths from the coronavirus pandemic. It made me feel life is nothing—it can be ruined at any time. I had lunch and prepared my uniform for work. I was scared to go to work, but everyone was continuing to work in the army barracks.

I went to my workplace. It was still in the same condition. There was not enough PPE. The staff was desperate for gloves and wiping clothes, and there was not enough disinfectant liquid and hand sanitiser. Luckily, I had taken my own gloves, mask, and hand sanitiser, so I worked without too much worry. Sky News was broadcasting 24 hours around the clock on the big screen, and we kept watching while working in the hall.

At 8 p.m., after dinner, the army was briefing outside of the college ground about the news of the prime minister announcing social distancing and lockdown measures. I came back home and had dinner with the family, which had all been cooked by my daughter.

✎ Tuesday, 31 March 2020
Ninth day of lockdown

I woke up early morning and brushed my teeth while my husband made breakfast for the family. I sat down at the computer to continue with my work to complete my ethics form for my dissertation, which I then emailed to my supervisor. It took me many times to complete that form. It gave me trouble again and again.

When I was on a short break, I checked Facebook and found the news about the death of one of the leading members of Rushmoor Borough Council, Frank Rust, the deputy mayor. I could not imagine how this could have happened, and what a coincidence—just two months ago, on 31 January 2020, our Greater Rushmoor Nepali Community (GRNC) team, along with Frank and many other councillors, had attended a special ceremony of sister cities establishing a relationship between the Gorkha Municipality of Nepal and the Rushmoor Borough Council UK at the Embassy of Nepal in London.

I was shocked and devastated to hear this sad news. Then I uploaded condolences for him on Facebook with lots of photos I had taken of the celebration programme.

I wanted to teach my son a few Nepali words, because he cannot speak and understand compared to his two sisters, but he wasn't interested, and I didn't want to force him. I had wanted to use my short break time to teach him some Nepalese, as I was a qualified teacher and head teacher in Nepal. Oh dear! Better luck next time!

My eldest daughter made an excellent Korean-flavoured lunch. She loves to cook food since she went to university. She learnt to cook so many different dishes.

I checked the BBC News, and the latest figures showed that the death rates for Covid-19 had increased by 381 instead of decreasing. The youngest victim was just 13 years old, nearly the same age as my son. The BBC News compared the UK and German health systems, in that the UK has only 48 labs for testing and Germany has 176. I realised that because of these 176 labs, there are fewer coronavirus cases and deaths compared to the UK and other European countries.

The news and statistics made me even more worried and fearful about the pandemic. I kept telling the children to wash their hands with hot water every time. I started to clean the house and bathroom two times a day instead of once. I saw a video of a person jumping out of a high building in the USA owing to this viral virus and lockdown. I just couldn't watch that suicide video again.

In the end, I tried to exercise for 40 minutes but still couldn't concentrate properly because of all the day's bad news, and the sad news in general about losing friends and relatives. I had dinner and then sat down for typing out my experiences of the day.

April 2020

✎ Thursday, 2 April 2020
Eleventh day of lockdown

Once I was awake, I could no longer remember my dream, so I got out of bed and started to clean the house before the children woke up and started to use the toilet, bathroom, kitchen, and TV room. I ate some fruits and drank a glass of water before starting to cook the potatoes for our special cultural dish (alu dam with dry fish) for the family. I boiled herbal water for my husband and myself. Then I sat down to work for an hour on planning my essay, which was about the London riots in 2011, which formed part of the Criminal Justice System module.

But I kept checking BBC News on my mobile. The death rate was increasing day by day, which made me so sad, and I was unable to continue writing my essay plan. I went into the kitchen to prepare dinner for my husband, because he was about to go on night duty. He is an essential worker (British Army), so he has no choice to stay at home.

I offered food to everyone, but the children were not ready to eat now, as it was just 4.30 p.m. They will eat later. It is the festival time, Chaite Dashai, called Ram Nawami in Nepali culture. I remembered my childhood days when I and my friends used to go to Ram Nawami (people go to have fun dating for one day). At that time, there was no such thing as Facebook or social media for young people to communicate with each other, so this particular day was a chance for youngsters to meet and enjoy each other's company. People used this occasion to introduce family members to friends, which was a way of making contacts between male and females in a congenial atmosphere.

At that time, the majority of people were very busy in farming and agriculture; this particular festival gave them an opportunity to meet relatives and to form relationships between unattached boys and girls. Some couples decided to marry after meeting at the bazaar and falling in love. People used to come from very far away to meet parents, family, friends, and relatives, because the schools and colleges were closed on that day.

There were no transport facilities like nowadays, and life was completely different. People had to walk miles and miles to go to this particular festival, so it was a very special occasion on the calendar. Sometimes Nepali New Year and this Chaite Dashai festival coincide.

My memories of attending one particular festival eighteen years ago still today makes me very emotional, because my second baby was only 2 months old at that time. I was celebrating this festival in my birthplace with my late grandma, siblings, uncles, aunties, neighbours, and friends. At that time, my eldest daughter was 2 years old, and my 2-month-old baby girl had been born in the Kent and Canterbury Hospital UK.

At that time, the British Army had a policy in place which stipulated those wives of Gurkha soldiers under the rank of staff sergeant were only allowed to stay with their husbands in married quarters for three years. This was very unfair and meant that we had to leave our married quarters when the three-year tour ended, although our baby was so little, only seven weeks old. Personnel of staff sergeant rank and above were allowed to have their wives and children with them for a second tour.

I had to make the long journey back to Nepal on two separate aircraft, although my baby was only 25 days old. I stayed a few weeks at Kathmandu, then we went via the night bus service back to my hometown. It was so difficult to travel with two little girls in those days, but once I reached my birthplace, it was so great to be home and with family. I wish to be there now, but everything has changed.

The number of deaths from coronavirus today is 569, and total deaths have risen to 2,921 in the UK. It is increasing day by day, and 1 million people are now affected globally. We are still in lockdown, and it feels more difficult than being a prisoner. But I focus on my beautiful children and family. I don't want to miss this time with my children.

Covid-19 is very frightening, and I worry constantly about their education and future lives. My children are still dependant on us, so I worry about their future and job prospects. Inside me, I feel very tearful, but on the outside, I have to be strong for them and my husband.

At 8 p.m., I heard clapping outside my house. My neighbour and my daughter were both outside and clapping as a thank you to the NHS doctors and nurses. I went outside to join them, and my eyes were full of tears. It was such an emotional experience, and I had to back into my house. My son came near me, and when I told him I was so emotional, he ran away from me. He's only 12 years old. Innocent boy.

I sat down near the bed and stayed quiet and speechless. I was thinking inside about this invisible powerful human attacker coronavirus and how it is destroying life all around the whole world. It made me feel very vulnerable, and I felt a great sadness well up inside me.

Saturday, 4 April 2020
Thirteenth day of lockdown

I woke up early this morning and went out to water the garden in the fresh air. I had not been able to sleep for forty-eight hours because of the pandemic. I was too tired even to write on the eleventh day of the lockdown.

Again I cleaned the house and disinfected all areas, including the kitchen, and had my usual glass of hot water and fruits. I focused on reading articles about the London riots in 2011 in order to have a historical perspective on that time. My eldest daughter made beef and chicken burgers for lunch. The whole family then gathered together to discuss the pandemic.

After lunch, we all went back to our studies for a few hours before my youngest daughter and my husband went out jogging. They were out for two hours before they came back home. My husband started to cook dinner.

In the meantime, I had checked the BBC News on my mobile in the short break and found that the total number of deaths from coronavirus had risen by 708, making a total UK death count of 4,313. This number made me feel very sad. Actually, I was so shocked when 10 people died in a single day two weeks before, but today's data added extra stress.

I checked the data of other countries' death rates, such as the United States with 7,803, Spain 11,744, Italy 17,365, China 3,330, Korea 177, and finally the UK with 4,313. It was quite upsetting to see how the UK compared with South Korea and China, which seem to have done much better in controlling the virus compared to Europe. As we all know, the USA and UK have invested billions in weapons of mass destruction, but they seem unable to control Covid-19.

So far, globally, 60,000 people have died as a result of contracting coronavirus, and 1 million people have tested positive for virus. It is more devasting and terrible than both world wars.

🖉 Monday, 6 April 2020 (20/12/2076, BC) Chaite Dashai Nepali Festival.
Fifteenth day of lockdown

> ➤ ***In the news***: PM Boris Johnson is hospitalised.

I woke up on tenterhooks because of the historic speech by the queen due to be broadcast that evening at 8 p.m. on news media and BBC News. I did the same jobs as usual—cleaning and washing the house before the children woke up.

I sat down to find articles about the London riots of 2011 and to read participants' perspectives, view CCTV footage, and listen to interviews with participants. I was very interested to discover that black people are more likely to be stopped and searched than whites. Another interview said that "I hate it because they shoot people for no reason". This article showed that policing was racially discriminating, and for that reason the London riots of 2011 happened.

My eldest daughter spent a long time making tacos (a Mexican dish) for lunch, and we had it together apart from my husband. He went shopping and took many hours queueing because of social distancing. Again, I set the alarm clock for two hours on the timer for study. The children and I had been busy all day following our schedules for online classes and assessment for school, college, and university.

Today was a special day: the second greatest day in the festival calendar of Nepal, called Chaite Dashai, celebrated by Nepali people the world over. I contacted my brother and sister at KTM Nepal, knowing they were planning to celebrate the festival at home in spite of the lockdown situation.

It reminded me of the same date 18 years ago. I was celebrating Chaite Dashai with my late grandma (my dad's mum) and all my siblings and parents in Oyam (Yangwarak) Pachthar, my birthplace. I had two little girls (ages 2 years and 2 months old). My family and I went to Oyam after landing at KTM from the UK.

Now, I won't ever experience that moment again, because Oyam is very far away from where all my siblings, relatives, and parents now are. I used to celebrate this festival every year in the UK, but at the moment, life is so uncertain—as if we are just counting the days and times to die. Therefore, I forgot to plan for the Chaite Dashai festival.

Rice Fields from my birth place in Oyam (Yangwarak) Pachthar - the eastern part of Nepal

I received an email saying we should keep a minute's silence for the late Frank Rust (the deputy mayor), and I stayed silent for one minute for him but could not go to sign the note at the council offices because of late information. The UK had 563 deaths from Covid-19 today, with 2,353 total deaths and 29,000 cases. This data made me feel speechless and made me lose hope about our survival. All the children studied turn by turn, but I only spent two hours reading today. I was too sad.

We decided to have dinner about 8 p.m. while watching the queen's speech on BBC One news. I felt so emotional about Her Majesty's speech, because she mentioned all the people who had lost relatives and were separated from their families due to Covid-19. Also, the news mentioned her previous special speech in 1948 with her sister. It reminded me that both of her grandsons, William and Harry, went to the Royal Military Academic at Sandhurst. Prince Harry joined on 9 May 2005 as an officer cadet. Every meeting, we workers were told that we were not allowed to talk about him with the general public. We should keep everything secret from the media and news reports, and the staff were not to talk publicly about him.

Prince William joined the RMA after his younger brother on 9 January 2006 as an officer cadet. The sovereign parade was attended by Queen Elizabeth and Prince Charles on 12 April 2006. I was serving pre-drinks in the old college at the sovereign parade when the queen was talking with her guard and took a glass water from my tray, saying "Thank you" with such a posh and queen-like sweet voice that I was quite overcome and thrilled that she had spoken to me She attended as the chief guest for the marching-past parade.

I thought so seriously about those people who were separated from parents, grandparents, children, relatives, and friends forever because of the invisible enemy, Covid-19. My eyes were full of tears while watching the news, and I went to the computer and told my daughter to order extra reusable and disposable masks. I explained that we had to prepare in case someone tested positive for the virus, and we would all have to isolate and might not get delivery quickly enough and couldn't buy this kind of PPE in shopping centres.

I decide to go out jogging with my husband after dinner, after we finished watching the queen's speech on TV. The time was about 8.30 p.m., and we started walking from Quetta Park through Humphry Park Redfield Garden, Crookham Village, and Tesco, then back home—about an hour and 20 minutes. We heard reindeer noises in the late evening, and it was so sweet, because I had never heard it before in that area.

The roads were so quiet and peaceful. No one was driving. We just saw babies and children jumping and playing through the windows inside of rooms like fish in tanks. I imagined how bored children must be feeling at this challenging time.

Near Tesco, I saw a hungry fox. He was going near to a bin, but the bin was empty. I talked to the fox, and he was coming over to me. I thought of him like a pet chicken or cat and wanted to take care of him. The poor fox followed me along the way. I was surprised, but it might have been owing to the lockdown that he was starving. He disappeared after a few minutes.

On my return home, I switched on the TV and heard on the news that the prime minister, Boris Johnson, was hospitalised today because he had tested positive for coronavirus. I checked BBC News on my mobile whilst I was taking a short break. The number of deaths by coronavirus today is 621, and the total deaths for the whole of the UK now stands at 4,934.

I have lost hope for life. My constant worry is for my family and how we would cope if we had to isolate. My husband cooks and my children cook, but if one family member had to go into isolation, it would be very difficult, because the virus is invisible.

It is 11.39 p.m. now, so I have to get ready for bed. I will be lucky if I can get to sleep this night.

Sunday, 19 April 2020
Twenty-eighth day of lockdown

I'm very upset because I lost thirteen days of diary entries—12,000 words accidently lost. I'm rubbish with technology, but the children are very smart. They are experts when using the computer, but I am not. I lost hope and did not want to record anymore, but luckily found half of what I thought I had lost recorded in a different diary.

I had kept it in a separate file where I recorded it every day with a diary name. I could not understand how I had deleted the rest of it. I had recorded some very important information and everyday statistics of Covid-19, and I regret losing my work. I cannot remember now what I said.

However, I was excited to be attending a yoga Zoom class online for a lockdown run by the Greater Rushmoor Nepali Community (GRNC). After yoga finished, we updated what was going on in our local community as regards voluntary workers to give extra support to elderly people who are in quarantine and unable to look after themselves or are unable to visit the local shops. Many Nepali people have so far died from coronavirus.

I prepared lunch for the family then sat down to study the Grenfell Tower Disaster on 14 June 2017. The reports on the Grenfell Tower Disaster indicated that the Met Police found that the "stay put" policy used by the London Fire Brigade had resulted in the deaths of 72 people. It is one of the UKs worst modern disasters. The fire spread rapidly because of the poor quality of the cladding panels. There were many factors involved in this incident, ranging from local borough councillors to inadequate oversight from the government inspectorate:

> This serious and major fire has quickly been acknowledged as a health and safety crime committed by the government and building contractors who caused so many deaths. The residents were utterly desperate as the fire swept through the 120 apartments in the Grenfell Tower Block in Kensington. There were no sprinklers or fire alarm systems. Residents had never been trained as to what to do in case of fire due to lack of fire safety systems at Grenfell Tower.

Smoke from The Grenfell Tower Disaster on 14 June 2017 in London UK.

I was also emotional over the death of a 28-year-old single mother and carer who had died leaving a 3-year-old daughter behind due to this pandemic. She was pleading with her mother to please look after her daughter. The grandmother now has to look after the child, which will be difficult for her. I couldn't imagine what it would be like for that innocent little girl left without a mother.

Two NHS nurses have died. They worked for the nation to make it safe for people like us, but sadly they died. One of them was and 84-year-old nurse who had come out of retirement to help out and support the NHS UK.

Today's death toll is 596, making a total of 16,060. In the beginning of the pandemic, I felt very emotional when 10 people died in one day, but now it has affected 185 countries and 161,000 people have died. Across the world now, 2.3 million cases have been recorded. I heard news about my relatives who have been hospitalised after testing positive for coronavirus.

✎ Monday, 20 April 2020
Twenty-ninth day of lockdown

At present, 100 NHS doctors, nurses, and front line workers have lost their lives as a result of contracting coronavirus in the UK. Every day on the BBC news, the government is criticised for its failure to provide sufficient PPE for front line workers and carers. This makes the UK look disorganised and shambolic around the world.

When HMRC opened after lockdown, millions of applications were uploaded within hours. I deep-cleaned all surfaces and disinfected the house early this morning. After that, I started work on my assignment for university.

This afternoon, my eldest daughter made delicious Korean food for the whole family. After that, I prepared for my afternoon class in criminology. The death rate has dropped down to 449 since last week, and the total number of deaths now stands at 16,509, but this does not include data from care homes and community death rates.

✎ Tuesday, 21 April 2020
Thirtieth day of lockdown

A bright morning. Birds were chirping outside; otherwise, it was all quiet and soundless everywhere. I brushed my teeth as soon as possible after waking up and getting out of bed because I had a class at 10 a.m. in Criminology. In class, we discussed the London riots of 2011. After that, I had a one-on-one with my lecturer, after which I started to type up my assignment. I set my alarm clock for one hour in order to measure my typing words per minute, as well as to control my time management.

Once I had typed 1,000 words, I had lunch, but I forgot to drink a glass of water. From reading the articles and typing the essay, I gained greater understanding of the real reasons behind the riots. According to the home secretary, Theresa May, "the 2011 rioters weren't trying to make a political or social statement; they were thieving, pure and simple." I now had a more in-depth understanding of the background to the 2011 riots, which took place in Tottenham after the shooting of Mark Duggan by a police officer on 4 August. This was the trigger for the riots.

The message about the shooting was widely shared on social media, and demonstrations started soon after this. The riots spread to 31 metropolitan cities, and 6,000 officers were on the streets. Riots took place within many cities of the UK. Millions of pounds worth of damage was done, and an estimated 1,500 people took part in the riots. This incident was very important to understand what happened in the past and what lessons can be learned for the future.

The police trying to control fire during the London riots in 2011

My and my husband's name were registered on behalf of the GRNC to support Nepali elderly people who are not able to speak English. During this lockdown, it is important to provide information for people who are self-isolating. The Nepali community decided to produce a leaflet which would set out how those in the community who were unable to speak English could access essential services to get help.

In this leaflet, there was also information of a "lockdown special" programme for free online yoga and meditation, which is organised by the GRNC. Many people, especially the elderly in our community, cannot access information online through email, Facebook, and WhatsApp. I felt happy after doing this volunteering job today. I continued to type up my essay after delivering the leaflets to many Nepali homes.

Deaths in England and Wales have nearly doubled the average number at this time of year and are expected to hit a twenty-year high. According to the Office of National Statistics UK, there were 823 deaths today, making a total of 18,500 overall. We have again sad news that we have lost a member of the Nepali community who was diagnosed with coronavirus. He was a contemporary of my husband, and I was so emotional.

I imagined if we died in this pandemic how our two elder daughters would have to look after and take care of their little brother. I could not think of any positive aspect today because of the high death rates in the UK. I could not sleep when I laid down on my bed. My thoughts and feelings were centred on my relatives scattered around the world. This included my relatives who had passed away and even some of my friends I had grown up with in my birthplace, Oyam-Panchthar, Nepal.

On the daily BBC News, the World Health Organisation (WHO) said that only two groups of people should wear masks at the moment: those working in care homes and front-line workers. This is to stop people buying medical masks that are needed for the NHS. Other countries have distributed masks, and tests for Covid-19 are available in many public places, like shopping malls. But here in the UK, I wanted to order masks but they take three to four weeks to arrive. I also wanted to buy a test kit for myself, but they are not available for the general public unless you have Covid-19 symptoms. This is a continuing worry while people are in lockdown.

✎ Wednesday, 22 April 2020
Thirty-first day of lockdown

I woke up early this morning, although I went to bed late last night. We, my husband and I, both attended online meditation. This programme was run by the GRNC.

I sat down at the computer for my assignment and typed 500 words to complete it. I did all the referencing and made it ready for uploading to my assignment folder at University of Surrey. Then we decided to go out walking as a family for two hours from Church Crookham to nearby Aldershot and Fleet and to Farnham Broader Field (army training area).

All the way walking there and back, we discussed the coronavirus situation. I convinced my two daughters that they should look after their little brother if we both died from Covid-19. They tried to me cheer me up and told me that would never happen. The number of confirmed coronavirus deaths has risen by 759 to 18,100. The figures were a little lower than Tuesday's rise of 823.

We cooked national food made from plan flour (*dhido*) and vegetable curry for dinner. It is the national dish of Nepal, and it was delicious. Everyone was interested in watching an Indian movie with the family after the lovely meal. Otherwise, nothing special to record for today.

Thursday, 23 April 2020
Thirty-second day of lockdown

> **In the news**: "The first human trial in Europe of a coronavirus vaccine has begun in Oxford. Two volunteers were injected, the first of more than 800 people recruited for the study."

The morning was very bright and chilly, although it is the third week of April. I brushed my teeth, had a shower, and cleaned the house. I was going to attend online yoga exercises via Zoom, which was organised by the GRNC. I met people from different part of the UK, greeted them, and asked them how they were before the start of the yoga session.

The yoga teacher came and started the yoga with a variety of postures and poses. She was also a volunteer helping to manage the lockdown quarantine situation fighting Covid-19. The session took an hour and a half: one hour of yoga and half an hour discussing community update news. I was interested in the yoga, because I used to do it two or three times a week before.

Today is a special day for mums in Nepal, similar to Mother's Day (it follows the calendar, not like the UK). I called my mum on video to wish her happy Mother's Day as soon as I had finished the yoga exercises.

Mum reminded me of many things from my childhood that I had

forgotten. For instance, I found someone's purse and showed it to my friend, who was a few years older than me, and she kept the purse. It belonged to a friend of my mother, who used to help us with domestic work. My mum told her that I found it and that my friend had kept it, and she complained because I had not given it back to her immediately. I didn't know that purse was that old woman's purse. I felt like I was baby again in my mother's lap!

My parents had been in lockdown in Hong Kong since coronavirus started to spread in China. I confessed my secret to my mum from thirty-six years ago: I was going to get drinking water from a small pond where people had to wait ages to get a gallon of water. I went with my younger brother, each of us carrying a gallon container (*okharbote-kuwa*). The weather was winter cold, so people used to boil water on the fire and have a shower there. I tried to light the fire for warmth whilst waiting to fill up the gallon container. By mistake, I set fire to the whole field while my brother was waiting for water at the pond.

The fire spread to all areas of the dry field and put all the small nursery and trees at risk. On top of that, it was going to burn people's houses down. People from the village got together and manged to control the fire. I ran away quickly with my little brother, and nobody knew that it was my fault. My mum was so surprised by my secret all these years later, laughing at me because if people had known at that time, they could have charged my parents for the damage or given me a severe telling off.

My relatives were so worried about the death rates from Covid-19 in the UK. I convinced them not to worry and told them if any family members in the UK did die, they would just have to manage their land and money and hire a carer or nurse to look after my parents. This would only be in the worst case, but it is always better to be prepared and have a future plan. News of more deaths each day is distressing to people across the country, as well as a tragedy for the families involved.

I spent three hours studying the University of Surrey link on the Grenfell Tower Disaster in June, 2017, and found the following report online:

Corporate Manslaughter and Corporate Homicide Act 2007 and Grenfell

The Corporate Manslaughter and Corporate Homicide Act 2007 came into force in April 2008 in so that companies and organisations could be charged and held accountable for corporate manslaughter, when they have failed to manage and provide of duty of care, which has caused serious crime. The offence of corporate manslaughter allows a corporation to be penalised for conduct that leads to a person's death. As stated above, the offence of corporate crime and manslaughter and related deaths can be a result of a direct result of corporate behaviour, for example where health and safety procedures have failed. One of the examples of this is that the council pacified the residents complaining about poor maintenance by paying for an external "facelift" of the building. This cost several million pounds and burned in the fire for 24 hours. However, this is difficult to prove because it is complex. It would not be easy to prove that a facelift of the building directly caused the fire.

Covid-19 continues to dominate the daily news headlines. The number of people now confirmed with coronavirus has risen by 616 to 18,738, but the figures are a little lower than yesterday. As a mark of respect for NHS doctors, nurses, and front line workers, we clapped hands, and some bonfires were lit to celebrate their continuing service to the community. I felt so emotional for all their hard work. Clapping hands cannot repay all their hard work or in any way compensate them for their selfless service. Some of them are separated from their own families and relatives at this challenging time.

My daughter ordered Indian takeaway for dinner because I was busy outside in the garden putting in vegetable seeds.

✏️ Friday, 24 April 2020
Thirty-third day of lockdown

I tried to complete my normal routine jobs as soon as possible so that I could focus on my studies for the next two hours. Afterwards, I cooked a traditional food, *pakauri* (made from onion, potatoes, and cabbage with spicy herbs and rice), for dinner. My husband helped me to prepare all the ingredients and did the washing up whilst I cooked the food. My eldest daughter had two coursework deadlines to meet, so I did not want to disturb her. After she submitted them online, I talked to my friends, and we exchanged experiences and feelings about the coronavirus.

With my children, I discussed with the arrangements I wanted to make if I died of coronavirus. My children did not take me seriously and said, "Don't say things like that," but it is such an emotional time, and being a mum, I worry about my family and how they will cope if anything should happen to me.

I saw this report in the *Guardian*:

> In the UK, the number of domestic violence killings has doubled during lockdown. In the first four weeks of lockdown, 13 women and four children are believed to have been killed by men in the UK, most of these murders took place with in their homes. That's double the (already mind-bending) average of two women a week. At the same time, women's frontline services are reporting record-breaking cries for help. Calls to domestic violence helplines have increased by 120% whilst traffic to their websites have tripled.

This news was very heartbreaking. People all over the world were dying from coronavirus, and now coronavirus was also responsible for deaths from domestic abuse and violence in the UK. I always thought the UK was the best place to live, but now I have lost hope of life in the UK due to the global pandemic of Covid-19. The reasons are that death rates are high compared to Asian countries. The coronavirus test is available everywhere in China and Korea, but London only allows front line workers and relatives to have the virus test. It is also not possible for the general public to buy PPE.

The number of people dying with coronavirus has now risen by 684 to 19,506, a little more than yesterday.

Saturday, 25 April 2020
Thirty-fourth day of lockdown … and my birthday

This morning, the sun rose early. I brushed my teeth, showered, and prayed, as Saturday is our day of prayer. I attended my yoga session for one hour, which was organised by our community. I prefer to attend because I'm also secretary of this group.

I talked to everyone online after we had completed the yoga for a lockdown special. I prepared breakfast and called my parents in Hong Kong to talk about my birthday. I started to focus on my assignment for my presentation on corporate crime responsibility.

My husband bought a bunch of flowers and a cake to celebrate my birthday. I was worried about the loss of many people from the virus; therefore, I was not ready to celebrate like past birthdays. I told everyone I did not want to celebrate, as the situation is now critical. Finally, my family lit the candles for me, and I just joined with them in eating the cake and the food. I did not let them take any pictures of me with the cake, or the gifts and flowers.

My article about the Nishan history of the Limbu tribe in the eastern part of Nepal has been published in many media. The article includes a video recorded with my dad's voice speaking about this unique history and holding a crown (*subhangi/subba*) with writing in an antique language I do not understand. This Nishan power was given by the late king Prithibi Narayan Shaw 264 years ago to show his strength and leadership. It is similar to the honorary symbols of a mayor in a county or ward.

My ancestors were part of this great tradition. My grandfather and my father used to hold this great power in the municipality, and my father still holds some part today, although nowadays it is contradictory in the Limbu tribe in the eastern part of Nepal. It is relating to a great festival Dashai (Hindu religion) in Nepal, and it is complex and paradoxical at the moment. In the past, the Limbu tribe (the indigenous people of Nepal) were forced to celebrate Dashai, but now most people are secular and have a choice.

The image of the Jangi Nishan flag is a symbol
of the Limbu subba (headman)

Covid-19 daily update: The number of people with confirmed coronavirus who have died has now risen by 813 to 20,319. The figures are a little more than yesterday.

I remembered that when the first woman age 70 died on 5 March 2020 after a positive test for coronavirus, I was very upset, but within 55 days there were 20,319 deaths in the UK. We have lost 33 Nepali people (Gurkha families) in the UK, whereas back home in Nepal, nobody has so far died from Covid-19. It is very shocking news—an awful experience of life.

My Facebook wall was covered everywhere with birthday wishes from friends and relatives all around the world. Unfortunately, people now in the UK are not allowed to attend funerals because of Covid-19 restrictions and social distancing rules.

🖉 Sunday, 26 April 2020
Thirty-fifth day of lockdown

I woke up quickly, as I wanted to clean the house before sitting down for yoga (lockdown special) as organised by the GRNC. I spend one hour doing yoga daily during this critical situation. Again, I started to do my work on my Grenfell Tower Disaster PowerPoint, as this was due very soon. I kept reading many articles relating to this topic, as it is very interesting. The fire erupted in Grenfell Tower in west London on 14 June 2017. It is the worst fire disaster in peacetime in the UK since the nineteenth century, with seventy-two people killed and hundreds left homeless. It is one of the UK's worst modern disasters.

Covid-19 daily update: The number of people confirmed with coronavirus who have since died has now risen by 413 to 20,732. The figures are less than yesterday. It is tragic and terrible to lose a such huge number of people in less than two months. The first death from Covid-19 was on 5 March 2020. I'm unable to smile since yesterday because of the over twenty thousand deaths from coronavirus.

Finally, after finishing my PowerPoint, I had to complete and upload the relevant documents for my dissertation proposal. It has taken up so much of my time, but I have now completed the proposal, and I emailed it to my supervisor at 11.30 p.m. I'm trying to write a few words in my diary, although I'm very busy with coursework during this critical lockdown period.

🖉 Monday, 27 April 2020
Thirty-sixth day of lockdown

I went into the back garden for some fresh air before carrying on with domestic jobs. I attended the dissertation writing class from 11 a.m. to 12 p.m. via Zoom. Regarding lunch, I made *selroti* (dough made from rice flour, ghee, and sugar), then I had a two-hour break before sitting down

down at the computer for my next class. It is the first day of class after the Easter break. I did not have a moment to draw breath owing to the many assignments and reading articles relating to my course. I also had a moment of panic due to Mr. Covid-19.

In addition, I completed my presentation about the Grenfell Tower. I was not able to be involved in my yoga group because I had a range of tasks today. I had dinner with my children, but my husband had already left for duty. Finally, I had a quick chance to listen to lecture slides on the recorder via SurryLearn. I'm crazy to check BBC News for information about the virus.

Covid-19 daily update: The number of confirmed coronavirus deaths has now risen by 368 to 21,092. The figures are less than yesterday, thankfully.

Tuesday, 28 April 2020
Thirty-seventh day of lockdown

It was a bright and quiet morning. I washed my face and brushed my teeth. I had a glass of hot water and then joined the group yoga, which was organised by the GRNC. It was the first week of class after the Easter 2020 break. My eldest daughter made lunch, but she too was busy with her deadlines for university.

My first class—the Crime and Offending module—started at 1 p.m. and finished at 3 p.m. From 3 to 5p.m., it was Law and Social Control. It was long day, and afterwards, I felt dizzy, so I went out into the back garden for fresh air. Then I went back to my study and had some fruit and a cup of tea while I took a short break.

I suggested to the family that they should have dinner while I did my last class, but they waited for me to finish. We had dinner late, about 9 p.m., because my class ended at 8.45 p.m. Luckily, the class was run online due to Covid-19—although all the students, myself included, were complaining about their difficulties in accessing the reading materials because the Surrey University library was closed.

The number of people who have died from coronavirus has risen by 586 to 21,678. The figures are higher than yesterday. It is tragic to lose such massive numbers of people such a short period of time. The first death from Covid-19 in the UK was on 5 March 2020. It has been a huge loss for so many families.

Wednesday, 29 April 2020
Thirty-eighth day of lockdown

> *In the news*: 4,419 deaths from Covid-19 in a day

A bright and quiet morning. I got up, washed, and had a glass of hot water before joining mindfulness concentration meditation organised by the GRNC. Just 25 minutes after that, I checked, and all was well with the PowerPoint for my class on the Surrey University learning site. I did not do much during the day because I was tired from the day before. Later on, between 5 and 6 p.m., I attended a short class. My husband cooked dinner and invited all of us into the TV room, and we had a family get-together watching TV and talking about the virus.

My heart felt broken today. The death toll has now risen by 4,419 to 26,097! The loss is impossible to imagine—and 60,000 deaths in United States!

Thursday, 30 April 2020
Thirty-ninth day of lockdown

> *In the news*: Captain Tom Moore's NHS appeal tops £32 million on 100th birthday

A chilly morning as usual. I got up, then started to research for my PowerPoint presentation. I was so busy, I even forgot to have a glass of water. All I had was a cup of tea until 5 p.m. because of the deadline for my coursework the next morning. I was experiencing a lot of technical problems with the new and old version of the computer system, so much so that I didn't even have time to cook lunch and dinner today, just focused on my PowerPoint work. Fortunately, my husband cooked dinner again.

I watched TV a few minutes whilst having dinner with the family.

It was very encouraging to see how Captain Tom Moore's NHS appeal topped £32 million on his 100th birthday. Captain Tom was a war veteran who had the wonderful idea of raising money for the NHS by walking laps of his garden on his Zimmer frame and was made an honorary colonel. He is said to have received 100,020 birthday cards from well-wishers.

By contract, some sad news again from India: the death of celebrity hero Rishi Kapoor in Mumbai.

The number of deaths today from Covid-19 in the UK has risen by 674 to 26,771.

MAY 2020

Friday, 1 May 2020
Fortieth day of lockdown

Early-morning sunshine outside the window greeted me as I got up and started to practice my PowerPoint presentation, because I had to present it to the class that day. I had technical problems such as the Zoom camera not working on my new computer, and I had to use my son's laptop, but I was not used to using it. I had a rush to set up for class. It was stressful.

This was the first day back in the Corporate Crime class after Easter break. We had to present online with Zoom due to Covid-19. My presentation went well, and many questions were asked by the lecturer, some of which were quite difficult to answer. We had the week 8 lesson—nearly the end of the second semester for this subject. I attended a second class from 2 to 4 p.m. for my Criminal Justice System subject. I felt stressed, so I asked my husband to come out jogging with me. After an hour and a half, we came back home.

This evening, I did not have to cook dinner, because my youngest daughter made traditional food like roti and curry gravy. I invited all the family for dinner in the TV room so that we could watch the TV together and talk about coronavirus.

I joined a Facebook live session to listen to Jeremy Corbyn's May Day speech on working together. May Day is a public holiday usually celebrated on 1 May or the first Monday of May. It is an ancient festival of spring and a current traditional spring holiday in many European cultures. Dancing, singing, and sharing food are usually part of the festivities.

In 1889, May Day was chosen as the date for the International Workers' Day by the Socialists and Communists in Chicago to commemorate the riots there in 1886.

✎ Saturday, 2 May 2020
Forty-first day of lockdown

> ***In the news***: Twenty protesters participated in a mass hugging against lockdown in London near the Houses of Parliament

Literally, I forgot to wake up on time. I nearly missed my fifteen minutes of Zoom online yoga. It was a clear day with early sunshine outside the window. We had a group conversation via Zoom for the Greater Rushmoor Nepali Community (GRNC), both members and volunteers from each area. I prayed as I normally do every Saturday as part of my religion, and I tried to focus on my new assignment.

My eldest daughter cooked Korean food for lunch and called everyone to have food. I went back to my university work for two hours, and later on I prepared dinner early, because my husband had to go on night duty. I read a chapter on illicit drug use for my assignment before having lunch. I had dinner with my children and watched TV. The children played a game of Monopoly for about an hour.

Spain has made mask-wearing compulsory on all public transport. The Spanish government will distribute 6 million masks to be worn on public transport and has allocated 7 million Euros to local authorities to cover the cost. By contrast, the UK government is still studying the advice from scientific experts on wearing face masks.

I'm scared to go out without a mask, but the UK government has still not reached a definitive decision on the benefits of wearing masks. The death toll from Covid-19 is increasing every day. The daily death toll has now risen 621 to a staggering overall total of 28,131, although the increase is less than the previous day. It is a tragic and terrible loss of human life, all within two months of the first death of Covid-19 announced on 5 March 2020.

Protesters in London have been seen taking part in a "mass hug" outside the Met Police headquarters in defiance of the Covid-19 lockdown. The crowds were close to the Houses of Parliament. Some of them were holding signs which read "My body, my choice, and no more lockdown". Around 20 people appeared, including young children.

I contacted my mum and dad in Hong Kong to update them on the virus. They are praying for all of us, including my siblings all around the world.

Time: 01.01 a.m.

✏ Sunday, 3 May 2020
Forty-second day of lockdown

I dreamed of my birthplace, Oyam Panchthar in Nepal. I was going uphill to my real birthplace home above the Gaukanchhi ghar. I was near my neighbour Tara's house under the main road. We used to work a lot together in the cornfields during the summer season. I still remembered working with her in the dade khet field and our field, and with many other workers, during my summer holidays after finishing my SLC exams.

In the dream, I was happy talking to her, and she was coming towards me and stopped me from going up. She persuaded me to go back with her to her house, which was between our rice field and the nearby bamboo field. I was looking at her land and my land. I was jumping up and down like I used to when coming back home from school in my childhood days.

I spent fourteen years at this house till we all moved to a bigger home, which was built by my parents. We stayed in that new big house for only two years. We then decided to rent out our house and move a little bit farther down to a more spacious home with a big field and more land, which was closer to everything.

In my dream, I was waving to the sunrise from the eastern part of our house when I accidentally woke up and found that I was in bed, but still my body and mind weren't in my bed. I revisited all my memories of childhood, and the flood of memories shook my heart and caused tears to rise from both my eyes. I nearly missed my 15 minutes of Zoom online yoga.

According to the Office of National Statistics, people who are living in more deprived areas of England and Wales are more likely to die from coronavirus than those in wealthier places. Higher death rates from coronavirus are more prevalent in deprived areas, as well as crime and antisocial behaviour, according to the health secretary Mr Hancock.

The death toll from Covid-19 has now risen by 315 to 28,446. The first recorded death from Covid-19 was on 5 March 2020. This is a huge loss of lives in the UK.

Time: 11.40 p.m.

Monday, 4 May 2020
Forty-third day of lockdown

I started to check my work before starting my dissertation-writing class. I had to miss my yoga class, although I love to join in. I read a chapter on the use of illicit drugs for my topic for a few hours. I had dinner with the children and had a shower. There was no time to watch TV today, because I had to submit my assignment one day before the deadline.

I emailed the assignment to the supervisor in charge of my dissertation, together with a few questions. I sent another question to the male lecturer in charge of the module for crime and offending.

I'm scared to go out without a mask, although the UK government is still going by the decision of the senior scientist, and the mask is not essential yet. The death toll is increasing every day. If I wear one, everyone looks at me with surprise, which makes me feel excluded and strange, but I stick to my guns. Lockdown is more stressful and terrible than life in prison.

I attended one lesson and submitted one essay, and then I happily joined the evening yoga for 45 minutes to refresh mind and body in order to be able to manage this lockdown situation.

The death toll from Covid-19 rose by 288 today, the lowest daily update since 29 March 2020. The total as of today is 28,734. It is tragic and terrible to lose such a massive number of people in such a short times. Today is almost two months since the first death from Covid-19 on 5 March 2020.

Time: 12.25 a.m.

✏️ Tuesday, 5 May 2020
Forty-fourth day of lockdown

> ***In the news***: The first death from Covid-19 was exactly two months ago today.

The day was clear. I could see the early sunshine outside the window. I washed and brushed, then joined the yoga class for one hour. I was nearly ten minutes late because I went to bed so late—1.30 a.m. I had drink and fruits at 10 a.m., and then I prepared the homework for Crime and Offending week 8, and White-Collar Crime, from noon to 2 p.m. Before the first lecture, all students, including students from around the world—from the USA, Denmark, India, South Korea, Hong Kong, and so on—were updated about the coronavirus situation.

I would like to include here some information from my studying which perhaps will interest you. Edwin Sutherland (1949) stated that White collar crime was a crime committed by a person of high status in the course of his occupation. This challenged existing criminological theory. Hazel Croall (2001) suggested that occupational crime is when offenders engaged in illegal/rule breaking activities for personal gain at the expense of consumers, clients, or employers. Organisational crime is crime, not directly involving personal gain, for the benefit of the organisation.

There was a lot of class discussion about this. I wanted to say something in the class, but I had a noise problem at home. For that reason, I stayed on mute for the whole class. It was a really interesting topic today.

I looked quickly at the subject of the next class. Then I had cereal with milk and a short break before the start of the second class. I joined the class again from 3 to 5p.m. This time, the topic was law, society, and social control. The subject was crime, including the media representation of violent video games and behaviour.

> There is consistent evidence that violent imagery in television, film and video, and computer games has substantial short-term effects on arousal, thoughts, and emotions, increasing the likelihood of aggressive or fearful

behaviour in younger children, especially in boys (Browne and Hamilton-Giachritsis, 2008).

When the two lessons were finished, I checked the Surrey University Learning email for the homework for the last class while on a short break. I asked my husband to cook the rice, and I managed to cook curry and pickle and salad for dinner during this short break.

I sat down for the last evening class from 7 to 8.30 p.m. It was an upper intermediate English class. There were a number of problems with Zooming and emailing homework, because the teacher herself was still gaining experience at it. She had to prepare for online teaching due to the pandemic and talked with international students, including a friend from Hong Kong who went back there just a few days ago and who attended the class at midnight HK time.

The children were waiting to have dinner at the same time as me, so we all had a late dinner at 9 p.m. After dinner, I had a cup of green tea and went straight back onto the computer to research illicit drug use. I set the time on my mobile for one hour and started to make notes, but I couldn't finish the reading. So I reset the alarm for 30 minutes and completed making notes. I felt a slight ache in my right arm due to writing all day on the computer and paper.

I hadn't thought much about Covid-19, but finally, again, my eyes went to the mobile news update of today. The death toll from Covid-19 rose by 693 today, more than yesterday, bringing the total to 29,427. That death toll of 29,427, as recorded by the UK government, is the highest in Europe.

I still remembered that the first death from Covid-19 was of a 70-year-old woman at the Royal Berkshire Hospital in Reading. It is not a joke to lose nearly 30 thousand people and have them separated from their loved ones and families.

I was able to contact my parents in Hong Kong for few minutes at 12.30 a.m. Mum was telling me that she was praying to God for us to be safe from the coronavirus. I thanked them sincerely, because they themselves are 72 and 74 years old now. They were worrying so much about the UK situation at the moment. I was able to manage to write my diary in spite of being very busy today.

Time: 1.12 a.m.

✎ Wednesday, 6 May 2020
Forty-fifth day of lockdown

> ***In the news***: The first death from Covid-19 was two months ago yesterday, on 5 March 2020. The number of deaths has now risen by a further 649 today, which makes the UK the first European country to pass 30,000 deaths. This is the second-highest number of recorded coronavirus deaths in the world behind the USA, which has more than 70,000.

It was a clear day with early sunshine outside the window. I joined the meditation class for one hour, from 7 to 8 a.m. I woke up on time even though I went to bed late, at 1.30 a.m. I did not have a chance to join in with the group conversation due to my class on Crime and Offending starting at 10 a.m.

I prepared lunch and had it with the children, after which I sat down to study my notes on illegal drug use. It is essential to understand illicit drugs, because they can create many underlying problems which harm individual lives and caused immense harm to society. There are many kinds of drugs which are not legalised by the government but which are used illegally by many people for different reasons. Using illicit drugs has negative effects, such as dependency, addiction, and unemployment, and can lead to criminal behaviour as well as death. Also, these drugs cause health problems, break up family relationships, and cause social harm.

I set up my alarm clock on my mobile for every hour in order to study journal articles that I received from my lecturer. It took two and a half hours. I went to walk in the long valley woodland which borders the towns of Aldershot, Farnham, and Fleet. It took two hours. I asked the children to go out, but they did not want to. Therefore, my husband and I went out. We saw so many people in the field walking with their dogs, cycles, and children.

My husband cooked dinner because he has the day off today. After dinner, I went straight back to work on the computer again.

I'm scared to go out without a mask, but the UK government is still undecided and waiting for a decision from the senior scientists. The death toll is increasing every day. I use full PPE, but people tease me like I'm a clown.

I was able to contact my parents in Hong Kong for a few minute at 12.30 p.m. I did not have a chance to talk to my mum, but I was able to talk with my dad. One member of the Nepali community here in the UK who was my dad's friend has died from coronavirus.

Time: 12.05 a.m.

✎ Thursday, 7 May 2020
Forty-sixth day of lockdown

At 8 p.m. tonight, there will be a collective neighbourhood clapping session for NHS and front line workers. Because testing was limited to hospital patients, NHS, and care-home staff workers until recently, the actual number of infections is estimated to be higher than what we currently know now.

Later on, I joined a Zoom class for two hours. It was to work on my dissertation protocol format and fill in a risk assessment. It has been a long process to complete since New Year 2020. I had to miss my yoga class with community members due to my class work. I completed all the forms and emailed them to my dissertation supervisor.

I went into the kitchen after class and cleaned all the first floor for a few minutes. I wanted to make sure the house was clean before the children started to use the facilities. Also, I had a drink and fruits. Then I attended my next class from 2 to 3 p.m. It was about how to prepare for a future career.

I prepared lunch for the whole family, after which I sat down to study illegal drug use again. In addition, I set up a second alarm clock on my mobile for one hour for typing up my notes. We ordered Domino's pizzas for our evening meal, although we had some rice and curry left.

I decided to go out for a walk with my husband at 8.30 p.m. for one hour after dinner. I contacted elderly Nepali people from our community to ask what they needed, and I found that one family needed a mask and hand sanitiser. I ordered extra and delivered to them free because they are in their 80s and can't speak or understand English very well. We advised them to stay at home and not go out.

I'm feeling incredibly sad because so many people are grieving as a result of Covid-19 and also experiencing the shock of losing a loved one, often after a very short period of illness. Government restrictions such as social distancing and self-isolation have meant that many people cannot spend time with their loved ones as they are dying.

The numbers of mourners are also limited at funerals and memorial gatherings. I cannot imagine how people can repeatedly cope with the sadness and shock leading up to a death.

The death toll from confirmed coronavirus cases rose by 539 today, less than the previous day, bringing the total to 30,615.

I was not able to contact my parents in Hong Kong, but I looked at Dad's Facebook page and wished a happy birthday to Lord Buddha. I remembered 22 years ago, back home, when I used to go to the Lord Buddha temple in Oyam, Panchthar, with friends, relatives, and all familiar people around the city. It was really enjoyable and festive at that time. It is officially a day off; therefore, I did not go to school for teaching. For that reason, I had fun as well.

Time: 12.05 a.m.

Friday, 8 May 2020
Forty-seventh day of lockdown

It was Easter Friday, and there was clear sunshine outside the window. I did not have to attend my online class today, so I participated in lockdown isolation meditation with the Lama Guru from 9 to 10 a.m. It was an amazing experience shared by everyone after completion of meditation. It enabled me to control my mind, because Covid-19 stress was affecting me psychologically.

I started to clean the house and decided to deep-clean the toilet and bathrooms. I disinfected with alcohol spray everywhere. It took two hours to finish the special cleaning before I could begin to study for just a short time.

I asked my husband to help prepare the ingredients in the kitchen whilst I made organic home-made bread (*alu paratha*). It is made with a mixture of onion, ginger, garlic, spices, salt, and pepper, all mixed into a dough and cooked in a big pan. Besides this, I cooked gravy soup, lentils (*dal*), and salad. Then we had a big family lunch on the round table. I spent most of the time in the house with the family today. I did not have to focus on study that much. That means my draft essay could not move forward more than 500 words of typing.

After dinner, I sat down to study the information on the DrugWise link sent to me by my lecturer. The Scottish Crime and Drug Enforcement Agency (SCDEA) suggests that heroin costs, on average, are £47.35 per gram. Thus, the total cost of Scotland's heroin market is estimated to be £550,939,291, or £11,002 per heroin user. This is an alarming amount of money as well as being one of the major causes of many deaths.

I'm scared to go out jogging today because the death toll is still increasing in the UK. The sad news, according to BBC news, is that "people living in more deprived areas of England and Wales are more likely to die with coronavirus than those in more affluent places, new figures suggest. Office for National Statistics analysis shows there were 55 deaths for every 100,000 people in the poorest parts of England, compared with 25 in the wealthiest areas."

Saturday, 9 May 2020
Forty-eighth day of lockdown

> ***In the news***: The UK now has the second highest number of recorded coronavirus deaths in the world and the highest number of deaths in Europe.

The alarm rang at 8.30 a.m. I woke up for my yoga lockdown isolation meditation programme. I set it because I went to bed at 1 a.m. The weather was clear sunshine outside the window.

I quickly contacted Mum and Dad in Hong Kong to update them about coronavirus deaths and to see how they were generally. Then I did a brief clean of the kitchen and the loo and disinfected them.

Dinner was cooked by my husband again today due to him having the day off from work. Everyone else was ready to eat dinner, but I was rushing to complete my essay draft and email it to my teacher. If I had not sent it today, it would have been delayed by another day. That's why I was working towards this all day.

After a big dinner, I felt very stressed and in need of exercise, so I went out jogging for an hour, from 9 to 10 p.m. After that, I contacted a friend of mine and talked about the death of a friend who died yesterday. Her husband was just one year senior to my husband in joining the British Army, and I knew his late wife many years ago when I was in Brunei with my husband's regiment.

I read in the *Mirror* about the NHS nurse who quit a London hospital due to the lack of personal protective equipment (PPE). It is true that if health workers are not safe, how can their patients be safe?

The UK is a world-leading country, and now it is leading in Covid-19 death rate. This makes me ponder and feel concerned all the time. The death toll from Covid-19 rose by 346 today, which at least is less than the previous day. The total as of today is 31,587. This pandemic has resulted in a huge loss of people in the UK and has been a terrible experience for everyone throughout the world.

Time: 12.18 a.m.

✏️ Sunday, 10 May 2020
Forty-ninth day of lockdown

The alarm clock rang at 7.30 a.m., and I woke up for the yoga lockdown isolation meditation programme. There was clear sunshine outside the window. I joined the class online for an hour. It was an amazing yoga experience due to the teacher using different varieties of the sun salute posture that enabled control of body and mind during this critical situation.

After the yoga session, I tried to start an article for a new topic on the Criminal Justice System module. I set the alarm clock many times to search on Google Scholar and Surrey University Library. I also did some of my usual chores today.

My eldest daughter made Korean fried chicken wings and Indian samosas, and we all had a family dinner together. I watched the BBC News at 7 p.m. and learned that the UK Prime Minister Boris Johnson "has unveiled a 'conditional plan' to reopen society, allowing people in England to spend more time outdoors from Wednesday" of the coming week:

> The PM also said people who could not work from home should return to the workplace—but avoid public

transport. He said a new Covid Alert System with five levels would monitor how quickly lockdown restrictions could be eased. He hoped the next step, "at the earliest by 1 June" would be for some primary pupils to return to school in England. ... He said these steps formed part of a "first sketch of a roadmap for reopening society". The PM added: "This is not the time simply to end the lockdown this week". ... Mr Johnson also confirmed that fines for the "small minority who break" lockdown rules will increase.

NHS and key workers are still pleading for enough personal protective equipment. The death toll from Covid-19 rose by 269 today, less than the previous day, bringing the total to 31,855. The UK has the second highest number of recorded coronavirus deaths in the world, and the highest number in Europe.

Time: 11.59 p.m.

Monday, 11 May 2020
Fiftieth day of lockdown

Testing in England and Scotland has been confined to people with symptoms who are key workers and their families, hospital patients, care-home residents, over-65s, and those who need to leave home to work.

No alarm time was set. I just woke up at 3 a.m. and typed my work until 6 a.m. to finish my assignments on time. I then went to bed again for two hours. I woke up at 8 a.m., but I missed the yoga. The weather was bright and clear sunshine outside.

I read and paraphrased the work of Cuthbertson (2017), which highlighted the great number of people who are sent to prison due to their criminal behaviour. Less than 8 per cent of custodial sentences were put in place for first-time offenders. A person who is sent to gaol should have at least 46 prior convictions or warnings, i.e. 10 per cent more than non-criminals, which I have learnt from my reading.

I watched the BBC news at 11 p.m. The PM said the new measures, including encouraging people in England to return to work if safe, were "baby steps". He also said employers should be sympathetic to workers who do not have access to childcare.

It came as new rules said people in England can soon meet one person from outside their household at a distance. People can now socialise in open spaces or play one-to-one sport, such as tennis with another person—as long as they stay 2 metres apart.

I am feeling incredibly sad. Many people are grieving as a result of losing a loved one suddenly within a very short period of time to coronavirus. Government restrictions to slow and control coronavirus include social distancing and self-isolation, which means that many people cannot spend time with their loved ones as they are dying. Neither can they spend time with their loved one's body afterwards, nor hold a normal memorial gathering. I cannot imagine how people cope.

The death toll from Covid-19 rose by 160 today, less than the previous day, bringing the total to 34,796.

Staff at a care home where 11 people have died in just two weeks say the horrifying impact of coronavirus is like nothing they have ever experienced. Workers and staff have spoken of the tragic impact of the deadly virus. An experienced nurse in Scotland with young children quit her job in a care home due to not having access to proper PPE. She said, "My children need me alive."

Time: 11.25 p.m.

Tuesday, 12 May 2020
Fifty-first day of lockdown

> ***In the news***: For the first time, people in England are being advised to wear face coverings in some enclosed places.

I woke up late, at 8.30, and missed yoga. The weather was cold, although there was clear sunshine outside the window. I had a glass of hot water, and from 10 to 11 a.m., I had to make notes after watching the Panopto recorded session from my university lecturer.

From 11.30 to 12.30 a.m., I had a Zoom meeting with my dissertation supervisor and discussed how to prepare protocol procedures. I had a snack quickly and then a drink before I prepared for my next class.

At 1 p.m., I attended a Crime and Offending class (week 9 session). We discussed the wide-ranging and ever-changing nature of criminal activities, which are difficult to regulate. For example, consider the new ways of committing familiar crime such as fraud—phishing, scareware, hacking, and so on.

I had a short break and then prepared for my next class. At 3 p.m., I began my Law, Society and Social Control module. This enabled me to see whether or not different social and political contexts can produce different responses to crime from the state, and how historical conditions can shape contemporary responses to crime in different nations. For example, in Switzerland, euthanasia is allowed under the law if a patient has a terminal illness, whereas in England it is illegal.

At 5 p.m., I took a short break to get fresh air, and then I joined in with yoga online for one hour. That made me feel fresh, after which I went out into the garden to water the new plants I had recently planted.

I was then ready to take the last class of the day. My English language class started at 7 p.m., again on Zoom. The teacher had technical problems, so, because of difficulties, it was decided to run a face-to-face class at the university. Finally, I completed all classwork, and then I typed up my 200-word assignment before dinner. This meant I had dinner late with the family.

The death toll from Covid-19 rose by 627 today, more than the previous day, bringing the total to 32,692. It is a huge loss of people's lives in the UK and a terrible experience for everyone.

Time: 12.14 a.m.

Wednesday, 13 May 2020
Fifty-second day of lockdown

There are now nearly 230,000 confirmed cases of coronavirus in the UK and more than 33,000 people have died, according to the latest government figures.

At 9 a.m., I started to type up my draft essay on illicit drug use for my Crime and Offending module. At 11.30, I had an online Zoom meeting with a friend for an astrology reading about my personal life and future prospects. At 5 p.m., I contacted all family members for an online conversation about our parents, who are in lockdown in Hong Kong.

After this, I needed to have a short break with some fresh air. Following this, at 6 o'clock, I joined a Rushmoor Healthy Living UK quarterly meeting. We discussed how we can help deprived local areas. Unfortunately, many members of the Nepali community very rarely attend exercise classes, which is a cause of concern for the whole community. It was found that Rushmoor Borough is the poorest borough in Hampshire and the most affected by Covid-19.

I typed up all the necessary sentences for my protocol format proposal. After this, I watched BBC News for 30 minutes to listen to an update on Covid-19 and changing the lockdown rules on Wednesday. Some people in England who cannot work from home were encouraged to return to their workplaces, as the government started easing some lockdown measures. People were urged to avoid public transport, if possible, but some commuters in London reported that the tube trains and buses were still too busy to observe social distancing rules.

The confirmed death toll from Covid-19 has now risen by 494, for an overall figure of 33,186. This makes me feel so sad and worried. The UK still has the second-highest number of recorded coronavirus deaths in the world and the highest in Europe.

Time: 11.35 p.m.

Thursday, 14 May 2020
Fifty-third day of lockdown

> ***In the news***: Community clapping for NHS and key worker at 8 p.m.

My alarm was set for 7 a.m., but I could not wake up today due to going to bed too late. I have just woken up at 8.30 and missed the yoga lockdown session. This was followed by an isolation meditation programme. The weather was cold, although there was clear sunshine outside the window. From 11 a.m. to 1 p.m. I had an online class for Crime and Offending essay writing. This was followed from 2 to 3 p.m. by a class on another topic.

At 5 p.m., I needed to have a short break and some fresh air before I joined the online yoga class for one hour. This class made me feel more relaxed and less stressed, and able to concentrate on my next and final class of the day. I watched the BBC news for an update on Covid-19. The daily updated number of confirmed coronavirus deaths is 428, which is less than the previous day. But the total number of confirmed coronavirus deaths now stands at 33,614.

Time: 11.35 p.m.

Friday, 15 May 2020
Fifty-fourth day of lockdown

> ***In the news***: Most recorded coronavirus deaths have been among the elderly. NHS England shows more than half the deaths have been among people over 80.

The weather was cold, although there was clear sunshine outside the window. I had a glass of warm water and began to type my essay, feeling a bit stressed due to the many assignments coming up. For a short time, I talked to my parents, and my dad was very worried because of the lockdown in Hong Kong. He said that he had lost hope for life due to his illness. I tried to calm him down by telling him it was not a big problem. Meanwhile, my eldest daughter was taking her university assessments from 9 a.m. to noon on Zoom.

From noon to 2 p.m., I attended class for Corporate Crime, week 9: Environmental Crime. We learnt about issues relating to the protection of the planet, which continue to capture media headlines and provoke public and political debate. The United Nations Intergovernmental Panel on Climate Change has referred to global warming as a weapon of mass destruction (IPCC, 2007). However, global warming is not the only earth-threatening issue; there is also an increasing amount of environmental crime.

I took a break for 10 minutes. Then, after two hours of class, from 3 to 5 p.m., I needed some fresh air, so I joined my online yoga for an hour. That made me feel fresh. I went out into the garden to do some watering and tend to my new nursery. Finally, I was ready to tackle a new reading topic.

I watched BBC News to update myself about Covid-19, feeling incredibly sad about the people grieving and who have experienced the shock of a loved one suddenly dying, often after a very short period of illness. Government restrictions to slow and control coronavirus—such as social distancing and self-isolation—have resulted in many people being unable to spend time with their loved ones, even if they are dying, or even to attend their funeral. I cannot imagine how people can cope with the repeated sadness and shock.

The death toll from Covid 19 has now risen by 384 to 33,998.

Time: 23.48 p.m.

Saturday, 16 May 2020
Fifty-fifth day of lockdown

- Prime Minister Boris Johnson unveiled a new Covid-19 Alert System on Sunday, with five levels to govern how quickly lockdown restrictions could be eased. Scotland, Wales, and Northern Ireland had their own powers over the lockdown and decided not to ease restrictions at that time.

I woke up earlier than usual, but unusually, the weather was getting colder and colder, although there was plenty of sun. I began to type my essay because there were plenty of other assignments coming up and I needed to get a move on.

With the change of lockdown rules on Wednesday, some people in England who hadn't been able to work from home were allowed to return to their workplaces, as the government started easing some lockdown measures. People were urged to avoid public transport if possible, but some commuters in London said tube trains and buses were still too busy for them to observe social distancing rules properly.

The death toll from Covid-19 has risen by 468, more than the previous day, bringing the total to 34,466. There are at least 3,378 deaths of Black, Asian, and minority ethnic (BAME) individuals in hospitals in England up to 5 May 2020. This represents 17 per cent of all deaths to this point.

Time: 11.20 p.m.

🖉 Sunday, 17 May 2020
Fifty-sixth day of lockdown

Sadly, the first Covid-19 death in my homeland of Nepal was the mother of a 10-day-old baby. How tragic to leave a tiny baby alone without a mum due to this horrible pandemic!

From 10 a.m. to 2 p.m., I was reading and typing for my essay—a new topic again, drugs and prisoners.

At 3 p.m., I had lunch, got a bit of fresh air outside, prepared my uniform, and went to work. It was my first day back to work at the Royal Military Academic College Sandhurst after the Easter holiday. At work, everyone was wearing a mask. That made me happy and made me feel as if I was back in the dental surgery where I used to work, although there we had to change our mask after every patient. I used 200 pairs of gloves and 30 masks. At that time, I was happy to take the mask off, as you can imagine, but now I was actually happy to put a mask on at work.

First of all, I was updated about all the new cases of Covid-19 among staff. It was established that some doctors' and nurses' families were in quarantine, and so they couldn't come to work. At work, it was very difficult to observe new social distancing measures because the new cadets have to quarantine for two weeks at the beginning of term. Sometimes I think I'm no longer human due to all these difficult situations. Everyone is scared to get close and has lost their trust of other people. This Covid-19 epidemic has ruined the dreams of millions of people!

The death toll from Covid-19 rose by 140 today, less than the previous day, bringing the total to 34,606 in the UK. The total in the US is 88,889. The UK still has the second highest number of coronavirus deaths in the world and the highest number in Europe.

There is a question as to why more people from BAME backgrounds are dying from coronavirus. Health Secretary Matt Hancock has said that people from ethnic minority backgrounds are "disproportionately" dying from coronavirus. Professor Chris Whitty, the chief medical officer for England, has said that while the evidence is not conclusive, "it is absolutely critical that we find out which groups are most at risk." There were at least 3,378 deaths of BAME individuals in hospitals in England up to 5 May.

This means that, where ethnicity is known, BAME people represented 17 per cent of all deaths to this point.

The 2011 census—the most accurate source—showed that 14.5 per cent of the English population were from BAME backgrounds, but clearly the proportion may have grown since then. Ms Smith said she was also concerned about protective equipment supplies. However, she said the "disproportionate ratio" of BAME communities being affected by Covid-19 was "particularly apparent amongst NHS staff and caregivers who have lost their lives."

Time: 12.30 a.m. Good morning, diary!

Monday, 18 May 2020
Fifty-seventh day of lockdown

I woke up earlier than usual at 3 a.m. and worked for three hours, then went to bed at 6 a.m. for three hours. The weather is getting colder and colder, although there is bright sunshine outside. I decided to give the yoga a miss today.

From 10 a.m. 2.30 p.m., I spent time reading and typing for a new topic again, drugs and prisoners—part of my essay work.

I read on the news that there was a concern about the lack of protective equipment supplies. Furthermore, it was said that a disproportionate ratio of BAME communities were affected by Covid-19. It was "particularly apparent amongst NHS staff and caregivers who have lost their lives". The analysis was that BAME people were mostly working class and worked in low-level jobs rather than in decision-making, and were therefore mainly involved in front line and manual work.

Time: 12.24 a.m. Good morning, diary!

Tuesday, 19 May 2020
Fifty-eighth day of lockdown

> ***In the news***: Chancellor Rishi Sunak has said the UK scheme to pay wages of workers on leave because of coronavirus will be

extended to October. In addition, he has said it's very likely the UK is in a significant the financial crisis.

There was bright sunshine outside the window again this morning, as if the weather is telling us that there is hope for things to come. From 10 a.m. to 11 a.m., I had to watch the Panopto recording of one of my university lectures. Just time to have a quick snack and a drink before preparing for my next class.

At 1 p.m., I attended the Crime and Offending class, week 10, and had a deadline for an assignment. There were no special topics in the class, but I enjoyed taking part in the group discussion and was able to upload the assignment afterwards.

At 3 p.m., the Law, Society, and Social Control class began. For the last module, there was a guest speaker on the subject of law and society, and it was very interesting to listen to his talk.

At 5 p.m., I needed to have a short break and fresh air, so I joined the online yoga for an hour and went into the garden to water the new nursery. Then I was ready to take the last class of the day.

I had to print out my homework for the 7 p.m. English language class on Zoom that I attended today. Students from all over the world attend this particular class, even though the time differences vary dramatically from midnight to early morning.

After finishing my classes, I checked the BBC News and extracted some relevant information on the subject of BAME deaths. Apparently, a disproportionate number of ethnic minority deaths and hospitalisation have been recorded during the pandemic in London.

There are many underlying reasons for this high rate of deaths, including health issues, living conditions, and low-paying work, often on the front line. While there is no conclusive evidence that minority groups are more at risk from the disease, some are more likely to have certain underlying health conditions like diabetes. Black people are more likely to be overweight than the rest of the population, according to the evidence gathered so far. Many Asian and Black people have been found to have a higher risk of heart disease, both of which have been linked to higher coronavirus death rates. This official national statistical data impacted heavily on my mind, leaving me feeling very insecure about staying in the UK, but we currently have no choice.

The death toll from Covid-19 rose by 545 today, more than double the previous day, for an overall total of 35,341.

Time: 10.40 p.m.

Wednesday, 20 May 2020
Fifth-ninth day of lockdown

It was announced today that the families of overseas NHS support staff and care workers who have died with coronavirus can now stay in the UK permanently if they decide to do so.

The weather was very hot today, with clear sunshine. I attended my protocol lesson from 10.30 a.m. to noon. After that, I cleaned and disinfected the house and ate my daily portion of fruits before I sat down to work on my assignment. There was no chance to draw a second breath. I kept reading and typing, although my right arm has ached since last week.

From 1 to 5 p.m., I spent time reading and researching information before typing it up. I completed a draft essay and then emailed it to my Criminal Justice System lecturer. I found that drug use in UK prisons was a huge problem.

According to the data from the UK parliament (2012), 70 per cent of offenders had a previous records of drug misuse, and 51 per cent were drug dependent. Another 36 per cent were heavy drinkers, and a further 35 per cent admitted injecting various drugs. Finally, 16 per cent had gone to prison for alcohol dependency. This is very depressing. Prison Reform Trust (2012) conducted a survey of prisoners and found that 19 per cent had used heroin the first time in prison.

At 5 p.m., I needed to have a short break and some fresh air. After that, I did yoga exercises for one hour.

From 6.30 8.30 p.m., I spent time on the protocol of my dissertation. I had dinner with the family before my husband went on night duty.

The number of confirmed coronavirus deaths rose by 363 today, less than the previous day, for a total of 35,704.

More than 35 councils in England have warned that not all of their primary schools will be ready to reopen on 1 June. I think I'm not ready to send my children to school so soon. But education and social skills are so important for children, and I recognise this.

Time: 12.00 a.m.

✎ Thursday, 21 May 2020
Sixtieth day of lockdown

Heat and sunshine early in the morning. The birdsong was lovely, but I could hardly hear it because of the shouting from the mothers and children outside. I just peeped out from the window, then started to do my normal housework.

I kept reading and typing, although my right arm has hurt since last week. I made a homemade smoothie drink with apple, banana, grapes, blackberries, and milk for my family in the short break.

I spent 90 minutes with my teacher from 2 to 3.30 p.m. for basic guidance protocol work which was pending since last week. I had been focusing on recent assignment deadlines and therefore, it was getting late. Currently, the title of my dissertation is as "Hidden domestic violence against Black, South Asian, and minority ethnic (BSAME) women in the UK". The aim of this proposal is to investigate and explore the issues underlying hidden domestic violence against BSAME women in the UK. This is a very topical issue at the moment, and the aims will be to examine the current strategies used by the government. Local services have suffered from recent cutbacks, and these measures have had an adverse effect on BSAME women who are subjected to domestic violence.

The objective of the final project will be to add to the academic literature already existing on the continuing violence against BSAME women and, in so doing, add to the growing amount of evidence from abuse victims and survivors. It will also hopefully provide greater opportunities for exploration of this complex subject.

Afterwards, I focused on the use of drugs in prisons in the UK for 30 minutes. I took a short break before preparing a light meal whilst on my break. Unfortunately, I had to miss yoga because of my protocol work.

I'm feeling so sad at the news that hundreds of thousands of people are losing their lives to coronavirus every day. Their ages range from 5 to 108 and cover a wide spectrum, from a retired policeman to a shoe designer to an eccentric aristocrat and a vicar. Their names are released and their stories all-too-briefly told by the heartbroken relatives left behind.

On the international scene, in the Brazilian city of São Paulo, they are apparently digging more graves than normal. On an average day, they bury about 40 bodies at the cemetery and 60 on the weekend. But now the municipality has bought 5,000 body bags, and they are hiring more gravediggers because of Covid-19.

Along with the rest of my road, we joined in the weekly clapping for NHS and front line workers.

The number of confirmed coronavirus deaths rose by 338 today, less than the previous day, for a total of 36,042. The UK now has the second highest number of recorded deaths in the world, with Brazil in third position.

Time: 10 p.m.

Friday, 22 May 2020
Sixty-first day of lockdown

> ***In the news***: It was revealed that Dominic Cummings, the prime minister's chief adviser, travelled hundreds of miles from London to County Durham during the lockdown when he had coronavirus symptoms. This is strictly against the current rules, but the prime minister refused to criticise him. Other people who have broken rules have paid hefty fines.

This morning, it was hot and sunny early in the morning. The birds were singing, and I could hear the children shouting outside again, as many of them still cannot go to school. I just peeped out from the window, then started to check my homework before starting my class. I played back the last recorded call on the answerphone and heard a message from my dad. He told me that he was in a great deal of pain. He is still recovering from his recent stay in hospital in Hong Kong.

From 10 a.m. to noon, I focused on drug use in prisons and treatment in the UK for my assignment. I found that an astonishing number of drug offences occurred due to outside suppliers smuggling drugs into prisons. In 2016, there were 102,000 drug offences, together with warnings for the use of cannabis. Of these, 9,000 out of 102,000 offenders were sent to jail, and 2.88 per cent went to prison for supplying drugs. According to the research, 71 per cent of prisoners were involved with class A drugs, 28 per cent with class B, and 1 per cent with class C.

From noon to 2 p.m., I joined my Zoom class, as it was the last week of this module (Corporate crime and Corporate Responsibility). The new furlough system, which came into effect because of Covid-19, will be studied after ten years as history. The lecturer ended the session by thanking all the students for their continued attendance and support during this difficult time.

From 2 to 3 p.m., I attended a Criminal Justice System class for the last week of this module. We had a guest speaker from another university.

From 3 to 4.30 p.m., I had to complete my protocol basic guidance in order to meet the deadline set by my dissertation supervisor. This made me feel stressed for the rest of the day.

From 5 to 6 p.m., I sorted out and organised all documents of protocol, then emailed them to my dissertation supervisor. After that, I went out for fresh air and checked the back-garden vegetables.

I have had a headache all day today. There was no chance to take a breath owing to my busy routine and the pandemic situation. I cannot imagine how people cope with the sadness and shock from the rising death toll. It makes me sad and depressed when I hear of every death.

The number of confirmed coronavirus deaths rose by 351 today, less than the previous day, for a total of 36,393.

Time: 12.06 a.m.

Saturday, 23 May 2020
Sixty-second day of lockdown

I cannot believe where the time has gone during these last sixty days of lockdown.

It is chilly and windy, with sunshine early in the morning. Today, there were no children in the street, although it is Saturday. I checked on

Facebook Messenger and found a miscall from my dad. I contacted him and had a chat both with him and my mum. This time, we were able to talk for longer, and I encouraged him to take his medication, exercise, and eat sensibly.

From 1 to 4 p.m., I joined in a global network conference on Zoom with Dr Marohang Limbu, a professor from the University of Michigan in the United States, together with many doctors, intellectuals, and academics from around the world. We discussed the history of Nepali literature from its early beginnings. I have learnt that Latin forms the basis for 120 different languages. We also discussed how the rights of certain indigenous people are being eroded on a daily basis. I wasn't able to attend yoga on Zoom today due to this conference.

After the meeting, I had a light lunch and then focused on work again. I learnt about the new UK drug policy. The House of Commons (2019) has now reclassified cannabis from class one to class two under the Misuse of Drug Regulation 2001 because cannabis is beneficial for therapeutic treatment. The chief medical officer and the Advisory Council on the Misuse of Drugs have conducted two reviews and legalised the use of this particular drug with medical approval. This means that it can be made available legally.

Medical cannabis is developed from the cannabis tree, and it is mixed with more than 100 chemicals. These are known as *cannabinoids*, *cannabidiol (CBB)*, and *tetrahydrocannabinol (THC)*. They are used to treat a wide range of medical symptoms and conditions—for instance, chronic pain in adults, induced nausea, vomiting chemotherapy, multiple sclerosis, and epilepsy. However, it is not easily available, and most of it is still unlicensed.

I went jogging with my family for 90 minutes, as we have not been able to do this for many days. Many people were walking with dogs and their families. The time was late evening, but we still managed to fit in a very lengthy run. People were scared to come near us, and on a number of occasions, we had to cross to the opposite side of the road to avoid people. It was a very strange situation, because everyone wanted to avoid contact.

After going jogging, I felt refreshed in my mind, and I didn't need to take any paracetamol today.

The number of confirmed coronavirus deaths rose by 282, less than the previous day, for a total of 36,675. The first death from Covid-19 was on 5 March 2020. It is now two months since lockdown started on 23 May 2020. So, it is a huge loss of people during that very short time in the UK.

✎ Sunday, 24 May 2020
Sixty-third day of lockdown

> ➤ **In the news**: The prime minister has confirmed that there will be a phased reopening of schools in England to start on 1 June as planned.

I went to work in the Royal Military Academy Sandhurst. There were all new officer cadets. We had to serve food, as they are in quarantine for two weeks. I had to wash my hands every time as well as use hand sanitiser and wear a mask. There was a clear understanding and adherence to the rules of social distancing. Some of the cadets, though, came too near when I was serving them. This made me feel nervous about me or them catching the virus.

There were no new disposable gloves, and staff had to bring them from home rather than reuse them. I was just thinking of Asian countries where governments distributed individual PPE and food for the public, but the UK government has not provided those kinds of facilities for the general public. Even Covid-19 tests are not readily available yet, although I'm a key worker for this company. It is very difficult to manage two meters social distancing at work and group or team work. I think if everyone had done a virus test and antibody test like in China, Korea, and Hong Kong, it would be easier and safer to work.

I did not eat any food and fruits at work, because I'm not 100 per cent sure how of hygienic the cleaning is in a big kitchen in a military camp. To be quite safe, I arrived home and disinfected my uniform and myself before going into the house.

I'm scared to send my children to school and university when schools reopen on the first of June. How do I know all the teachers and children have no coronavirus? The general public have not been tested for the virus yet, although nearly 37,000 people have died so far.

The death toll from Covid-19 has now risen by 121 to 36,796

Monday, 25 May 2020
Sixty-fourth day of lockdown

> ***In the news***: Dominic Cummings, adviser to UK PM Boris Johnson, is facing calls to resign after he travelled 260 miles during lockdown.

It's warm and sunny early this morning. Birds are singing, but there are no children and mums out due it being a bank holiday Monday. Between 9 a.m. and 2 p.m., I focused on coursework because I had an essay deadline. I uploaded my submission into Turnitin before 4 p.m. This shows whether there are too many similarities of work in the essay to the original sources. I had to rush to complete this essay and start a new one for the next assignment.

I joined yoga on Zoom for an hour to breathe in some fresh air through the open windows and practice good breathing. It's hard to maintain one's peace of mind at the moment; one is always thinking about the virus and is scared to go out unless for a special reason.

I wanted to be tested for antibodies but couldn't just buy it from a shop. My thoughts and feelings are always with the victims of Covid-19. We keep on with the family hygiene routine.

The UK PM's chief adviser Dominic Cummings has said he doesn't regret his behaviour during lockdown. His statement follows allegations that he broke lockdown rules by travelling 260 miles with his family to be near relatives when his wife developed coronavirus symptoms. The PM Boris Johnson has attempted to draw a line under the row, but MPs have continued to call for Mr Cummings' dismissal.

The death toll from Covid-19 rose by 118 today, less than the previous day, bringing the total to 36,914. Perhaps I should mention, though, that on Mondays, the death toll is usually lower because not all the figures have come in. The USA has the highest number of recorded coronavirus deaths in the world with 97,460, the UK has the second highest, and Brazil the third—22,666 within a very short time. At least 4.3 million people are known to have been infected with the coronavirus worldwide, and 295,671 people have died.

These figures, collected by Johns Hopkins University, are, they say, likely to be a great underestimate of the true scale of the pandemic. To think that the first death from Covid-19 in the UK occurred just under three months ago, on 5 March 2020. Since then, so many people have died from this horrible disease.

🖉 Tuesday, 26 May 2020
Sixty-fifth day of lockdown

> ➢ ***In the news***: Conservative Junior Minister Douglas Ross has resigned after Dominic Cummings' defence of his trip to County Durham during the coronavirus lockdown.

The weather was very hot and dry. I set the alarm clock, and I started research relating to the Grenfell Tower disaster and Corporate Crime, my first task of the morning. My cat was playing outside in the garden and caught a baby bird. My son rescued the baby robin, brought it inside, and asked me how to look after it and save its life. He started to search on Google as to how to look after birds. I reminded him that the baby robin would really be missing its mum, and its mum might be coming back with a full beak of food for her baby.

I submitted my assignment on drug use in prison, part of the Criminal Justice System module. I took a short break and went out into the garden to pick vegetables and check the nursery.

I started to write 300 words for an assignment for a case study about Grenfell Tower. The Grenfell Tower disaster, which took place on 14 June 2017, caused 72 deaths, and 227 people escaped the blaze. This was the worst disaster during UK peacetime since the nineteenth century.

From 7 to 9 p.m., I attended a Zoom English class, and then I had dinner with the family. I contacted my youngest brother in Nepal to update the family about Covid-19.

I heard very bad news on Nepal News about the killing of a young boy of low caste who fell in love with a higher-caste girlfriend in the western part of Nepal. Not only was the young boy killed but also some of his friends. In remote areas of Nepal, acts of caste discrimination are actually condoned. This is tragic, and the acts must be punished by law.

I wish I could get a coronavirus test or an antibody gene injection from the chemist shop or from my GP. I wonder why people stare at me when I wear a mask and they don't bother, although the UK is the second-worst Covid -19-affected country in the world.

Every day, there is more news from 10 Downing Street about this critical situation. I always check the late news to update the death toll. Today, the death toll from from Covid-19 rose by 134, bringing the total to 37,048.

Wednesday, 27 May 2020
Sixty-sixth day of lockdown

> There have been more than 260,000 confirmed cases of coronavirus in the UK and more than 37,000 people have lost their lives, according to government figures. It is heartbreaking and humbling, this tragic story of lockdown.

Dad called me on Facebook messenger from Hong Kong and updated me about his health, and I talked with Mum a bit longer before lunchtime. I have begun the second phase of my research. I have learned about the Corporate Manslaughter and Corporate Homicide Act, which was introduced in 2008 across England and Wales. This act can be used to prosecute companies suspected of an individual person's or a number of persons' death.

The police investigated the Grenfell Tower disaster and reported that there were "reasonable grounds to suspect" Kensington and Chelsea council, and senior management of the organisation, of wrongdoing. They will have to submit to a police interview regarding their possible committing of the crime of corporate manslaughter. It is a fairly new crime act under UK law. For prosecution to be successful, the company needs to be proven accountable rather than an individual.

I felt so tired, and my neck and right hand were aching, so I joined yoga on Zoom for an hour and 15 minutes. The meditation and yoga exercises helped me to feel fresh, happy, and optimistic. My youngest daughter cooked dinner because she didn't have a class.

Many preschool children are making noise and celebrating a lockdown-free day. My house is near to the preschool, so I can always hear all the activities of the children and the teacher. This reminds me of my experience back home teaching and head teaching in a primary school in Nepal. I still remember my students and their names and how they always looked forward to Teacher's Day once a year. I really miss them and my job there!

The death toll from Covid-19 has now risen by 412 to 37,460.

Thursday, 28 May 2020
Sixty-seventh day of lockdown

> ***In the news***: It's the first day back for children at preschool; Coronavirus UK's tenth—and possibly final—clap for NHS and key workers; lockdown restrictions are gradually being eased in parts of the UK.

It was a warm and sunny morning; birds were singing a lovely song. The weather was so hot and dry. I washed and brushed my teeth, then I started to read and type my assignment relating to the Grenfell Tower disaster for my Corporate Crime module, step by step, from morning until 1.30 p.m.

I took short break for lunch and went out for fresh air for around an hour. My dad called me on Messenger and told me that he has not been getting any better. I suggested to him to have regular medication, and that would help him to settle down.

From 2 to 3 p.m., I looked for the link for the email address to upload my proposal and documents. I listened to the BFBS Gurkha Radio and include a few pieces of information.

The caste system and patriarchal culture is still playing vital role in certain communities in Nepal due to the Hindu religion (four types of Barana system: Brahaman, Kshetri, Baishna, and Sudra). I heard some very sad news from the western part of Nepal about the deaths of five Dalit (low caste/untouchable) youths in the District of Rukum.

The Nepal chapter of Amnesty International has called on the Nepali authorities to immediately and effectively investigate the deaths of five Dalits youths in Rukum (West) and ensure justice to the victims. The same day, in Rukum (West), a group of 18 young men, many of them belonging to the Dalit community, was attacked by a village mob from a dominant caste who chased them to the edge of the Bheri River.

The bodies of five men were discovered over the next five days. One other man remains missing. Human rights is still not established in this area, and therefore many communities and tribes are suffering from hierarchy. That mean only 135 out of the whole population of tribe people have ruled Nepal since Nepal became a named country.

There are so many social activists who are working very hard to abolish this inequality and unfairness in Nepali society. I also have been concerned about this matter for a long time, and how it has happened throughout this Covid-19 lockdown time.

Lockdown restrictions are gradually being eased in parts of the United Kingdom. From this coming Monday in England, we will be able to meet with up to six people from different households outside, either in parks or now in private gardens, as long as we remain 2 meters (6 feet) apart. For example, you could have a barbecue in someone's back garden.

I do check the news late at night to see what the updated death toll is. It rose by 377, and the total as of today is 37,837. USA is the first in the world, and the UK has the second highest number of recorded coronavirus deaths in the world. Brazil is third in the world.

I still remember the first day I heard that someone had died from Covid-19. It was in the Royal Berkshire Hospital in Reading— a 70-year-old woman. It is tragic and terrible to lose so many people within the past three months. The first death from Covid-19 was 5 March 2020, which was three months ago.

Time: 12.03 a.m.

Friday, 29 May 2020
Sixty-eigth day of lockdown

> ***In the news***: First day of open preschool after lockdown.

I set my alarm clock, and I had to miss Zoom yoga. I felt so stressed due to my assignment deadline and continuing everyday life.

I checked the news later that day to see the updated death toll. The Covid-19 death toll rose by 324 today, less than the previous day, for a total of 38,161. It is huge loss of people in the pandemic time.

Time: 1.09 a.m.

✎ Saturday, 30 May 2020
Sixty-ninth day of lockdown

> ***In the news***: The private rocket company SpaceX has sent two NASA astronauts into orbit. It's the first time since the retirement of the shuttles nine years ago that an American crew has made the journey from US land. Two US astronauts are set to make a world first when they launch to the International Space Station (ISS) aboard a spacecraft built by Elon Musk's SpaceX. BBC News profiled the crew members.

I cannot imagine: how did we go all these sixty-nine days of lockdown in the UK?

The weather was very hot, and the sun was shining very early in the morning. On one side, I can hear the birds are singing, and on the other side, I can hear the children playing outside with their mothers.

I just took shower and worshiped as usual, although I'm very distracted due to regular deadlines of my assignments. My right arm has been aching for the last two months, but I have no time for rest due to my assignment deadlines.

I set my alarm clock for every hour to speed up my work. I have to finish my research and draft by today, so I really concentrated on my work to the point that I forgot to have a glass of water until 4 p.m.

I had fruit after I completed my reading and making a draft of my assignment. I went outside and had some fresh air for 30 minutes. I checked the garden to look at my vegetables. I cooked dinner and sat down and ate it with my family. I always follow my time-planning and priority-setting, depending on the situation and my work schedule. I missed yoga exercise on Zoom due to my priorities.

After my cleaning job was done, I cooked lunch as well. My husband was off today.

I was able to research the Grenfell Tower fire, which happened on 14 June 2017. Based on the Corporate Manslaughter and Corporate Homicide Act 2007, there was a public inquiry to look into the disaster, accompanied by public and media pressure. They needed to act and look at what had happened.

According to the latest figures from the CPS, nineteen companies have been charged with corporate manslaughter since the law was established in 2008. New guidelines have been introduced in the last year, and this act is expected to lead to high-level charges for bigger companies and organisations that may lead to convictions.

Lawyers have been carrying out the public enquiry for the past 18 months, and the second phase of the inquiry is ongoing. This includes enquiries into the primary refurbishment, cladding products, complaints, and communication with residents; the management of Grenfell Tower; and compliance.

The act of prosecuting for corporate manslaughter over the Grenfell disaster would be a tough task. Prosecutors would have to be convicted in the court that "the council or the tenancy management organisation owed a relevant duty of care", a public body would be working out public functions, and a statutory corporation would be set up for handling social housing. They would have to demonstrate that a gross breach happened with a particular person. He/she could be a councillor or director who has been acting the way that straight led to the deaths.

The NHS and key workers are still pleading for personal protective equipment. It is true: if health workers are not safe, how will they save patients?

It's incredibly sad that people grieving for friends or family taken by Covid-19 are also experiencing the shock of a loved one dying suddenly, often after a very short period of illness. Government restrictions are attempting to slow and control the coronavirus. Social distancing and self-isolation have caused many people to be unable to spend time with their loved ones who are dying, or spend time with their loved one's body afterwards, or hold a normal memorial gathering. I cannot imagine how they can cope with a situation like this.

The death toll from Covid-19 rose by 215 today, less than the previous day, bringing the total of 38,376.

🖉 Sunday, 31 May 2020
Seventieth day of lockdown

> ➤ **In the news**: George Floyd's death: Lawyer calls it "premeditated murder" in USA.
>
> Violence has broken out again in the US as protests continue across the country over the killing of an unarmed black man by police in the state on Minnesota on Monday. It reminds me of the London riots of 2011 as to why and how this protest was breaking out. George Floyd died in police custody while an officer kneeled on his neck to pin him down.
>
> A lawyer for the family of George Floyd, whose death sparked unrest across the US, has accused a police officer of "premeditated murder". For many the outrage over George Floyd's death also reflects years of frustration over socio-economic inequality and segregation, not only in Minneapolis.

I woke up earlier than usual. The weather was getting cold, although there was clear sunshine outside the window. I was concentrating on my current assignment, but luckily, I remembered the previous module and quickly checked my diary and found that the deadline is also the same as the latest essay.

I had to give myself five minutes and just change my dress and get ready for work. New officer cadets are coming back from quarantine, but we have to be careful and make sure that we use double masks and gloves and continue to carry on our work. I could not talk to them and be friendly and happy as usual. No time to talk to parents and families today.

At 2 p.m., I finished work, and I came back to home at 3 p.m. I started to focus on my coursework without talking to my family. I just kept searching and typing constantly until 9 p.m. Then I had dinner, which was made by my husband. I spent thirty minutes with my family whilst I had dinner.

At work, everyone had a mask, and that made me glad. It reminded me of when I was in a normal dental nursing job. Back then, I wouldn't want to wear a mask outside of work. Why? Because I wore 200 pairs of gloves and 30 masks at work. Therefore, I did not want to wear one outside of the surgery.

I have updated all new cases of Covid-19 between staffs. It was found that doctors' and nurses' families are in quarantine and they could not come to work. At work, it is very difficult to control new social-distancing maintenance because new cadets have to quarantine two weeks at the beginning of when their first term starting point to save each other.

Sometimes I think I'm not anymore human due to all these situations. Everyone is scared to come close and has lost trust. This Covid-19 has ruined millions of people's lives and dreams.

The death toll from Covid-19 rose by 113 today, less than the previous day, bring the total to 38,489.

I'm able to type a short diary, although I'm very stressed due to my many assignments. It must mean I really love doing it.

Time 11.58 a.m.

June 2020

🖉 Monday, 1 June 2020
Seventy-first day of lockdown

I woke up earlier than usual. The weather was getting colder, although the sun was shining outside the window.

I was concentrating fully on my current assignments. My right arm and neck were aching seriously, and I had no time to talk to my parents and family today. I even forgot to eat a sliced apple which was made by my youngest child and offered to me.

I started to focus on my work without talking to family and just kept searching and typing constantly from 7 a.m. until 9 p.m., then I had dinner, which was made by husband. I spent 20 minutes with my family whilst I had dinner and went back to work until late, 12.30 a.m., then uploaded on the university similarity check.

I'm not good at IT skills. Therefore, sometimes I make mistakes without knowing, and I get myself upset. I was not born with it.

I cannot think of any good thing today. I have tried to put a few words in this diary to keep a regular record of my typing and making it a habit.

The death toll from Covid-19 rose by 111 today, just two less than the previous day, bringing the total to 38,600.

Time 00:10 am

🖉 Tuesday, 2 June 2020
Seventy-second day of lockdown

> ***In the news***: President Donald Trump has threatened to send in the military to quell growing civil unrest in the US over the death of a black man in police custody. He said if cities and states failed to control the protests and "defend their residents," he would deploy the army and "quickly solve the problem for them." Protests over the death of George Floyd have escalated over the past week.

Presidential candidate Joe Biden criticised Mr Trump on Tuesday for "serving the passions of his base ... We're not going to allow any president to quiet our voice," the Democrat said, referencing the US constitution, which guarantees protestors' freedom to assemble.

On Tuesday, the Las Vegas sheriff said an officer died in a shooting after police attempted to disperse a crowd. Dozens of people have been injured as authorities used tear gas and force to disperse protests, which have swept more than 75 cities.

This incident made me feel scared to be part of an ethnic minority group and what will happen in the future in the 21st century. We created laws to stop death from racism happening, yet it still happens.

I woke up earlier than usual. My right arm and neck continue to ache seriously. I emailed many departments within the university to inquire about resubmitting my assignment. Because I thought today was the last deadline, I was panicking. I could not find the email notice and assessment folder; therefore, I kept emailing my personal supervisor, class teacher, and help desk at the sociology department all morning until 11 a.m.

Finally, I reached my module teacher, and he clearly told me that it was 100 per cent not today. It will be in August, so I am now less stressed. I focused on my final essay for four hours. There was a lot to do at this time. I typed continually whilst I kept checking the time on my computer, and the time was flying faster than the wind. I needed another two or three hours, but it was not possible.

I even forgot to pull the curtains open on the near window and did not realise how hot it was, and I was constantly sweating. My husband helped to close the curtains to make me feel cooler, and my son brought me a cold glass of water. I did not have any food, apart from the glass of water, because there is so much work to be completed.

At 4 p.m., I submitted my essay and went out to the back garden to look after my vegetables and play with the cat for a few minutes. I grabbed some fresh air and then went back inside.

At 5 p.m., I checked all the reading links for my next essay that was due on the same day next week, and I did my homework for 30 minutes. I joined my Zoom class for English. After my class, the family was waiting for me to have dinner with them.

The death toll from Covid-19 rose by 324, almost three times more deaths than the previous day, bringing the total to 38,924.

I'm able to type a short diary today, although I was busy with many new assignments, and I really love it. Now it's time for me to brush my teeth and have a shower and go to bed.

Time: 12.45 a.m.

Wednesday, 3 June 2020
Seventy-third day of lockdown

> ***In the news***: Thousands of mostly young protesters have marched through central London in an overwhelmingly peaceful Black Lives Matter demonstration that culminated in passionate crowds gathering at the heart of Westminster. They persuaded two police officers to "take the knee" outside the gates of Downing Street in a mark of respect to American George Floyd and other black victims of police violence in the late afternoon, prompting cheers from the crowd present.

It is the twenty-first century; can you imagine that people are discriminating against people of race and colour? I feel insecure to be a British citizen and a person with an ethnic background and life within the UK at this current time.

I set my alarm clock for 7.30 a.m., and then at hour intervals, to account for my studies and get more information. I have to work really hard to complete my essay due to the short time span. At 2 p.m., I went out to the back garden to look after vegetables and play with the cat for a few minutes. I went back into the house to prepare a mixed fruit, which had strawberries, blackberries, and apple with milk, and I ate it whilst I was typing.

At 5 p.m., I checked all my reading links for the essay due next week, and I did homework for 30 minutes. I was tired from reading and typing on assignments during the whole lockdown time; both my arms and neck were sore, and I lost concentration, so I asked for help from my son to copy the book for a few pages.

Due to lockdown, I could not access the reading material enough. I tried to search according to the teacher's reading list, but most of them I could not find online. There are very limited resources when I cannot access the library at the university.

I checked BBC News at the end of the day to see the daily update for the number of people with confirmed coronavirus who died. The number has risen by 359, more deaths again than the previous day. The death toll as of today is 39,283.

I'm able to type a short diary today, although I'm very busy with my assignment. I had a thirty-minute rest whilst my son helped me to copy 3,000 words. He is a lot quicker than I am because he is used to using technology.

Time: 1.11 a.m.

Thursday, 4 June 2020
Seventy-fourth day of lockdown

I realised that I did not wash my face this morning and began laughing out loud due to waking up and straight away beginning to work on a 3,000-word essay. I completely forgot.

I set my alarm clock for 8 a.m. and at hourly intervals. I do this to make me conscious of my time, and to make me work harder and faster. I have to work really hard to complete this essay due to the short time frame for this assignment.

Whilst I was writing my assignment on how the media influences us, I was reading a news article in the *Guardian* (2020) and found that the media plays an important role in what news is distributed and what the public sees and takes in. For example, the case of George Floyd is an example of the ideal criminal and the ideal victim. The video clearly shows that the officer wanted to kill him with a plan, because Floyd told the officers that he could not breath twelve times and he was about to die. He called out his mother, although the officer has not stopped punishing him.

The death of George Floyd at the hands of a white policeman led to outcries from the public and calls for justice. However, since then, riots and looting has overtaken the news and media reporting. With reporting changing its perception of the ideal victim and the ideal criminal and by covering stories of lack of social control, vandalism, violent protests, and anti-police attitudes, the self-fulfilling prophecy takes place, in which the public, protesters, and those calling for justice are branded as the troublemakers.

This relates to Cohen's theory about the "folk devils", as the protesters and those speaking up against police violence are seen as a threat to social values and morals and social order, and this is reinforced by news reporting.

I wanted to include this knowledge from what I was currently doing. It will remind me what I was doing at this time and also, I might forget all the knowledge that I learned from my university course.

The George Floyd incident was a big influence on my assignment, due to it being very relevant to me personally. The fact that racism and social disorder is still happening in the world caused this man to die. We are told that people are protected from discrimination, but the George Floyd murder shows that this isn't true.

The death toll from Covid-19 rose by 176, less than the previous day, bringing the total to 39,459.

Time: 1.26 a.m.

Friday, 5 June 2020
Seventy-fifth day of lockdown

> ***In the news***: The World Health Organization (WHO) has changed its advice on face masks, saying they should be worn in public to help stop the spread of coronavirus. The global body said new information showed they could provide "a barrier for potentially infectious droplets."
>
> Some countries around the world already recommend or mandate the wearing of face coverings in public. The WHO had previously argued there was not enough evidence to say that healthy people should wear masks.

However, Dr Maria Van Kerkhove, the WHO's technical lead expert on Covid-19, told the Reuters news agency that the recommendation was for people to wear a "fabric mask—that is, a non-medical mask." Yet the total death toll today is up to 40,261.

The weather was getting and colder and colder, although it was quite sunny outside. I was concentrating too much on my current assignment, and my right arm and neck were aching badly. No time to talk to parents and family today. I just didn't have enough time to relax and devote to family due to regular deadlines.

I set the alarm to ring every hour from 8.30 a.m. to 12.30 p.m. to account for my study and getting information. I had to work really hard to complete my other essay due to the lack of time. I wanted to include a little information from my daily studies. My research for today was *Tough on Crime* by Tim Newburn (2020), which explored tough-on-crime theory and tendencies in crime and punitive policy procedure in England and Wales. The key issue in this period was political and concerned with media after the Second World War. Crime was regularly on the increase until the mid-1970s, and dual-party penal policies and law and order were beginning to unravel. Reiner (2000) suggests that crime continued to increase in England and Wales until the mid-1990s, and violent crime continued to rise.

Two-year-old James Bulger was brutally murdered in February 1993, and the majority of the public were worried about the increasing crime. The murder was shocking news for both political parties and encouraged them to come together with a tougher approach to crime. Moreover, Tony Blair had been appointed shadow home secretary in 1992 and delivered a powerful "speech-cum-sermon". Furthermore, Michael Howard at the Conservative Party conference in 1993 had outlined the government's new criminal justice policy.

The death toll from Covid-19 rose by 357 today, more than the previous day, bringing the total to 39,816.

Time: 1.06 a.m.

✎ Saturday, 6 June 2020
Seventy-sixth day of lockdown

> Today, thousands turned out for the UK anti-racism protest in London and in many other places in the UK. The protests, sparked by the death of George Floyd in the US, were held in cities including London, Manchester, Cardiff, Leicester, and Sheffield. In London, protesters knelt for a minute's silence before chanting "no justice, no peace" and "black lives matter".
>
> The majority of the day's protests were peaceful, but, in the evening, there were disturbances outside Downing Street. BBC correspondent Chi Chi Izundu said some demonstrators started throwing bottles and a riderless police horse bolted, trampling a demonstrator.
>
> The Metropolitan Police said 14 people were arrested and 10 officers were injured after a smaller group became "angry and intent on violence." It is lockdown because of the Covid-19 pandemic, but people are protesting that racism is much worse than coronavirus.

I woke up, had a shower, and worshipped for a few minutes—my normal Saturday routine. I set the alarm clock at hourly intervals to pace for my study and getting information. After I had managed to write a draft of my essay, I decided to join the yoga class, because I had been missing it for a long time due to continuing coursework.

Here is another part of my research from today: A key feature of contemporary societies is the omnipresence of mass media of communication, in rapidly proliferating new forms. A significant part of each day is devoted by most people to media consumption of various kinds. This comes home to me particularly now as well when we sometimes sit glued to our TV screens listening for information about Covid-19.

My research states furthermore that crime narratives and representations are, and have always been, a prominent part of the content of all mass media.

The death toll from Covid-19 rose by 204 today, less than the previous day, bringing the total to 40,020. The UK still has the second highest number of recorded coronavirus deaths in the world and the highest in the Europe.

Time: 1.58 a.m.

Sunday, 7 June 2020
Seventy-seventh day of lockdown

> - Second day of protest in the UK after death of George Floyd in the US. "A slave trader's statue in Bristol has been torn down and thrown into the river during a second day of anti-racism protests across the UK. Metropolitan Police Commissioner Cressida Dick urged protesters to find another way to make their views heard. But thousands of protesters in London are protesting outside the US Embassy for a second day. Protesters in Bristol used ropes to pull down the bronze statue of Edward Colston, a prominent 17th Century slave trader."

The ongoing power struggle, with democracy, and the ongoing education of the public, is needed. History is a constantly changing factor, and the public should be listened to on these issues.

The weather was getting colder, although it was clear sunshine outside. I brushed my teeth, took a shower, then started to type for my assignment. It was giving me so much stress. I was able to join on the Zoom programme with Dr Yogi Bikasananda's wellness programme speech from Nepal. I left the group early to join another Zoom group.

My daughter came back from her university and told me that she went to the protest about the death of George Floyd in the US. I was proud of her. At least she represented and showed her support for the fight against racism.

I started to focus on typing from 3 to 6 p.m. I was concentrating too much on my current assignment. I did not have enough time to do housework at this time due to regular deadlines. Here is some part of my research from today;

"Ideal criminal" is constructed by the media the case of Ahmaud Arbery is one example. According to *The Independent* (2018) an investigation of a videotape released that he was walking unarmed into an open building area with before jogging away but he was shot dead. It took three months for an arrest to take place once video footage was released of him innocently jogging and being shot dead. Between the incident and the arrests stories were circulated by the media about him being involved in criminal activities, creating a perception of him being "the ideal criminal". This is an example of how news reports and media amplify moral panic and can influence how the public see the victim, perpetrating a belief that a "criminal" is dangerous, even if he is innocent of a crime at the time. In relation to this, the way that the media creates moral panic and social regulation can be seen when exploring the issues of terrorism. The way that a Muslim terrorist is presented in the news is completely different from the way it reports incidents involving white terrorists. In the reporting of terrorism acts in which white people are involved, they are presented as having mental health issues. Because of this, they are not called terrorists in the news and this leads to the public creating an idea of the "ideal terrorist" being a Muslim terrorist.

Whilst I have been studying, I have found that many issues are relevant to what we see in the news today.

The death toll from Covid-19 rose by 77 today, bringing the total to 40,097. Today is the 100th day since the virus started. We have lost over 40,000 people within 100 days. It is a very serious life and health matter.

Time: 1.58 a.m.

✎ Monday, 8 June 2020
Seventy-eighth day of lockdown

> ➢ Boris Johnson has urged the country to "work peacefully, lawfully" to defeat racism and discrimination.

I decided to wake up a bit later today because I have been busy for the last three weeks on the same assessment and coursework. I cleaned the house, had tea, then sat down for work again, giving my essay its final check before uploading it to the university folder to check for similarities and submitting the real assignment.

After I had finished all my work, I sat down and began to watch the BBC News. It focused on UK Prime Minister and how he urged the country to "work peacefully and lawfully" to defeat racism and discrimination.

The PM said the government could not ignore the anger and "undeniable feeling of injustice" sparked by George Floyd's killing. But he said the cause was at risk of being "undermined" by a minority of those attacking police and property. The prime minister continued and said Mr Floyd's death had "awakened an anger and a widespread and incontrovertible, undeniable feeling of injustice, a feeling that people from black and minority ethnic groups do face discrimination: in education, in employment, in the application of the criminal law."

People riot and protest to express their feelings about social, economic, and political disorder, and there are many underlying reasons for this to happen in these incidents and events.

The killing of Georg Floyd is a symbol of social disorder in the UK and US which needs to be addressed and action taken quickly. It reminds me of a time in 2000 in the UK when there was barely an Asian face around the Kent area. I was discriminated against by many residents in a care home where I used to work at that time. I worked as a care assistant until one week before having my youngest daughter. Some residents were very rude and racist towards me. They used to call me the "black hair lady" as well as "half pint" all the time.

Society has changed so much compared to twenty years ago in the United Kingdom. This is due to people developing an understanding of what racism and discrimination are. Twenty years ago, it was OK to be openly racist to me, and this upset me. Today, due to people's education, this very rarely happens.

All the family decided to go for a walk to Long Valley Forest for two hours. There were more people than last time. We were scared to approach another person, so we just tried to walk on the opposite side of the road and field. The family dynamic will never be the same again, once you've separated from your loved ones in this situation.

The death toll from Covid-19 rose by 286 today, bringing the total to 40,383.

Time: 1.30 a.m. good morning, diary!

Tuesday, 9 June 2020
Seventy-ninth day of lockdown

> George Floyd's funeral hears calls for racial justice. The funeral for African American George Floyd, whose death in police custody caused global outrage, has heard impassioned pleas for racial justice. Texas lined up to remember a man whose "crime was that he was born black."
>
> One of Mr Floyd's nieces, Brooke Williams, called for a change in laws which, she argued, were designed to disadvantage black people. The laws were already put in place for the African-American system to fail. And these laws need to be changed. No more hate crimes, please! Someone said 'Make America Great Again,' but when has America ever been great?" His little daughter was there, the one who said "Daddy's going to change the world."

George Floyd's crime was being black. It was touching that his little girl spoke, but she had to lose a father for the world to change.

Birds were singing outside; a few cars were moving around because of the second phase of relaxed lockdown. I cleaned the house, had a glass of warm water, then sat down for work again. I focused on my proposal documents, but there were so many documents to write up today.

I had to inform my participants for my research entitled "Hidden domestic violence against Black South Asian minority ethnic (BSAME) women in the UK". I read and typed all day today until 7.00 p.m., then went on Zoom for my two-and-a-half-hour English class at 7 p.m. After that, I had dinner with my family. I watched the news and a documentary while having dinner. I did not have any free time for yoga and jogging today.

The death toll from Covid-19 rose by 286 today, more than the previous day, bringing the total to 40,669. I know this is a repetitive part of my diary, but the virus death toll changes every day. It is a constant reminder that this is what we are all battling.

Time: 11.49 pm.

Wednesday, 10 June 2020
Eightieth day of lockdown

> ***In the news***: Single people can stay the night with loved ones announced by the UK PM.

> People living alone in England will be able to stay at one other household as part of a further easing of coronavirus restrictions. No 10 said the change aims to help combat loneliness and that people are being trusted to observe the rules. Finally, grandparents could see their grandchildren, but cannot hug them.

> According to the Office for National Statistics, there were 8.2 million people living alone in the UK last year, with just under half aged 65 and over. There were also 2.9 million single-parent households.

It was another sunny but cold day, just like the rest of June. I cleaned the house, had tea, and then sat down for work again. I checked my proposal documents and wrote the gatekeeper request letter for the university ethics team.

I focused on the proposal documents, although there were so many documents to write up. I had to email my supervisor today. I read and typed all day today until 5.00 p.m., then went on Zoom for yoga exercise with the group. Then I started to research for the literature review. This literature section will show a range of sources which provide information and evidence supporting the underlying reasons behind domestic violence against BSAME women in the UK and suggesting alternative theories and strategies to support the aims I hope to achieve.

Under the BSAME section, I will explain BSAME women's experience of domestic violence, as well as the underlying reasons why they are unable to come and speak up and report their traumatic pain to the right agency. The dissertation will be divided into two categories: Black minority ethnic women (BME) and South Asian minority ethnic women (SAME), which will then create a working acronym of BSAME. This acronym is suitable because it captures the conditions of both categories of women in the UK.

Furthermore, the literature review will summarise some of the reading materials, journal articles, and texts used to conduct research and write my dissertation. It will also look at the interventionist work that has been carried out and how this can work for the future of BSAME women in the UK.

I had dinner with family whilst talking to friends and relatives to update them about coronavirus. The death toll from Covid-19 rose by 245 today, less than the previous day, bringing the total to 40,914. That's a loss of nearly 41,000 people in 103 days. This is a very serious matter of life and health. Even though the death rate is slowing down, it is still a worry for many people, including myself.

Time: 11.05 p.m.

Thursday, 11 June 2020
Eighty-first day of lockdown

> **In the news:** A report containing measures to protect ethnic minority groups from coronavirus has been drawn up for the government, BBC News has learned. This was in response to the Public Health England (PHE) report published last week confirming that coronavirus killed people from ethnic minorities at disproportionately high rates. However, a senior academic told

BBC News a second report, containing safeguarding proposals to tackle this, also existed. The PHE now says this report will be published next week. Labour described the decision not to immediately publish the second report as "scandalous and a tragedy". The PHE review already published had shown that people of Bangladeshi heritage were dying at twice the rate of white Britons, while other Black, Asian, and minority ethnic groups had a between 10 per cent and 50 per cent higher risk of death. However, the report had been widely criticised by MPs for not including any recommendations to protect these communities.

This report made me feel worried, being a person of ethnic background myself.

I woke up at 7 a.m. this morning and joined the lockdown isolation yoga for one hour. The weather was bright but breezy and with some rain. Birds were singing and sheltering under the trees, and my cat was on the prowl for birds.

I took shower after the yoga exercise and had a cup of tea and a bottle of water. I contacted Dad in Hong Kong, but he was still not very well. He had checked in many times at the hospital but was still not getting better. I can't stop thinking about him.

Again, I started to manage my folder of documents for my proposal because my supervisor had commented on a few points. I needed to correct them, and it took all day. I prepared the letter for the gatekeeper regarding my project interview. I have to do this to gain access whenever I interview participants for my dissertation.

Millions of people who have not been able to touch loved ones since lockdown began will be allowed to reunite with them from Saturday. It is true that people have lost trust with other people and family friends due to Covid-19.

I cooked a variety of foods for dinner, such as pork fry curry, green vegetables, dal soup, egg fry with mixed vegetables, salad, and drinks. We had ice cream for dessert. We watched a film while having dinner, but I could not finish seeing the full movie. I left halfway through because I had other stuff to do.

The death toll from Covid-19 rose by 151 today, less than the previous day, bringing the total to 41,065. The UK still has the second highest number of recorded deaths in the world.

Time 10.46 p.m.

✏️ Friday, 12 June 2020
Eighty-second day of lockdown

> ➤ **In the news**: Regarding Black Lives Matter, the police imposed conditions ahead of anti-racism protests.

It was already 7 a.m. when I woke, but I didn't feel rested, so I went back to bed for a while. I woke from my second sleep and started to clean the house.

I had to arrange for all my research participants to sign a consent sign form, which I then had to scan and send to the university ethics team. In actual fact, it took me all day to manage all the documents and my folder.

Restrictions have been placed by the police on several groups ahead of the planned protests in London this weekend. The Metropolitan Police said several protests are scheduled in the capital on Saturday, including a Black Lives Matter demonstration. But the police force warned protesters to reconsider attending at all due to the coronavirus pandemic.

"We are asking you not to come to London, and let your voices be heard in other ways," Met Commander Bas Javid said. The restrictions came in the wake of violence and serious disorder in Westminster at the end of protests the previous weekend. The demonstrations were on the whole peaceful, although there were dozens of arrests and 27 police officers were injured. Many people felt that protests and demonstrations should not take place in such a critical situation, and this was a symbol of social disorder and the disgrace for the nation.

Calls to remove "racist" Gandhi statue in Leicester: A petition to remove a statue of Mahatma Gandhi in Leicester has received nearly 5,000 signatures. The online petition accused the Indian independence campaigner of being "a fascist, racist and sexual predator".

Last year, students from Manchester called for a similar statue of Gandhi to be removed.

Time 11.22 p.m.

🖉 Saturday, 13 June 2020
Eighty-third day of lockdown

> ➢ ***In the news***: The Queen's official birthday has been marked with a unique ceremony performed by the Welsh Guard at Windsor Castle. The traditional Trooping of the Colour parade was cancelled because of the coronavirus pandemic. It is only the second time in her 68-year reign that the parade in London has not gone ahead. The Queen, flanked by officials, sat alone on a dais for the ceremony. It was her first official public appearance since lockdown began. The Queen celebrated her 94th birthday in April, but it is officially—and publicly—celebrated on the second Saturday of June every year.
>
> It is typically accompanied by the annual announcement of the Queen's Birthday Honours' List. However, this year she has "graciously agreed" to postpone publication of the list to the autumn. Prime Minister Boris Johnson said the delay in the honours list "will allow us to ensure that the list, agreed before this public health emergency developed, reflects the Covid-19 effort, and comes at a time when we can properly celebrate the achievements of all those included".

It was nice to have something other than the pandemic on television to watch, I enjoyed the change in the social media and routine, and it was nice to see Her Majesty on tele.

Weather was not too hot, and the sun was shining early in the morning. Birds are singing with a lovely song, and the mums and children are outside.

I cleaned the house, took a shower, and worshiped as usual. My eldest daughter prepared lunch for me, and I attended the global network Zoom interaction. The presentation was limbu chum lung cultural (mundhum), the holy part of South Asian indigenous culture. This was presented by Dr Kamal Tigela from Kathmandu Nepal. There were many doctors and senior position-holders from Nepal—for instance, former Journal of Nepal

Army, former CDO, scholars' rituals, and Kirat Yachting Chumlung Nepal EC teams. The aim of the presentation was to renovate a historic ritual holy book for all Limbu tribes in Nepal. The global network was hosted by Dr Marohang Limbu.

The death toll from Covid-19 rose by 181 today, bringing the total to 41,662. It is nearly the end of lockdown, but still people are dying from coronavirus, nearly 200 every day, and fear is still in our hearts. It feels scary to walk freely outside.

Time 11.42 p.m.

Sunday, 14 June 2020
Eighty-fourth day of lockdown

> ***In the news***: PM Boris Johnson has commissioned a review into the 2m social distancing rule, the chancellor has confirmed. Mr Johnson said there was "margin for manoeuvre" in the 2m rule as the number of coronavirus cases falls.

I heard on BBC radio news about third anniversary of the Grenfell Tower fire today. The survivors of Grenfell Tower fire, which killed 72 people, have said "nothing has changed" three years after the disaster. Those who escaped from the west London tower block said they feel "left behind" and "disgusted" by a lack of progress in making other buildings safe. Some 246 buildings still have aluminium composite material (ACM) cladding. Churches across London will ring their bells seventy-two times to mark those who died. The inferno at Grenfell—the biggest domestic blaze since the Second World War—started as a small kitchen fire.

It is very apt that this is the topic of today, as this is the main focus of my assignment. This is part of corporate crime. Many people lost their lives when they didn't need to, and no one has been held to account for this horrific crime. This is a very bad modern disaster, but it has taught corporations that they cannot get away with this situation.

I woke up 8 a.m., brushed my teeth, and had a shower, then got ready for work. My husband went to work early in the morning also. It was very quiet outside today, due to it being Sunday. I prepared the PPE in my bag, then drove to work at the Royal Military Academic Sandhurst. It was the first time I saw one of the staff members have a mask on in the college town gate office, but the rest of the people still have not worn one yet. The UK government has announced that compulsory mask wearing is to start tomorrow.

The staff prepared a special meal—dhido and sukiti gravy. That is a lockdown special organic meal, which is called national food. We took a picture to share in our group network.

All the staff workers were excited and had the food after they finished work, and everyone went home for three hours. I preferred to stay, because I took my laptop with me to do the research work I am currently working on:

> Women and girls from black and minority ethnic (BME) communities who have higher (some evidence suggests disproportionally higher) levels of domestic homicide, so-called "honour" killings, and abuse driven suicide. (Siddiqui and Patel, 2008) While cuts in legal aid, housing, policing, social services and welfare benefits have had a disproportionally negative and discriminatory impact on women, BME women and girls have faced the brunt.

All these points show that there is a negative view in the ethnic community to come forward and talk about these issues. They feel they have nowhere to go and no help.

I am concerned about social distancing and coronavirus. This is not possible due to the nature of my job.

All the staff came back to work from their break and worked another four hours, which was very intensive, and then we went back home.

My husband and I got home at 8 p.m. and decided to go out jogging with the three children. We saw many people in the field, and we always went in the opposite direction. We are scared to approach people due to the virus, and we have not meet close family, siblings, in-laws, or relatives since lockdown started. It has been 85 days since the beginning of lockdown.

We decided to go near the local area of Crookham Park Lake and Field in Fleet for one hour. I took a shower, and I felt very tired from my very long day at work. My hands, legs, and fingers are aching due to the very long hours of working.

The number of Covid-19 deaths rose by 36, much less than the previous day, for a total of 41,698.

Time 11.42 p.m.

🖉 Monday, 15 June 2020
Eighty-fifth day of lockdown

> ➢ ***In the news***: Non-essential shops opened for the first time in three months, and they attracted a lot of people to stay in queues for a long time. Some shoppers waited for more than an hour at retailers such as Primark, TJ Maxx, and Foot Locker. Retailers have taken safety measures familiar in supermarkets, such as plastic screens at tills and 2m floor markings for queueing.

Today we found out that domestic violence killings appeared to have more than doubled during the coronavirus lockdown. Karen Ingala Smith, who has been tracking the numbers of women killed by men for an annual census on femicide in the UK, has identified at least 16 suspected domestic abuse killings that occurred between 23 March and 12 April.

Ms Ingala Smith said the number of women killed by men during the first three weeks of the government's lockdown is the highest it's been for at least eleven years. It is double that of an average twenty-one days over the last decade.

When lockdown happened, this created a prison for people living with domestic violence. They couldn't escape to go to work or for a walk outside. Therefore, the government kept domestic abuse victims trapped. This is both saddening and shocking to me.

I woke up at 8 a.m. and peeped out the window. The majority of the cars were not there. This is because today was the first day of shops re-opening after eighty-six days of lockdown. The weather was bright but began to rain, and I heard a loud noise of birds, including doves.

I set up my alarm clock for every two hours and started to read articles about sexual-orientation questions on a survey drawing on theoretical ideas expounded by Foucault, amongst others. The study explores how recent changes to legislation (Equality Act 2010) defining sexual orientation as a protected characteristic and calling for sexual orientation knowledge to be produced may be placing the LGB community at higher risk of being subjected to disciplinary power and norms. If this is the case, there is a need for better understanding on how and when it is appropriate to include sexual orientation questions on surveys.

Certain sectors are to explore their reasons for including or excluding sexual-orientation questions and to discuss for what purpose sexual orientation data would be collected. The main finding was that, amongst private and third-sector researchers, there is very little appetite to include sexual orientation questions on surveys.

This is all research for part of my assignment.

The death toll from Covid-19 as of today is 41,698.

Time 11.42 p.m.

✏️ Tuesday, 16 June 2020
Eighty-sixth day of lockdown

> ➤ ***In the news***: Coronavirus, Dexamethasone proves first life-saving drug. A cheap and widely available drug can help save the lives of patients seriously ill with coronavirus.
>
> The low-dose steroid treatment dexamethasone is a major breakthrough in the fight against the deadly virus, UK experts say. The drug is part of the world's biggest trial testing existing treatments to see if they also work for coronavirus.
>
> It cut the risk of death by a third for patients on ventilators. For those on oxygen, it cut deaths by a fifth. Had the drug had been used to treat patients in the UK from the start of the pandemic, up to 5,000 lives could have been saved, researchers say. *And* it could be of huge benefit in poorer countries with high numbers of Covid-19 patients.

This news about the new Covid drug gave me hope for the future, but I am still worrying uncontrollably due to the pandemic. Will we ever see the end of this?

I woke up at 7 a.m. and peeped out of the window. White and dark mixed fog was in the sky. Very few cars were left in the car park. The wind was moving the tree leaves, and it was a cold and chilly morning. The dog was barking, and doves were peeping back from one side of the field.

I joined the lockdown meditation yoga at 7 a.m., which was organised by the Greater Rushmoor Nepali Community UK (GRNC). I took a shower and had a glass of water after I finished meditation.

I talked to my parents and got updated about my dad's health condition. He is still not very well, and he is worried so much about the family, who are all around the world. I searched for a few pieces of information for the university form filling and update, and then had lunch.

I did yoga at 5 p.m. for one hour and had a short break while watching TV. I had class for upper intermediate at 7 p.m., and the family ordered pizza from Domino's for dinner.

Not a very busy day today.

The death toll from Covid-19 has now risen by 223 to 41,921.

Time: 12.00 a.m.

Wednesday, 17 June 2020
Eighty-seventh day of lockdown

- ***In the news:*** There are new Covid-19 rules for days out at theme parks and museums. Theme parks, museums, and leisure centres are working out how they can reopen safely, as lockdown restrictions ease. Riding on a roller coaster is going to require a face mask and social distancing when attractions open up again.

- A report from the Creative Industries Federation says 400,000 jobs are at risk, and the cultural and creative economy is losing more than £1 billion a week in revenue.

When I read the news, I found that the number of women being killed by domestic violence has risen to a high of three a week during lockdown. This makes me upset and sad.

I woke up 8 a.m. The morning was much brighter than the day before. The sky was clear, and very few cars were left in the car park.

A dog was barking, and birds and doves were singing from the back side of the field. I came out the back door into the garden to check on the vegetables and flowers for a few minutes. I put oil on my hair and massaged it for 10 minutes, and left it for 10 hours to set on my hair.

I missed the morning meditation yoga due to going to bed late the previous night. I read an email from my university supervisor advising me to apply for an ECS form. I looked on the link and emailed her about it, as I did not understand. I set up my alarm clock to go off between 2 and 4 p.m. for four hours of research on car parking articles on the university's learning log-in. I found very interesting data about car parking system and issues in the UK.

There are several unique dimensions within this topic, including resident experience, Trust staff experience, and the Trust parking management process, which requires equal consideration when evaluating the relevant literature, such as the following article:

> Parking spaces in the UK: According to research conducted by the British Parking Association (BPA, 2014), there are 11 million regulated parking spaces in the UK (including spaces at hospitals), with an approximate total figure of 17 million spaces when including residential spaces, such as garages and driveways. They also state that there are approximately 29.6 million licensed cars in the UK. ... the number of parking spaces available and as the BPA state "every car requires a parking space at the beginning and end of the journey" (2014).
>
> This resonates with the situation at the local hospital, as the organisational director is quoted as saying "We simply do not have enough parking spaces for a hospital of our size and our car parks are a constant battleground, on a daily basis" (Get Surrey, 2014).

By looking at this research, I can see that people need to forward-think about the use and amount of car parks that will cover the UK in the next 100 years.

I kept hearing noise of some building or plumbing work outside of the house or some area behind my house, but I could not recognise where the noise was coming from. It was echoing around the whole neighbourhood and was very distracting.

I went to jogging in Long Valley Field, which is between Farnham and Aldershot. It took an hour and a half. I could see many young couples after the slight easing of lockdown and the introduction of the social bubble by the UK government.

Everyone was facing opposite ways when walking in the fields. Coronavirus has had a bad impact on human beings, because people have lost trust in each other. I was scared to approach and be in front of another person. Also, the people all went along with antisocial behaviour due to the fear of talking and greeting one another.

I cooked a variety of Nepali food for dinner, and we ate a bit late today. My number-one priority is to feed the family. Today it was just a little later than usual.

The death toll from Covid-19 has now risen by 184 to 42,105.

Time: 12.00 a.m.

Thursday, 18 June 2020
Eighty-eighth day of lockdown

I woke up at 8 a.m. and peeped out of the window. It was light and bright this morning, and the sky was clear.

I had a dream last night that I was in my real birth house in Oyam-6 (Yangwarak 3), Panchthar) in a big building. I met a student of Oyam school; she was in the class above me. I was happily talking to her and was telling her my story of how my birthplace house was built thirty-two years ago in my beautiful dream world.

I feel that the house is very meaningful because I had to work very hard to complete that house, although I was small. I took much responsibility to manage the house, and to make lunch and dinner for the workers at that time, when my mum was gone to her father's funeral and final ritual ceremony for one week. I used to help the workers paint the colour for this house.

I stayed for two years in this house. Then we moved farther down to another house. My dad had bought a big amount of land and the house, and it was closer to school. Many students and teachers used to live in this house after we moved to a new house and new area.

I went to visit my birth house two years ago, twenty years after I had left. I cried for a few minutes standing behind this house; the reason is that I remembered my late friend who was the same age as me, and who I used to go to school, play with, and work with all the time. I visited the next-door neighbour and friends, elderly people who used to love me while I was going to school and on my way back home.

The sun was rising over the khanakle jungle through the sky, and I was talking to a senior friend from school. She was in a white T-shirt and blue skirt and looking like a young person enjoying student life. I was inside the house near the kitchen and dining area, and I was planning to go from the second to the third floor up the stairs, but I woke up before I got upstairs.

I was very happy all day due to my dream. My conscious mind, heart, and homeland are tightly connected to each other, and for that reason, I used to dream of my birth house sometimes. It put me in a very good mood for the rest of the day.

I talked to my parents, and they updated me about my dad's condition. He was still not very well and was worried so much about the family all around the world. I wrote down the news of the historic points of the Limbu subhangi (headmanship) system in Nepal Limbu Community, which is led by my father:

> In the case of Limbus (indigenous peoples of Nepal), both chieftaincy and headmanship existed prior to the treaty in 1774 between Gorkha rulers and Limbu chiefs. Subhas, Limbu clan headmen, were subordinate to the Limbu chiefs. Later, the Subhas emerged as a strong institution and again, gradually became weak and disappeared in 1964. This paper explores how the Gorkha rulers once treated Subhas as equal to their nobles in order to control their own territory through "indirect rule," and how the Gorkha rulers ignored the Treaty of Salt Water ("Nun-Paani Sandhi") in 1774 in order to displace and destroy

the Subhangi in Limbuwan (the homeland of the Limbus). The Gorkha rulers were previously unsuccessful in establishing direct rule over Limbuwan, so they gradually adopted a policy against the Subhangi to weaken the system.

I checked my email from the university supervisor who had advised me to apply for the ECS form, and she suggested I ask my module leader.

I am studying domestic violence and South Asian women in the UK and found that very factual data from ONS (2018) presented data of domestic violence victims, women who were burned in South Asia countries—for instance, Bangladesh Afghanistan, Bhutan, Maldives, India, Nepal, Sri Lanka, and Pakistan. There are many ways to suffer domestic violence for South Asians, such as non-physical abuse, force, threats, or sexual assault carried out by a spouse/ex-partner and family member. However, it was found that there was less domestic violence against women from Bangladesh than women from other countries in South Asia

Crime Survey for England Wales (2018) stated that 6.9 per cent of age 16–74 women experienced domestic violence more than once in the previous year. It was found that 3.4 per cent of age 16–74 women who were born in South Asia experienced domestic violence.

I wanted to highlight this because of the news, and this is currently part of my thesis.

My eldest daughter prepared Korean-style food for dinner. She cooked rice, eggs, fried chicken wings, and bacon on table gas. We ate it with salad with kimchi. I cooked momo and chutney (pickle), which is specialty for Nepalis everywhere. It was so delicious to have with the family.

The death toll from Covid-19 rose by 135 today, less than the previous day, bringing the total to 42,240.

Time: 12.16 a.m.

✏️ Friday, 19 June 2020
Eighty-ninth day of lockdown

> ➢ ***In the news***: The government is planning to relax its travel quarantine rules in early July for some countries. UK officials are talking to their counterparts in Portugal, France, Italy, Greece, and Spain. However, the UK hopes to make an announcement on 29 June that it has secured a number of "travel corridors". The government had previously said that the quarantine would be reviewed every three weeks, and 29 June marks the end of the first three-week period.
>
> A travel corridor would mean that two people travelling in both directions between two countries would not have to self-isolate after they travel. The first travel corridors could come into force on 4 July, although that date is by no means confirmed.

A few key worker parents and children are walking with their school bags to school. The birds were having food from cages under the trees near my back garden.

I cleaned and washed the house before the children woke up, and I started to study and do my research about my coursework. I looked for the information on the student finance support documents and wrote a letter, then posted it. I checked for email from my university supervisor, and she had emailed me many forms with comments that I have to correct and amend a few things before sending them again.

I went jogging around Long Valley Field with my husband. We walked 10 kilometres within two hours. We came back home and had dinner. My husband opened an old Nepali film, but I could not finish it because it was too long. Only my husband watched until the end of the film.

I was able to read some news regarding Nepali and the MCC, and this is part of my study subject for corporate crime:

> Millennium Challenge Corporation (MCC) has been a disputed topic in Nepal's politics for quite a time now.

If Nepalese politicians decide to sign this contract, this would bring challenging situation in Nepal. Although our politicians have denied MCC being a part of Indo Pacific strategy, US defence's website tells a different story. MCC is not a US government but a profit-oriented corporation. It is similar to East India Corporation that entered in India few centuries back. It took almost 200 years for India to get out of it, and it is said that India still hasn't been able to get out. Signing MCC will bring Nepal's sovereignty at risk. The so-called Federal Democratic Republic of Nepal that has never been colonized may be under the control of the US military under certain conditions. MCC is said to be a donation to develop the infrastructure of our country. It is said to focus mostly on electricity and road networks. Amount of Nrs 55 Arba will be given to Nepal as a donation, and Nepal will have to invest NRs 13 Arba. Even though it is said to be a donation, there is a clause in the document which mentions about interests in this donation. This treaty is a direct threat to Nepal's sovereignty, and we have been fooled by our politicians into believing it is for the benefit of Nepal.

My youngest daughter prepared simple Nepali-style food for dinner.

The death toll from Covid-19 rose by 173 today, more than the previous day, bringing the total to 42,413.

Time:12.22 a.m.

Saturday, 20 June 2020
Ninetieth day of lockdown

> ***In the news***: Hundreds of people have gathered for Black Lives Matter protests in cities across England today. Peaceful protests took place in London, Coventry, and Newcastle—the latest in a series of anti-racism demonstrations in recent weeks. The gatherings are in breach of coronavirus lockdown rules and many in the crowds wore masks and observed social distancing guidance. The

government has previously warned against protesting during the pandemic. In London, protesters assembled at Speakers' Corner in Hyde Park amid a heavy police presence. Another group of people marched from Vauxhall to Parliament Square in London.

I came downstairs and put oil massage on my hair, then cleaned the house and disinfected every corner of the room. I took a shower, brushed my teeth, and worshiped as I usually do on a Saturday. My husband made *aludum* (item of potato), and I helped him make it taste better than it did last time. It was delicious, and I had some with a cup of tea.

I was ready to join a Zoom meeting with the global network organised by Dr Marohang Limbu, a lecturer at Michigan University in the United States. The presentation was about a Limbu cultural, ritual, and historic area that was being overtaken by mainstream society or the Nepal government. The Limbu tribe is group of indigenous minorities. They used to own land, and we were the landlord and had a king in our previous history. Many Limbus are campaigning to get equal rights and have human rights, including doctors, professors, and academic intellectuals, all from different social backgrounds.

I am very fortunate that as part of my master's degree, I was able to meet people from my community all over the world who are held in high esteem for being academic and intellectual.

The death toll from Covid-19 rose by 128 today, less than the previous day, bringing the to 42,541.

Time: 12.22 a.m.

Sunday, 21 June 2020
Ninety-first day of lockdown

> ***In the news***: The man held on suspicion of killing three people at a park in Reading was known to MI5, security sources say. Khairi Saadallah, 25, from the town, was arrested on Saturday, and police say they are not looking for anyone else over the terror incident. Sources told the BBC he is originally from Libya and came to the attention of MI5 in 2019. One victim has been named as teacher James Furlong—described by his family as "a wonderful man".

> Paying tribute to Mr Furlong, 36, head of history, government, and politics at The Holt School in Wokingham, his parents Gary and Janet said: "He was beautiful, intelligent, honest, and fun." PM Boris Johnson said he was "appalled and sickened" by the attack in Forbury Gardens on Saturday evening.

This is shocking, because we are all supposed to be staying inside and keeping one another safe, yet a crime has been committed.

I woke up at 9 a.m., late morning, because I went to bed at 2 a.m. The weather was nice, and the sky was clear. All the cars were in the car park, and it looked like midday. I got ready to go to work. The international yoga day programme was hosted by Greater Rushmoor Nepali Community, but I had to miss it due to my work.

On my way to work, at the Royal Military Academy Sandhurst college town gate, my pass was renewed by the guard, who asked me about furlough payments. But I had never stopped working throughout the pandemic, as I'm key worker.

I hurt my finger with a small knife I was using to cut off a milk pipe at work. I kept hold of my finger until I found small plaster. I looked in the first-aid box, but there were no plasters. I went to check in the office and found a small roll of tape and put it on my finger, but I could not control the bleeding. Blood ran all over my hand and the paper on the table. I was crushed, because there were not enough materials, such as bandages and plasters, for the staff. Finally, I took two pairs of gloves. One pair was dropped in the bin because of bleeding from the cut on my finger, and the remaining pair I used during my work.

I used to wear a mask at all the time at work, but most of the staff are not wearing any still. I wanted to keep the people safe as well as myself. All army officer cadets and staff are still not wearing masks, and it is difficult to manage social distancing, although we try very hard because we have to serve food to them morning, afternoon, and evening.

I decide not to have food from that kitchen. I came back home to take a shower, get changed, and have food at home. It was Father's Day. I contacted my dad in Hong Kong to wish him happy Father's Day. The children prepared a cake, ordered takeaway food, and celebrated. We had to celebrate at home in this critical situation, and then my husband went on duty.

It is also the longest day of the year. In the Northern Hemisphere, the longest day of the year is always on or around June 21. This is because on this date, the sun's rays are perpendicular to the Tropic of Cancer at 23°30' North latitude.

I watched the news while I was having dinner for few minutes and was scared by the story on the stabbing at Reading incident.

The death toll from Covid-19 rose by 43 today, less than the previous day, bringing the total to 42,584.

Time: 3.30 a.m.

Monday, 22 June 2020
Ninety-second day of lockdown

> *In the news*: The UK has recorded its lowest number of daily confirmed coronavirus cases, 958, since the lockdown began. The number of daily virus deaths also fell to 15, the lowest figure since 15 March, the day before the government began its daily televised briefings. However, the number of deaths are often lower on Mondays due to reporting lags over the weekend.

I woke up at 3.30 a.m. because I went bed early at 10 p.m. The weather was warm, but the sky was not bright. I sat at my computer and realised that I forgot to record my diary, so I caught up on some paragraphs from yesterday. It took me about one hour, then I talked to my parents. I went back to bed again for two hours and woke up with the sun shining.

I got ready as soon as possible and put tea towels and hand-cleaning cloths into the washing machine. I disinfected all surfaces in the house and then sat down at the computer to correct the basic proposal part of my dissertation until 2.30 p.m.

I had a cup of tea with fruit as a snack. I was stressing myself for few minutes due to not being able to understand some of the words from the teacher's comments—but after a second try, I got it. I spent quite a long time correcting my documents today.

If anyone sneezes or coughs at home, all the family thinks about the coronavirus.

The death toll from Covid-19 rose by 15 today, so much less than on previous days, bringing the total to 42,599.

Time: 10.47 p.m.

✎ Tuesday, 23 June 2020
Ninety-third day of lockdown

> ***In the news***: Prime Minister Boris Johnson said people should remain 2m apart where possible but a "one metre plus" rule would be introduced. Two households in England will also be able to meet indoors and stay overnight—with social distancing. The prime minister warned that all the steps were "reversible". Theatres, cinemas, libraries, museums, theme parks, and zoos are among other businesses that can also reopen.

I woke up at 7 a.m. to join the yoga class, but I could not stay for long due to the poor network connection. I went back to bed again and slept for a bit longer.

When I woke, I cleaned the house. My husband made breakfast and lunch. I sat on the computer for an online class for my proposal. It took about an hour, and then I talked to my sisters to update them about the global pandemic.

I went back to the garden for an hour for fresh air and looked after my vegetables and flowers. Preschool children are playing in school and making noise and screaming. I always do listen to this noise, because I live near the local school. My husband went shopping and organised a BBQ, and our children helped to make organic pickle sauce for the BBQ.

I joined my evening language class for two hours. The family waited to have dinner with me, so we had mini party with a BBQ dinner. For dessert, we had ice cream.

I had a shower as soon as possible and then typed a few words in my diary.

I read in the news from the World Health Organisation (WHO) that domestic violence is already a deadly epidemic. One in three women around the world experience physical or sexual violence, mostly from an intimate, according to WHO. As WHO notes: "This makes it the most widespread, but among the least reported human rights abuses."

Gender-based violence tends to increase during humanitarian emergencies and conflicts; "women's bodies too often become battlefields".

Due to the pandemic, domestic violence has risen, and it makes me feel sad and upset that other women have to feel like this and go through this kind of situation.

The death toll from Covid-19 rose by 171, more than the previous day, bringing the total to 42,770.

Time: 10.38 p.m.

Wednesday, 24 June 2020
Ninety-fourth day of lockdown

> ***In the news***: Wednesday is officially the hottest day of the year so far, with people flocking to beaches and beauty spots. The Metro police office said the temperature hit 32.6C on Wednesday, beating the previous record of 28.9C set at the end of May. A level three heat-health alert has been set for parts of England, with advice to take extra care in the sun.

I woke up at 9 a.m. because I couldn't sleep through the whole night due to my thyroxine making me feel hot and sweaty. A friend of mine contacted me and told me that her 17-year-old son passed away. That made my heart sink, and I was so shocked. I was speechless all day, and I couldn't imagine how she could survive at this critical time, and I shared this sad news with my children and family.

My husband made breakfast and cleaned the house, because I wanted to get into my work proposal to amend my typing. I spent all day until 6 p.m. doing this. I emailed it to my teacher, and then I felt free for a few minutes, but my right arm is aching so much.

My project that I am working on will explore hidden domestic violence against Black and South Asian ethnic minority women in the UK. The acronym BSAME will be used to describe this group.

BSAME women face many barriers when accessing support from domestic violence services. For this reason, BSAME women are more at risk of "honour based" abuse, which is a type of abuse connected to honour and shame in the community. Honour and shame are significant factors in some communities because of the way that women are seen within the culture and family unit. BSAME women are afraid to report their husband's abuse due to cultural pressure.

I felt very stressed after I finished typing my basic proposal format. So I asked the family to go jogging. We went to Long Valley Field again. I ran for an hour and a half, nearly a 10k distance. We saw beautiful reindeers, birds, and lakes. At 9.15 p.m., late evening but still bright, we could see very clearly a view of the sun setting in the sky, and the sky was a lovely golden colour. We had dinner after we came back from jogging. I had just salad and fruit for dinner. I had a shower, brushed my teeth, read the news, and typed in my diary.

This is a small part of my research, which is an observational skills scenario in my local café:

> On the left-hand side of the counter four customers were having a drink, and they looked like non-English speakers but their body language and facial expressions were very happy. They all looked middle-age, and everyone was obviously enjoying themselves. Their facial expressions and body language were very happy and excited. Most of the tables had two or three customers, but only one table had four men around it. The researcher noticed that when they came out from the café, they were talking in their own language, which was not English.
>
> They talked loudly, gesturing with their hands as they came out from the café and walked on the street. They spent a longer time in the café compared to other customers. Two of the men had long beards and two were shaven, and they were all dressed in casual jeans and tops, for example, white, blue, and brown T-shirts.
>
> It was easy to notice that many people spent a shorter time inside the café while they had coffee. The ethnic minority group on the other hand showed a greater degree of bonding and sharing and feelings compared with other

customers. As it had not been possible for them to meet in their individual environments during the pandemic, the researcher noted that they found the café environment a place where they could share their feelings openly.

The death toll from Covid-19 rose by 171 today to 42,941. Time: 10.38 p.m.

Thursday, 25 June 2020
Ninety-fifth day of lockdown

> ***In the news***: South Asian people are the most likely to die from coronavirus after being admitted to hospital in UK. "South Asians are definitely more likely to die from Covid-19 in hospital, but we don't see a strong effect in the black group," Prof Ewen Harrison, from the University of Edinburgh, told the BBC. People from South Asian backgrounds were 20 per cent more likely to die than white people. Other minority ethnic groups did not have a higher death rate.

I woke up at 8 a.m. this morning. The weather was so hot, and the sun was shining. I couldn't sleep the whole night because my thyroxine made me feel hot and sweaty.

I studied a sample of a dissertation about car parking problems in the UK before lunch. My eldest daughter cooked Korean BBQ chicken wings with bacon, and she filmed it for her YouTube channel. I ate too much, and my tummy was full up. I emailed my teacher about my work, and she told to me to send documents to the university ethics team.

I went jogging with my husband again in Long Valley Field. We met so many people: cyclists, fishers, and picnic groups at the lake. All the people are scared of us, and we also feared to go near them because of Covid-19. I feel like the pandemic is creating antisocial behaviour, because people have lost trust in others in these situations.

We saw beautiful reindeers and birds collecting for their babies. It took an hour and half to get back home. Then all the family gathered and had a heavy dinner.

I decided to do research for my literature review for my proposal. This project will explore hidden domestic violence against Black and South Asian ethnic minority women in the UK. The acronym BSAME will be used to describe this group. I tried to highlight one particular reason for domestic violence for BSAME women in the UK:

> Honour is considered as a spoken in cross-cultural norms and values in patriarchal societies. This limits women's physical, sexual, and psychological freedom controlling by their behaviour and choices (Meetoo and Mirza 2007; Patel 2017; Gill et al. 2018, cited in Gill and Harrison (2018)). The concept of honour and shame is based on unrecorded codes that promote men's control and power over women under the appearance of admiration and protection (Payton, 2014). Meetoo and Mirza (2007) and Payton (2014) have investigated that what many scholars have defined as "honour" is linked between family and community which control their women. An issue of sex is known as the main cause of "shame" because an individual woman's behaviour is strongly connected with her whole family's pride and honour in South Asian communities. Therefore, most of women from this group do not want to report sexual violence that leads to domestic violence. Honour- based violence plays an important role in creating domestic violence for this community of women.

The death toll from Covid-19 rose by 147 today, less than the previous day. The death toll as of today is 43,088.

Time: 11.23 p.m.

✏️ Friday, 26 June 2020
Ninety-sixth day of lockdown

I woke up at 9 a.m. The weather was so hot, and the sun was shining. I slept better than the previous night. I can hear the noise of the cars moving away and parents and preschool children walking to school. Birds are enjoying food and feeding their babies too. Green tree branches and leaves are waving at each other with the wind blowing.

I spent the whole morning looking for a link on how to write a dissertation on the course module and had a few ideas to write it up. I spent the whole afternoon researching about domestic violence against women:

> Crime Survey for England Wales (2018) stated that 6.9 per cent of age 16-74 women experienced domestic violence more than once in the previous year. The data was found that 3.4 per cent out of 6.9 per cent of women who experienced domestic violence were born in South Asian families. This is a huge proportion of abuse for these women compared to mainstream society of women in the UK.

I contacted my parents in Hong Kong. They were ready to fly back after a long time trapped in lockdown. I was worried so much about my dad's health. He is suffering with constipation problems after he went to Hong Kong on holiday.

My youngest daughter made Korean kimchi fry for lunch, but it was very spicy. I decided to go for a walk with my husband again, then we went to Long Valley Field for two hours. We met many people and friends from the same roads where I lived in the fields.

We saw many reindeers that were running away from the walking path. They looked very scared to see so many people, because they were used to having freedom in their territory, lands, and field. They were distracted by many people walking during the lockdown. The reason is that all families and children had no way to spend time, so everyone was going to the same place to walk every day to pass the time and to have fun.

People are escaping from people, and animals are escaping from people. It was an interesting and strange experience with people living in Covid-19 times. I felt like the pandemic would create antisocial behaviour and depress people and make them lose trust in these situations. We saw beautiful reindeers and birds collecting for their babies

The children were waiting for us for dinner, so we all sat at the dinner table, and my eldest daughter cooked Korean BBQ chicken wings with bacon for dinner but did not do any filming at this time. We had too much food, and my tummy was full up. All the family gathered and had dinner.

The death toll from Covid-19 rose by 186 today, more than the previous day, bringing the total to 43,274.

Time: 11.00 p.m.

✎ Saturday, 27 June 2020
Ninety-seventh day of lockdown

> ***In the news***: Thousands of people gathered across England to mark the first anniversary of the death of a 12-year-old refugee girl who drowned in a river last year. Shukri Yahye-Abdi, who came to the UK in 2017, died in Bury's River Irwell, in Greater Manchester, on 27 June 2019.
>
> An ongoing inquest was told in February that an unnamed child had confessed to threatening her to "get in the water". The case has been highlighted by supporters of the Black Lives Matter movement, including *Star Wars* actor John Boyega. Violence against women from minority ethnic and refugee women's issues are ongoing in the UK. It is very serious crime for women.

I woke up at four in the morning, and the weather was cool and raining, I was wondering why the birds were chirping so early in the morning. The wind was blowing, and the environment was very different from yesterday morning. I woke up early due to going to bed early last night.

> I cleaned the house, took a shower, and did worship for my ancestor God called Yuma Theba. I played religious music (part of Hindu classical) as well. I had a glass of water and started to check my email from the university and worked out the new form and the correction of ethical documents of dissertation, and the signature from my supervisor and myself on the EGA form. I did a printout, completed my

form, and scanned and included it. This took me such a long time to do.

At 2 p.m., I joined a Zoom conference of the global network organised by Dr Marohang Khawahang from the USA. The presenter was Professor Arjun Limbu, and the topic was Limbu traditional headmanship in the eastern part of Nepal 200 years ago in 1774-1964. Subhas, as a Limbu headman, had a traditional leader's authority based on customary law. Subha and Subhangi have significant roles in Limbu history in Nepal.

After a short time, I contacted my parents who were in Nepal, having arrived from Hong Kong. They were ready to fly back after a long time trapped in lockdown. They were trapped for six months in total.

I decided to go for a walk with friends because the social bubble rule allowed us to walk with six people from different households. I went with another five ladies to Long Valley Field for two hours. We did not meet that many people and cyclists as in previous days. We did not see any reindeers in the field.

My husband and children were waiting for me for dinner when I got back. So we all sat at the dinner table, and my youngest daughter cooked dinner.

The death toll from Covid-19 rose by 100 today, less than the previous day, bringing the total to 43,374.

Time: 11.48 p.m.

Sunday, 28 June 2020
Ninety-eighth day of lockdown

> ***In the news***: The family of a man shot dead by police following multiple stabbings in Glasgow say they are shocked and saddened by what happened.

Currently there is no human life without crime. Many deaths are happening, such as stabbing, arrests, and discrimination issues. These concerns are ongoing in this lockdown time and with the ongoing global pandemic.

I woke up at 6 a.m. this morning. I brushed my teeth and got some fresh air for a few minutes outside. The weather was cool and raining, birds were chirping, and wind was blowing. The environment was very different from yesterday morning.

I prepared my PPE and then went to work. There was not enough PPE at work, and all the staff had to buy PPE for themselves. It was very difficult to manage social distancing at work, although I tried to manage my space. I came back home from work, disinfected my uniform, and took a shower to control coronavirus. I had some fruits and sat down on the computer to recheck six documents for my proposal.

I went with another two ladies to Long Valley Field for two hours. On the way to jogging, we saw beautiful rabbits (brown colour). I did not realise that we were gone so long when I walked with friends because we talked about coronavirus, including relatives and friends, and shared our feelings and views, so the time passed easily. I did not see reindeers and birds today.

It started to rain halfway to home, while we were jogging. We all gathered at 8 p.m. and had dinner with the family.

The death toll from Covid-19 rose by 36 today, less than the previous day, bringing the total to 43,550.

Time: 11.48 p.m.

Monday, 29 June 2020
Ninety-ninth day of lockdown

> ***In the news***: The UK was the hardest hit of all the G7 major industrialised nations in the weeks leading up to early June, according to BBC analysis of the first wave of the coronavirus pandemic.

I woke up at 7 a.m. The sky was not clear as before; half of the sky was covered with a dark fog, and the wind was blowing. A cold breeze was coming through the window. I put my jacket on and got some fresh air for a few minutes outside. The birds were busy picking up food. I had some fruits and a cup of tea, then sat down to research my subject on the computer.

I paid the General Dental Council annual fee online and also donated towards three other charities—small help for members of the community, friends, and relatives.

Today was a special celebration of Nepali (Ashar-15). I prepared some different types of food, like bitten rice yogurt (curd) banana, and BBQ with curries. We watched the news on the TV while we were having dinner.

I decided to go for a walk with my husband in Humphry Park Church Crookham Fleet after dinner. We met many reindeers and dog walkers along the way to jogging at that time.

As part of my literature review, I found some interesting research about the cost of domestic violence:

> Domestic violence costs the UK economy £16 billion (Walby, 2009) and yet austerity and political measures have reduced services and rights of survivors to escape abuse. Domestic violence is a high-volume crime, which often escalates over time, and can result in extreme outcomes such as domestic homicide or suicide. One in four women experience domestic violence in their lifetime, although official reporting and recording processes mean this is likely to be an underestimate. On average, two women are killed by their partner or ex-partner every week in England and Wales. Indeed, it is estimated that a homicide costs £1 million. These costs mainly relate to the expense incurred by the criminal justice system. More investment in early intervention, prevention of, and recovery from abuse would not only save lives, but also reduce the economic and human costs to society.

This is a high cost to rescue someone from domestic violence, and more funding is needed.

The death toll from Covid-19 rose by 25 today, less than the previous day, bringing the total to 43,575.

Time: 11.48 p.m.

🖉 Tuesday, 30 June 2020
100th day of lockdown

> ***In the news***: Boris Johnson has said now is the time to be "ambitious" about the UK's future, as he set out a post-coronavirus recovery plan. The PM vowed to "use this moment" to fix longstanding economic problems and promised a £5bn "new deal" to build homes and infrastructure.

I cleaned the house and cooked breakfast. I planned to research information on domestic violence against Black minority ethnic women, and Southall Black Sisters supporting these women:

> Southall Black Sisters (1979, cited in Ackerman (2020)) is situated in West London, which has been helping the minority ethnic and immigrant community, children, and women who are facing gender-based abuse. There has been an increase of 20 per cent in calls on helpline service during the lockdown.
>
> Multi Agency Risk Assessment Conference (MARAC) referrals have shown that domestic violence victims have a high risk of serious harm, and there were 17 MARAC referrals of women from the BME community within a week in May 2020.

I didn't go out for a walk due to my online class today. I taught my son how to make home-made bread for dinner before I attended class. He prepared and baked the bread, and we had it as a meal with verity of curry, salads, and drinks with all the family.

The death toll from Covid-19 rose by 155 today, more than the previous day, bringing the total to 43,730.

Time: 11.58 p.m.

July 2020

✎ Wednesday, 1 July 2020
101st day of lockdown

> ➢ *In the news*: More than 12,000 people in the UK are set to lose their jobs after a raft of firms announced cuts in the past 48 hours.

I woke up at 9 a.m. It was cold and raining this morning. The sky was not as clear as before. I massaged my hair with herbal oil and started to clean house again—only the downstairs kitchen, dining room, living room, and toilets for today.

I made a cup of coffee after I took a shower, but I spilled it on the table, over my books and notes. I swore at myself and made another cup of coffee. I am usually not a fan of tea and coffee apart from warm water. My husband came back from food shopping, and my eldest daughter made Korean fried rice for lunch and we had it together in the late afternoon.

I checked my email from the university and found that my proposal was accepted by the ethics team, and they told me to carry it out as soon as possible. I felt really excited and happy for this good news.

I began to research information of hidden domestic violence against Black South Asian minority ethnic (BSAME) women in the UK for my literature review. I found the following:

> Over the last 15 years, the state had witnessed bigger intervention on domestic violence against BME community womens' issues, although there are harmful cultural practices among these women, for instance, female genital mutilation and "honour-based" violence and forced marriage. Civil Protection Act 2007 was introduced to guidance for forced marriage as a criminal offence. The criminal offence of forced marriage has incorporated in the "Anti-Social Behaviour, Crime and Policing Act 2014". However, the above acts have dropped

tackling the main cause of violence against BME women, and the women have been experiencing a lack of resources.

I did yoga for one hour and decide to go out jogging. We all went out jogging, but it started to rain 10 minutes after I left home, so we decided to come back home.

We had home-made bread and Korean fried rice pickle and roast pork curry for dinner. We watched the Nepali film *Jhole* for two and a half hours. It was quite a long movie. It was based on an interesting social-change theme relating to culture, class, caste, gender, and social hierarchy issues in Nepal.

I'm worried about life and my job due to the coronavirus pandemic. UK Prime Minister Boris Johnson announced that more than 12,000 people in the UK are set to lose their jobs. Up to three million Hong Kong residents are to be offered the chance to settle in the UK and ultimately apply for citizenship, Boris Johnson has said. The PM said Hong Kong's freedoms were being violated by a new security law, and those affected would be offered a "route" out of the former UK colony. About 350,000 UK passport holders and 2.6 million others eligible will be able to come to the UK for five years. And after a further year, they will be able to apply for citizenship.

The death toll from Covid-19 rose by 176 today, more than the previous day, bringing the total to 43,906.

Time: 12.18 a.m.

✎ Thursday, 2 July 2020
102nd day of lockdown

I had an appointment this morning with a participant for an interview for my research, so I contacted her at 10 a.m. exactly on time. I took the interview remotely under a control situation within 30 minutes. The question was about domestic violence against BSAME women in the UK. The participant was a police officer specialising in domestic violence (rape and sexual assaults). I finished taking the interview and transcribed half of it. I left the rest for later.

I had a 12.40 p.m. appointment at the general practice for a blood test for myself, and I went with my husband. I had to wait outside for 20 minutes in a queue outside of the GP due to Covid-19. A nurse came out to collect me, and she was from Italy. She was a very lovely nurse and a post-graduate in 2019 from Reading University. I discussed with her my dissertation topic. I had a very nice conversation with her. It was a fasting blood test, so I had lots of food after I came back from the GP.

I had another appointment with a second participant, who I interviewed for 30 minutes. I was able to reveal supporting points for my topic. It was a professional support worker for domestic violence victims and survivors who answered questions about anything that heightened these issues, such as language barriers, culture, background, gender, and displacement. The correct answer was received from the interviewee:

> Language barriers, family, and community, because they do not want to talk about the violence issue, victimize. They do not want report due to a victim-blaming culture, and family does not want to talk about the victim due to culture and gender issues. With surging domestic abuse incidents during lockdown, ministers must provide proper support for victims.

I found another piece of research that agreed with this:

> The Covid-19 lockdown is believed to have caused an increase in the incidence of domestic abuse and violence. Mandy Thomas, a survivor ambassador for Women's Aid, has said, "This pandemic is an abuser's paradise. We all need to act to burst their bubble." Others talk about "walking on eggshells" as the abuser is at home twenty-four hours a day, giving victims no respite. Karen Ingala Smith, the founder of Counting Dead Women—a pioneering project that records the killing of women and their children—has identified at least sixteen such deaths in the UK between 23 March and 12 April.

I did not do yoga today and decided to go out for a jog with friends from my area. It took two hours to walk in a group and come back home. I tried to manage with social distancing and put my mask on every time. All my friends are healthcare workers, therefore I put on my mask, and I was scared to approach them owing to coronavirus. I have badly lost trust due to the virus.

The death toll from Covid-19 rose by 89 today, less than the previous day, bringing the total to 43,995.

Friday, 3 July 2020
103rd day of lockdown

> ***In the news***: The easing of lockdown rules in England is the "biggest step yet on the road to recovery", the prime minister has said.

I'm very excited to welcome easing lockdown because human beings have been trapped in since 23 March 2020 due to Covid-19. On the other hand, I fear coronavirus because many people are still dying with the virus.

I woke up at 9 a.m. on a cold and bright morning. A strong wind was blowing, and it pushed down my letter shelf inside the room due to me leaving the window open wide.

The mums and babies were walking around the preschool. Many carers drove out, and only a few cars were left in the car park.

My husband made breakfast and I had some while I took a short break from my research work. A cold breeze was coming through the window. I quickly checked my emails, all from different departments, and I did not have that many important ones, so I just checked and signed out.

I started to transcribe my interviews from the previous day in my Word documents. I thought I needed to take a short break and went downstairs and lightly cleaned house again. I went out to the vegetable garden for 20 minutes. I'd had enough fresh air and went back to my work. I picked a few vegetables for my family and relatives.

I did some research on the British Academy (2006) and would like to share my knowledge here:

The British Academy (2006) carried out a study of women from India, Bangladesh, Pakistan who married UK citizens and faced domestic violence due to immigrant issue and forced marriage. Much evidence shows that women with this background experienced more domestic violence than wider community (white) women in the UK owing to many factors, for instance, culture, language, and immigration status. This study interviewed a range of South Asian women using many languages—for example Hindi, Panjabi, Urdu, and English—to reveal victims experience.

I read BBCUK News and saw the following story:

Calls to a national domestic abuse helpline rose by 49 per cent and killings doubled weeks after lockdown, a report by MPs has revealed. Researchers at the Counting Dead Women Project told MPs fourteen women and two children had been killed in the first three weeks of lockdown.

It is very sad to know about this news.

My husband bought McDonald's from the drive-through for the children before dinner. My eldest daughter cooked Korean BBQ for dinner again. I cooked rice and vegetables, and the whole family had dinner with a range of food. We had a really great time together as a family with the three children.

I have never been bored during lockdown due to my studying and family activities. We will really miss the amount of time spent together after the lockdown eases in the UK.

The death toll from Covid 19 rose by 137 today, more than the previous day, bringing the total to 44,132.

Time: 11.36 p.m.

🖉 Saturday, 4 July 2020
104th day of lockdown

> **In the news**: People across England are beginning their first night out in three months, after coronavirus restrictions eased. Hospitality venues such as pubs and restaurants as well as hairdressers, cinemas, and theme parks have reopened with strict social distancing rules.

I woke up at 8 a.m. It was a cold and bright morning. Nobody was outside because of Saturday weekend. Quickly I took a shower and worshiped with my Nepali music. I set up my alarm time from 10 a.m. until 12 p.m. and paraphrased my writing. Afterwards, I again set up another alarm for two hours, then joined the global conference virtual meeting

My husband made breakfast and lunch. I had some while I took short break from my research. I found something interesting:

> The BBCUK (2012) stated one particular case centred on the young Asian girl named Shafilea Ahmed age 17 who was murdered in 2003 by her father for refusing to an arranged marriage. Shafilea was born in the UK but the cultural phenomena still remained part of her family's beliefs that she was her father's property. In fact, her brother and mother both took part in the murder. Her parents concerned regarding shame in their community was greater than their concern for their daughter (BBCUK 2012).

Through my research, I found out that both the mother and father are in prison living out a 25-year sentence for the honour killing of their daughter. I included this in my dissertation thesis, as it is very relevant to what I am doing.

The death toll from Covid-19 rose by 67 today, less than the previous day, bringing the total to 44,199.

Time: 11.19 p.m.

✏️ Sunday, 5 July 2020
105th day of lockdown

> ***In the news***: The NHS at 70; second day of bars, pub, and shops being open.

I woke up at 5.30 a.m. and brushed my teeth. The weather was bright and warm, and birds were chirping. My cat was hungry and asking for food, and I fed him.

I prepared my uniform and mask and gloves and went to work. I always put my mask on, but the rest of the staff did not use a mask. It was difficult to manage social distancing.

In honour of the National Health Service turning 70 on 5 July, a request went out for memories and pictures from around Scotland. When the NHS was founded in 1948, hospitals, doctors, nurses, pharmacists, opticians, and dentists were all brought together to provide services that are free at the point of delivery.

I came back home from work, had a shower and disinfected my uniform, and then started to do research for my literature review:

> Clare Wipe (2012) conducted research responding to domestic violence against South Asian women in the UK. Due to complexity and sensitivity of the problem under review, some of the research has been simplistic and some of it is been misunderstood. It has been largely based on stereotypes and therefore lacking in-depth investigation. The review outlined that Radical Feminists (1970s and 1980s) had concentrated too much on South Asian women, mainly Muslims, and gave no credibility to Black Asian minority ethnic (BAME) women's suffering. However, more recent research has shown that the views of BAME feminists had completely changed this situation (Crenshaw 1991, Bryson 2003, cited in Clare Wipe, 2012).
>
> Paradoxically, South Asian feminists had brought forward how their lives were controlled through emotional,

physical, and financial constraints by the patriarchal influences within their individual cultures (Mee too and Mira, 2007). This aspect made it even more difficult for South Asian women to challenge their cultures. This led in turn to a dangerous and unsupported idea of South Asian women being passive victims. (Volpp 2003, Sanghera)

My husband cooked dinner, and we all ate together. Then I decided to go for a walk with friends, and it took about two hours. We met many people at the field, but still we are scared to approach them. Friends discussed their children's school reports and their excellent grades. I also talked to them about my children's GCSE results, and my eldest daughter achieved 8 As (4A* and 4As) and youngest daughter had 9 distinction * and b +. We celebrated their achievement after their results. All parents and family will be happy if their children achieved good result from their study and exams.

The death toll from Covid-19 rose by 38 today, less than the previous day, bringing the total to 44,237.

Time: 12.00 a.m.

Monday, 6 July 2020
106th day of lockdown

> ***In the news***: Hong Kong—Chinese ambassador warns UK.

I woke up at 8 a.m. I cleaned the kitchen and toilets downstairs. I did yoga today because I had missed it for ages. I could clearly see dead trees in the middle of other trees. Such was my life compared with dead trees and children compared with live trees while I was doing yoga exercise. My husband and I cooked *alundum* (potatoes) and chiura furauni fried bitten rice.

I had an online class for an hour, and I also made an appointment with my participants for interviews to support my project. My participants expressed a very nice answer about my topic. One of the questions I asked was, "Are these issues heightened for any reason, such as language barriers, culture, background, gender, displacement etc.? If so, please explain." I think that cultural shame is very high in this community. Displacement happens if a daughter or wife has asked or reported for help from services and agencies due to culture and gender background.

Another question I asked is, "What other factors add to these difficulties?" In this society, middle-aged women suffer more violence, because they think about their children's future, and they don't want to raise their child as a single mother due to cultural shame. Due to lack of education and literacy, few elderly BSAME women can even type 999. These women also have suffered financial abuse.

My supervisor for my university course found this very interesting, due to the nature of the questions being asked about the older generation of BSAME women.

I again went jogging with friends. We spent a long time out because we went to visit a friend's allotment. We had fun visiting friends' vegetables gardens in the Church Crookham area.

The death toll from Covid-19 rose by 16 today, less than the previous day, bringing the total to 44,253.

Time: 12.35 a.m.

Tuesday, 7 July 2020
107th day of lockdown

> ***In the news***: Rishi Sunak to unveil "kickstart jobs scheme" for young people. The fund will subsidise six-month work placements for people on Universal Credit, between the ages of 16 and 24, who are at risk of long-term unemployment.

I woke up at 8 a.m. My cat went out, and the birds started to raise their voices to each other, just like they were communicating about the strange creature in the garden. My cat just sat and watched. I cooked breakfast and lunch for my family.

I didn't do yoga and had no exercise today because I was very busy with my literature review. I was writing during the day, and I joined my online English language class in the evening.

I did some research on my university log in and read some samples of many dissertations that were uploaded by my lecturer. The topic was interesting: the study was to explore survey designers' understanding about the inclusion of sexual-orientation questions in surveys. Drawing on theoretical ideas expounded by Foucault, amongst others, the study explores recent changes to legislation (Equality Act 2010) defining sexual orientation as a protected characteristic. Reading these samples gave me an idea on how to set up my thesis structure.

The death toll from Covid-19 rose by 155 today, more than the previous day, bringing the total to 44,408.

Time: 12.35 a.m.

Wednesday, 8 July 2020
108th day of lockdown

> **In the news**: Chancellor Rishi Sunak unveils £30 billion plan to save jobs in the UK. Sunak is to cut VAT on hospitality as part of a £30 billion plan to prevent mass unemployment as the economy is hit by coronavirus. The government will also pay firms a £1,000 bonus for every staff member kept on for three months when the furlough scheme ends in October.

I woke up at 7 a.m., and my husband I cooked breakfast and lunch for the family.

My eldest daughter went to collect her stuff from her university accommodation with my younger daughter, because they are going to a different house from September 2020. They are 18 and 20 years old and both have driving licences, so they decided to drive, taking turns when going and on the way back to home.

I had a meeting online with my English language teacher from my previous college.

I focused on my research design and methodology all day. Both my daughters came back from university, and they cooked dinner for us, which was Korean chicken wings and fry chips. I cooked a traditional dish of rice and spicy pork curry dal salad for dinner.

It looked like it was about to rain. I quickly checked the weather forecast and put on a raincoat before going out for a jog with a friend from my residential area.

It took me two hours to come back home from jogging. The coronavirus fear is still locked inside of my heart, so I was scared to approach other people. I always do put my mask on for my own safety and for others' as well.

Regarding part of my research, I saw some very interesting findings:

> Women's Aid and other respondents in this study have welcomed the introduction of the Domestic Violence Rule into the Immigration Rules, but many have cited its shortcomings and inadequacies. The domestic violence rule enables BME women who have experienced domestic violence whilst residing in the UK with their male partner (spouse or durable partnership), to remain in the UK by virtue of their victim status. However, it is applicable only to married women or women in a durable relationship with a British national or "settled" man living in the UK. It also dependent on the woman not having "over-stayed" her visa requirement. Women who are victims of domestic violence as the partner of asylum-seekers; spouses, partners or fiancées of students or temporary workers in the UK; durable partners of EEA nationals; or women who have entered without permission are not protected under this rule.

This is a very interesting issue, and a very specific point which falls under the umbrella of domestic abuse, which is needed for my thesis.

I was very keen to read news about the daily death rates of Covid-19. I found out that the death toll from Covid 19 rose by 126 today, less than the previous day, bringing the total to 44,534.

Good night, diary. See you tomorrow.
Time: 11.55 p.m.

Thursday, 9 July 2020
109th day of lockdown

> ***In the news***: Leisure facilities and beauty services in England will be allowed to reopen, the government has announced. Pools,

gyms, nail bars and tattooists will be able to open their doors again, and team sports—starting with cricket—will be allowed to resume. Announcing the changes at a briefing at No 10, Culture Secretary Oliver Dowden urged people to "work out to help out".

I woke up at 8 a.m. this morning. The weather was cloudy and neither cold nor to hot. I could feel it inside my bedroom.

I thought about my dream after I woke up from sleep. I was walking near my house and school in my homeland, Nepal. The small river was so clean on the way to home from school. I remembered all my school friends and relatives and the next-door neighbours. I was in a very happy mood in the whole dream world.

I contacted my parents and family in Nepal to update them about coronavirus. My parents have been in quarantine since they came back from Hong Kong. Dad is still not very well, but he has been taking medications since going on holiday to Hong Kong. I asked him about our family tree—Seling, my surname, a generation history—and he told me the true history of Seling surnames in types of Nepali. It is a 1,200-year-old history. My dad has a headmanship box (Limbu Subba) that contains all of the information he has found.

My cat wanted to go out for fresh air, so I let him go out. The birds were starting to raise their voices again in chirping. My husband cooked breakfast, and I prepared fruit and salads for lunch. I spent time on my coursework for two hours to research and make notes for my dissertation.

I typed my transcription after my research interviews. These were semi-structured remote interviews, and participants were encouraged to take their time and think about their responses. Explanations were provided, and there was an opportunity to ask questions if needed. In addition to this, the researcher explored responses in order to gain clarity. The semi-structured interviews were listened to several times, notes were made, and responses were interpreted and recorded.

I attended my online class at 3 p.m. for one hour regarding my dissertation.

All the family decided to go out walking because my husband had the day off today. My husband and I decided to take the children to

Firmly Field, 11 years after we left the place. Both my daughters studied at Lakeside Primary school until year 4 and year 2 in that school.

The place has changed so much. It is situated between Deputy and Frimely Green, and the lakes there are so beautiful. There were lots of bushes, trees, and reindeer. Birds were chirping and singing very late into the evening. I used to drive my both daughters for 40 minutes—a total of 80 minutes a day—from Fleet to Firmly for them to go to their schools for six months after we moved to Fleet.

We have talked about our family attachment, and my eldest daughter realised that if there was not a pandemic, we would not have the time to take a family walk like this. I said yes, family attachment and good relationships are very important for human life and society. In this case, I felt some positive aspect of coronavirus, although people did run away in an opposite direction from us at that field.

We spent more than three hours walking and went to view our home in Frimley Camberley. My youngest child, a son, was born at that house but hadn't been there for eleven years. We took him there to view his birthplace. Our daughters were taking pictures and videos while we walked to the field.

Due to the long walk and time, we planned to have Chinese takeaway for dinner. We watched a documentary movie while we were eating dinner. It was a very family-orientated day today. I enjoyed finding out more about my family tree and spending quality time with my family in a place we use to live in.

The death toll from Covid-19 rose by 85 today, less than the previous day, bringing the total to 44,619.

Time: 11.55 p.m.

Friday, 10 July 2020
110th day of lockdown

> ***In the news***: Sixth day of bars, pubs, and shops open; No. 10 considering mandatory face masks in shops in England. Making face coverings mandatory in shops in England is being considered by the government to slow the spread of coronavirus. Speaking

in a Facebook Q&A video, Boris Johnson hinted at the change, saying, "We are looking at ways of making sure that people really do have face coverings in shops." This is being put into place to make everyone safe when out shopping.

I am concerned about mask wearing all the time, and I do wear masks when I go out for walks with friends and relatives.

I woke up at 8 a.m. The weather was a mixture of hot and cold. It was hard to know how the weather was going to be.

I massaged my hair with herbal oil and left it in while I cleaned the kitchen and toilets, and disinfected all surfaces of the house. After I washed the oil out of my hair, I brushed my teeth as usual and took a shower.

My husband cooked breakfast for the whole family. I started to do my literature review and read information in the book about violence against women in South Asian communities, and I typed 1,300 words.

I noticed that Black and South Asian women face more domestic violence than white women in the UK. According Thiara (2005, 2006, cited Thiara and Gill, 2010):

> A study indicated that South Asian and BME women have experienced more severe domestic abuse over the long the period than mainstream society of women in the UK. Statistic has shown that 59 per cent of BME women … homicides from London in 2005 to 2006.

> However, very few mainstream researchers focused on exploring different backgrounds of women, which distresses in real practices, and this caused death of women in the UK. An essential part of investigation of domestic violence against women has emphasised racial women's experience relating to forms of domestic violence, control, agencies, housing authorities, social services, the police services, and criminal justice system processes. This investigation had found that women have experienced double victimisation (Gill 2004, Razack 1998, and Stark1995).

Hence, "collective victimhood" has led to silent at worst situation and limited attention on the problems of BME women and violence against women in the wider society of feminist literature in the UK.

This is part of my research for my literature review. It highlights the difference in help between women in the UK and BSAME women. Everyone who experiences domestic violence is a "collective victim", but those who need help have different experiences, and this basically boils down to the cultural language background.

My eldest daughter prepared Korean kimchi fry for lunch again, and we had this during the day.

I went jogging with friends for around four hours again. On the way to walking in the field, we met many groups of people. Cyclists were everywhere. Still, people have not built up trust with each other due to the coronavirus. We just waved to each other and walked off.

I had dinner with the family and watched YouTube videos about domestic violence against a young South Asian Nepali girl who had been suffering in silence for ages. The video was recommended to me by my two daughters. They sat and watched it with me. It was very relevant to what I was studying and nice to share my subject with them. It was the first time I had seen a video regarding a young (under 30) Nepali lady. She had recorded this herself and uploaded it onto YouTube. Technology is a fantastic and accessible thing.

The death toll from Covid-19 rose by 48 today, less than the previous day, bringing the total to 44,667.

Time: 11.50 p.m.

Saturday, 11 July 2020
111th day of lockdown

> ➢ ***In the news***: Jack Charlton, a World Cup winner with England and former Republic of Ireland boss, has died at age 85. One of English football's most popular characters, he was on the team that won the World Cup at Wembley in 1966, alongside his brother Bobby. He died peacefully in his sleep at age 85.

I woke up at 8 a.m. The weather was so bright, with a slight breeze. I spent quite a long time cleaning the house and had a shower and fed the cat. I cleaned the worship area, played ritual music, and worshiped.

My husband cooked breakfast for the family. I started to log into my university module and checked my email from university of Surrey and the teachers. I printed out some important information that was in the form of a PowerPoint presentation for my assignment's guideline and read the samples of some old dissertations from the master dissertation module.

On my Master degree (post-graduation) ceremony at the University of Surrey with my family around me

This gave me a few ideas about sampling (purposive sampling and convince sampling) for my research topic. My husband made some delicious food, such as *aludam* and dry fish mix. I joined the global network episode with Dr Som Dhimal. He presented a nice subject.

I remembered that five years ago today, I was attending as a judge for a poem competition in Reading which was organised by Reading Nepali Community to save and promote our Nepali language and culture within the UK. It was a special birthday celebration of the great poet, the late Bhanu Bhakta Archarya from Nepal.

I went jogging with my friends for a couple of hours again. I am concerned about mask wearing all the time, because not many people wear them and adhere to the rules set out. I do wear my mask when I go out for a walk with friends and relatives, as I want to protect myself and other people.

The death toll from Covid-19 rose by 148 today, more than the previous day, bringing the total to 44,815.

Time: 11.50 p.m.

Sunday, 12 July 2020
112th day of lockdown

> ➤ ***In the news***: Senior minister Michael Gove has said he does not think face coverings should be compulsory in shops in England; saying he trusts people's common sense.

> ➤ As India struggles with Coronavirus, Bollywood's Biggest Star Tests Positive—Amitabh Bachchan, whose face is everywhere in the country, checked into a hospital with mild symptoms. His son, daughter-in-law, and granddaughter have also become infected.

Doesn't matter where in the world you are, the coronavirus is affecting everyone, whether in the UK or, like above, in India.

I woke up at 3.30 a.m. It was dark outside, with a slight breeze. I got up and washed and brushed my teeth as soon as possible and prepared my uniform, then went to work. As always, there is a lack of PPE at work, although the government announced compulsory face masks for everyone. I do have a mask myself and carry it all the time and wear it when it is needed.

I came back home earlier than normal due to starting early at work today. I took a shower and disinfected and rested for a short time. I began to read an example of an article while I had to join a Zoom meeting for the Nepal Indigenous Society UK, for which I'm a vice president.

The main aim of this virtual meeting was to celebrate the 26th World Indigenous Day on 10 August. There was a very important agenda, and many issues were discussed and decided upon. The meeting took quite a long time and lasted longer than expected. People who attended included the ambassador of Nepal from London and many important leaders from around the world who were representing this society. I was busy with the meeting as well as typing work for my course. I was multitasking throughout. I had the role of secretary throughout some points in this meeting.

I spoke to my parents and family quickly in Nepal to get an update on Dad's health and found that he was getting better than before, which made me feel very happy.

My eldest daughter was busy cooking Mexican food for lunch, and my husband was deep-cleaning the house. They prepared everything and invited me for lunch. I had a lovely lunch with the family. My plan was to complete some work by today; therefore, I did not go out jogging. I told my friends this.

The death toll from Covid-19 rose by 21 today, less than the previous day, bringing the total to 44,836.

Time: 11.50 p.m.

Monday, 13 July 2020
113th day of lockdown

> ***In the news***: Face coverings in England's shops to become compulsory from the 24th July. Those who fail to comply with the new rules will face a fine of up to £100, the government is to announce. The move will bring England into line with Scotland and other major European nations like Spain, Italy and Germany. They are designed to minimise the spread of coronavirus and also encourage people to return to the shops safely. Data of face mask wearing countries: In Singapore, where it is an offence not to wear a mask outside your home, 90 per cent of people do so—the highest rate in the world. In Europe, the proportion of people wearing masks is highest in Spain (86 per cent), followed by Italy (83 per cent) and France (78 per cent). In the UK, just 36 per cent of people say they wear a mask in public, although this has been steadily increasing. In the US, the rate is 73 per cent, which is slightly higher than its neighbour Canada (60 per cent).

This shows that the UK has the lowest number of people wearing masks compared to the rest of the world. Everyone should be doing their part when fighting this virus, and it shows the UK needs to do more.

I woke up at 8 a.m. The weather was lovely—warm sunshine. I got up, had some tea, set up my alarm, and started to study the book *Crime and Women*. I found one of the important theories of domestic violence against women is the patriarchal culture:

> This theory states that in patriarchal culture, women are controlled by male power. They are hugely restricted and limited in their choices. Married women are likely to be smacked, shoved, and harshly beaten, murdered, and raped. Many witnesses have confirmed that "wife-battering" is "an assertion of patriarchal authority". Historically, a husband had the right to chastise his wife. However, in the late nineteenth century, that rule was slowly refused by legal process. (Dobash and Dobash, 1979, cited in Heidensohn, 1996)
>
> Furthermore, Dobash and Dobash (1979, cited in Heidensohn (1996) conducted a study among police officers and found that police officers were very reluctant to take custody when the husband is involved in domestic violence against his wife. In general, the police believe that they should not interfere in a situation between husband and wife. In patriarchal authority, many women are controlled and governed at home by domestic violence.

It shows that within history, any woman can experience domestic violence, and this has been a constant throughout society.

I went out jogging for about 80 minutes and talked to my mum for a long time whilst I was on the walk in the field. My husband came home from work, and he had dinner, took a shower, then read the news about the coronavirus update for today.

The death toll from Covid-19 rose by just 11 today, less than the previous day, bringing the total to 44,847. The death rate is the lowest it has been since the pandemic happened.

Time: 11.50 pm

✎ Tuesday, 14 July 2020
114th day of lockdown

> ➤ ***In the news***: Duchess of Sussex urges young women to challenge leaders to create positive change. The Duchess of Sussex has urged young women to "push" humanity in a "more inclusive" direction. Speaking to a gender equality summit, Meghan called on delegates to challenge "lawmakers, leaders, and executives" and make them "uncomfortable". It comes after she and her husband, Prince Harry, spoke to young people about equal rights. Last week, the pair spoke to young leaders during the Queen's Commonwealth Trust (QCT) weekly video call, which focused on responding to the Black Lives Matter movement.

I woke up at 7 in the morning. I decided to go for haircut today, because I haven't had a cut since before lockdown in March.

I had an appointment with the plumber and electrician. They came on time, fixed what they needed to, and left.

I joined the class for my dissertation for two hours. I finished typing my draft literature review and then emiled it to my supervisor for comment.

I took a short break, had some fruit and water, went out into the back garden, and picked some green vegetables for dinner.

I had another class in the evening for my English language course from the language department of the university. After I had finished class, I cooked dinner and fed the family.

I had to miss going out jogging due to having so many classes today.

The death toll from Covid-19 rose dramatically by 138 today, 127 more than yesterday, bringing the total to 44,985. It is very worrying that there has been a dramatic rise in deaths over the past 24 hours.

Time: 11.50 p.m.

✎ Wednesday, 15 July 2020
115th day of lockdown

> *In the news*: Boris Johnson has for the first time committed to an "independent inquiry" into the coronavirus pandemic. The PM said now was not the right time for an investigation but there would "certainly" be one "in the future" so lessons could be learned. Sir Keir Starmer is calling for an immediate inquiry into the government's handling of the pandemic.

I woke up at 8 a.m. The weather was warm, and the sun was shining. The birds were singing and having food.

I researched the topic of *hakpare*, a historic cultural practice which belongs to the Limbu tripe in Nepal. It is linked with ritual practices among Limbu cultures, such as sadness, happiness, and festival times from the eastern part of Nepal. It took a long time to do today.

I had lunch, which was made by the children, and sat down and ate it with them. I felt so tired today. I went out to the garden and picked some green vegetables for dinner. I especially like to eat fresh and organic vegetables with lunch and dinner.

I went jogging with my friend for a couple of hours. We met so many people, cyclists, dog walkers, runners, but everyone was maintaining social distancing. We saw some beautiful reindeers, rabbits, and birds. The weather was bright with no rain today, but we had a little rain when I came back home.

The death toll from Covid-19 rose by 85 today, a lot less than the previous day, bringing the total to 45,070.

Time: 11.50 p.m.

✎ Thursday, 16 July 2020
116th day of lockdown

> *In the news*: The NHS in England will get an extra £3bn of funding to prepare for a possible second wave of coronavirus, Boris Johnson is set to announce.

I woke up at 8 a.m. in the morning. As soon as I woke up and got myself dressed, I had a cup of tea and quickly cleaned the house. I talked to my friends for a few minutes.

I prepared a short talk about *hakpare* based on my research from yesterday. I added some details about its mythological history and its value in Limbu society in Nepal. I gave a talk that lasted a few minutes; this was done live on Facebook also. We used to celebrate this in the field every year in the UK with more than 5,000 Limbu people, including many other Nepalese, but this year we are unable to meet face to face due to the pandemic.

A picture of myself wearing Limbu (Nepali) cultural jewellery

I was able to do some typing, managed to get a dissertation draft done, and then emailed it to my supervisor at university. I decided to cancel jogging because I had to cook my festival food for Saune Sakrati (Sisekpa Tangnam), a Nepali festival. I cooked all the festive food: BBQ, *selroti*, *alu pakauri* (made from potatoes, pickles, rice curry paste), salad, and drinks.

We watched a Nepali movie while we were eating dinner. Usually, we would celebrate as part of the community. We used to organise a programme in the field, something that was very big and involved businesses, and we had many hand-made things available. But this year, we had to just stay with the family due to the pandemic.

This reminded me of my childhood, when I used to celebrate with my mum, dad, siblings, family, and relatives. This festival had unique value. People would work farming in the field during monsoons, and today was supposed to be the end of work and a new month of the Nepali calendar.

I still remember one of my best friends since childhood. We used to go to school, walk, play, and work together all the time, but unfortunately, she passed away last year. She left four children and a husband behind. I cried a lot when I heard the message of her death. It made a lot of memories come flooding back. They are constantly popping into my mind, and I can't rid of them. Most of the time, she came to my house for sleepovers, and she used to help me with my housework too.

The death toll from Covid-19 rose by 66 today, less than the previous day, bringing the total to 45,136.

Time: 01.23 a.m.

Friday, 17 July 2020
117th day of lockdown

I woke up at 7.30 a.m. and contacted my parents and my sister at Kathmandu. We talked for quite a long time. I updated them about the festival and talked to my mum and dad about celebrating the festival when I was a child. Childhood memories are always great. I had a dream that I was in my homeland and my family was there too.

I reviewed my course, which is part of the field method. I viewed the module guide and downloaded some important reading relating to my next research. It is about observational skills, and I printed out my old work for a sample.

I asked my husband to come to the café with me for my research work. We went to a café in Farnborough, but that café was drive-through only, so we went to another café in Aldershot town. We got in, and my husband ordered two cups of coffee.

I was starting to write up my notes at the table. There were not many people about, and it was the first day out for coffee in a café for 118 days, since the beginning of lockdown. Unfortunately, the staff from the café informed us that they were closing the shop within five minutes, so we had to go out with the coffees and go back home.

It was too late to go jogging with friends. Instead, I did yoga at home for around 90 minutes and had a shower. We had dinner and started to read the news update, and I started to type my diary for a few minutes.

Boris Johnson gave a coronavirus briefing on Friday, accompanied by Lady Harding, who is in charge of the NHS test and trace system for England. Here are some of the claims that were made about PPE:

> Boris Johnson: "We have substantially increased the pipeline of personal protective equipment [PPE] for the NHS and social care constituting over 30 billion items of PPE over the course of the pandemic".
>
> However, government figures show that only 2.3 billion items have actually been delivered to health and social care services in England, up to 12 July. This includes 1.4 billion gloves (which are counted individually as opposed to in pairs). It's not immediately clear where the 30 billion number comes from, but it could include future deliveries.
>
> On 26 June, Lord Deighton who's leading the government's PPE efforts, said there were 28 billion items on order.

Even though the government had promised a lot of PPE to be delivered out to people, we are still struggling to find PPE. From personal experience, I can say that we ended up using a lot that was bought from Asian sources.

The death toll from Covid-19 rose by 144 today, much more than the previous day, bringing the total to 45,280. The daily toll is over 100 for another day, and this continues to worry me.

Time: 01.08 a.m.

Saturday, 18 July 2020
118th day of lockdown

I woke up at 8 a.m. to lovely weather. Again, the birds were singing. I had some tea, and I was annoyed by my children because they had a sibling argument. I contacted my parents, spoke to my dad and brother at Kathmandu, and talked for quite a long while.

I prepared some questions about my assignment and did an interview with three participants.

We were invited for the graduation party of my eldest daughter's friend, and we were all excited to joined in with a small party. My daughter and her friend have been friends since her childhood. It was the first time we went to someone's house for a party since the lockdown started. Therefore, all family and friends were excited and happy to have a change, to see other people, and to celebrate something happy and deserving.

I missed jogging today due to the party. We had dinner, and I started to read the news update and typed my diary for a short time.

The death toll from Covid-19 rose by only 40 today, less than the previous day, bringing the total to 45,320. The death rate was less than 50 today—a lot better than the previous day, when it was over 100.

Time: 01.08 a.m.

Sunday, 19 July 2020
119th day of lockdown

> ***In the news***: Boris Johnson does not want second national lockdown. Speaking to the Sunday *Telegraph*, the PM compared the option of a nationwide shutdown to a "nuclear deterrent", adding he does not think the country "will be in that position again". But the UK's chief scientific adviser said there is "a risk" such measures could be needed as winter approaches. This comes as councils in England have been given "lightning" lockdown powers.

I woke up at 8 a.m. The weather was different from yesterday; it was raining but warm. I got up and washed and brushed my teeth as soon as possible, had a cup of tea, and went to work.

I came back from work, had lunch, and changed my dress. I went to Costa Coffee in Aldershot town with my husband. I ordered my drinks, found a table, and opened my laptop to start reading for the observational part of my research. I started to take field notes as part of my observational skills research.

Many seats were locked away to maintain social distancing, and half the amount of seating was available for customers. I saw many types of customers and observed and wrote down my observations for around an hour.

I went out jogging with friends for around 90 minutes. I tried to come home as soon as possible, because I had to attend an online meeting with KYC Rushmoor branch (Limbu Nepali community UK). We had to discuss a second property investment on behalf of all of the community members.

We had dinner with my son only. My two daughters went to their friend's birthday party. I started to read the news, and updated and typed my diary for a few minutes.

The death toll from Covid-19 rose by 27 today, a lot less than the previous day, bringing the total to 45,347. The death rate has come down over the past couple of days, first being below 100 then below 50 and now today below 30, which fills me with hope.

Time: 11.49 p.m.

Monday, 20 July 2020
120th day of lockdown

> ***In the news***: A coronavirus vaccine developed by the University of Oxford appears safe and triggers an immune response. Trials involving 1,077 people showed the injection led to them making antibodies and T-cells that can fight coronavirus. The findings are hugely promising, but it is still too soon to know if this is enough

to offer protection and larger trials are under way. The UK has already ordered 100 million doses of the vaccine.

I woke up at 8.30 a.m., and the weather was warm. The birds were singing and having food.

I visited the University of Surrey website and downloaded the field-method handbook for guidance to do my assignment. I talked with my dad for his health update, and I also contacted my brother. I found a study that focuses on

> the café spaces as part of a wider qualitative project on everyday, living multi-culture that aims to interrupt the associations of cultural difference and social problems through a focus on negotiation of cultural difference.
>
> Without marginalizing everyday racism, exclusion, and inequalities, our research aims to examine micro-narratives and routine encounters of cultural difference that are part of the lives of a growing majority of people in England.
>
> Partly this is a response to the new geographies of ethnic diversity in England, in which multiculturism is becoming a feature in smaller cities and suburbs and already multicultural places have become more so. New levels of migration and migratory populations with little or no connection to previous migrants are one aspect of this (Vertovec, 2007; Wessendorf, 2014). Mixed ethnicity populations are also increasing and established migrant populations are becoming more socially and economically diverse and fragmented (Neal et al., 2013).

This is part of my research for part of a project. It is very interesting how the diversity of café culture has begun to be focused on cultural differences and the geographies of the ethnic minorities.

I went out jogging with my husband for two hours along the Basingstoke Canal. There were many people around. Some were fishing in a tent for the whole day and night. They were preparing their bed and food for the night.

We saw a few people having pizza. Some people were having fun and talking on a boat trip. It was an amazing environment to be in.

I tried to maintain my social distancing. Everyone was giving way to each other to avoid direct contact. I was scared to approach other people, because I did not wear my mask today. I tried to come home as soon as possible because I had to cook dinner.

I started to read the news and updated and typed my diary for a few minutes. The scene of the canal was so beautiful. The birds were about to sleep, and ducks were there with their small ducklings. It was magical. I felt spellbound after viewing this very picturesque scene at the canal.

The death toll from Covid-19 rose by 11 today, a lot less than the previous day, bringing the total to 45,358. This has given me hope, with the death rate being so low.

Time: 11.03 p.m.

Tuesday, 21 July 2020
121st day of lockdown

> ***In the news***: The UK will be living with coronavirus for many years to come and even a vaccine is unlikely to eliminate it for good. Prof. Sir Jeremy Farrar told the House of Commons' Health Committee "things will not be done by Christmas". He went on to say humanity would be living with the virus for "decades".

I began my day as usual and gave myself some time to watch YouTube channels and Facebook information from Nepal. My husband made the family a full English breakfast, but the children had not woken up yet. This is due to them going to bed late. I had breakfast and then started to check my observational work from the previous visit to the café.

I went on a second visit to the café at around midday today. I felt that I had started to gain lots of experience in the social manner of café culture.

I bought a cup of green tea and mango juice and sat down in the middle of the hall in the café. I was very busy, observing and taking notes for my research, and I spent an hour there. My husband and daughter went to an Asian shop to buy food, and they waited for me in the car in Aldershot town.

When I came back home from the café, I prepared dinner. I had my English language class from 4 to 6 p.m., then went jogging with friends for a couple of hours and did around 10k. We saw beautiful rabbits and reindeers in the fields while we were jogging through the forest. I had a really joyful jog.

When I got home with my friends, I let them come into the back garden. This was possible due to the new rule change. I did not let them into my house, however; they were only allowed in to use the toilet. I didn't let them in at all today because the coronavirus makes me very scared of other people, especially when I know what they do as a job.

The death toll from Covid-19 rose by 110 today, much more than yesterday, bringing the total to 45,468. The UK has the third highest number of recorded coronavirus deaths in the world, after the USA and Brazil. This is very embarrassing for a small country, to be very high up on the world total.

Time: 1.08 a.m.

Wednesday, 22 July 2020
122nd day of lockdown

> ➤ ***In the news***: Care home residents in England can begin to be reunited with one of their loved ones, the government has said, as it publishes new guidance. Residents will be limited to seeing the same one visitor, where possible, the guidance says. Some providers began allowing outdoor, socially distanced visits in June, in the absence of government guidelines.

My day started with a lovely dream; I was in my birthplace with my best friend in my homeland of Nepal. The dream made me feel happy and smile all day. The weather was warm; the birds were singing and having food. An aeroplane was flying in the sky. I heard echoes of the plane but could not see it.

At 11 a.m., I started to study at my computer. I set up an alarm clock before I began to study about café culture and found that:

Jones et al. (2015) conducted a study of exclusionary towns and found that public spaces were a mixture of strangers because of the wide range of materials that form a coffee house. This idea is linked to (Habermas, 1989, Jones et al., 2015, Hall, 2012, Watson, 2006, and Wilson, 2011). They suggested that the nature of societal attendance and exercise inside gathering places is co-constitutive of broader public change, collaboration, and creations of belonging. Similar to Hall, they shared a concern about how local cafés were connecting with diverse people, and they meet one another and use spaces in café culture.

Furthermore, Poland Aneta Piekut (2013) carried out research in café and restaurant environments and found that chains of cafés and restaurants have been identified as "familiar points"—straightforwardly familiar places of cultural assurance and public comfort. An ethnomethodological study of cafés has demonstrated that they are a meeting points where an individual or group of people are accessible for their comfort. (Eric Laurier and Chris Philo, 2006). This investigation has raised question about conversations, motions, temporal rhythms, the design of cafés, and the public's choice of seating. All of these notions can be picked up from ethnography study. However, this context of studies have tended to concentrate more on the meanings involved in these chains of local café spaces, their services, socialites, "etiquette rather than as spaces of ethnic diversity and mixing".

This research has taught me many things, especially about behaviour in a formal setting. It has given me so much experience where observational studies are concerned. A lot of social aspects happen within the café culture, mainly that of trust of one another.

Again, my eldest daughter made Mexican food for lunch, and we had it together. I decided to go jogging for a couple of hours, which was great after a day of working on my research. When I got back home, I had a shower, had dinner, and updated myself on the BBC News UK.

The death toll from Covid-19 rose by 79 today, less than the previous day, bringing the total to 45,547.

Thursday, 23 July 2020
123rd day of lockdown

> ***In the news****:* Full guidance on wearing face coverings in shops in England has been released, less than 12 hours before the new rules come into force. Coverings will be mandatory in enclosed public spaces, including supermarkets, indoor shopping centres, transport hubs, banks, and post offices. Those who break the rules could face a fine of up to £100. Police will be able to "use force" to remove customers from shops if they do not wear face coverings, as well as prevent them from entering.

In Nepal, it is the first day of the lockdown being eased. The release of lockdown measures isn't due to the coronavirus being gone, but due to mass hunger. There was no help for anyone, and people need to work in order to eat. Many people died due to landslides in this monsoon season. On average, 200 people have died every year in Nepal. It is so sad to know about this statistic that was found by Dr. Tuladhar.

I woke very early in the morning. I was up too early—even the birds hadn't gotten out of their nest—so I decided to go back to sleep and woke up a few hours later. The weather was warmer than earlier, and the birds had started to sing, which made me want to get out of bed.

A friend of mine came to see us, and we stayed outside and talked for a few hours, then she left. It was nice to have someone to talk to other than my own family. With the weather being so nice, she stayed longer than intended.

At midday, I started to correct and paraphrase the field method part of my observational research on the computer. I spent two hours working on my research and had lunch, which was cooked by my husband. I prepared some salmon and fried it for dinner. My eldest daughter cooked dinner with the salmon fry, dal, rice salad, and curry.

I participated in my yoga exercise for a few hours at home. After yoga, I went into the garden to do some gardening and to collect some vegetables. I nursed and watered all of the plants. I had dinner with my family and washed up the plates, then I cleaned the whole house. It took me a couple of hours. Afterwards, I wanted to update myself on the BBC News, something that I continue to do daily.

The death toll from Covid-19 rose by 53 today, less than the previous day, bringing the total to 45,600. Life and health matter.

Time 11.39 p.m.

Friday, 24 July 2020
124th day of lockdown

> ***In the news***: Face coverings are now compulsory for customers in shops in England, after new coronavirus rules came into force within 12 hours of the government issuing guidance on the change.

I woke up at 7 a.m. A cool wind was blowing, and the birds were chirping in their nest. I can now see this nest from my window. The mother bird is sitting on her nest.

I joined a meditation session organised by the Greater Rushmoor Nepali Community (GRNC). The meditation took about an hour, and it was great to have this online meditation. It made me feel ready for the day.

Between 10 a.m. and noon, I spent time paraphrasing my café culture observational field work research. Here are some lines from my work which I find interesting:

> On the left-hand side of the counter, four customers were having a drink, and they looked like non-English speakers but their body language and facial expressions were very happy. They all looked middle-age and everyone was obviously enjoying themselves. Their facial expressions and body language were very happy and excited. Most of the tables had two or three customers, and only one table had four men around it. The researcher noticed that when they came out from the café, they were talking in

their own language, which was not English. They talked loudly, gesturing with their hands as they came out from the café and walked on the street. They spent a longer time in the café compared to other customers. Two of the men had long beards and two were shaven and they were all dressed in casual jeans and tops, for example, white, blue, and brown T-shirts. It was easy to notice that many people spent a shorter time inside the café while they had coffee. The ethnic minority group, on the other hand, showed a greater degree of bonding and sharing and feelings compared with other customers. As it had not been possible for them to meet in their individual environments during the pandemic, the researcher noted that they found the café environment a place where they could share their feelings openly.

The fact that cafés and pubs are now open fills a lot of people with happiness and hope, even though social distancing has made this very limited. It shows that through it all, people are happy to see one another after so many months inside.

I did some yoga exercise for a couple of hours at home whilst my three children went out for a jog. I waited for them to return, and then we had dinner with the children.

The death toll from Covid-19 rose by 123 today, more than previous day, bringing the total to 45,723.

I have been very busy today and achieved so much.

Time: 11.00 p.m.

Saturday, 25 July 2020
125th day of lockdown

> ***In the news***: Travellers returning to the UK from Spain after midnight will have to quarantine for 14 days, the government has said. The decision came following a spike in coronavirus cases in Spain, with more than 900 new cases of the virus reported on Friday.

I woke up at 8 a.m. with a cool wind coming through the window. I could see the birds chirping in their nest. I had a shower, brushed my teeth, and worshiped as normal due to it being Saturday, then had a cup of tea. I was ready for my English class, which was for a couple of hours. I had a late lunch, and we had Korean BBQ again, which was cooked by my eldest daughter.

At 3 p.m. I attended the global network conference and presentation by Dr Taramani Rai from Tribhuwan University Kritipur KTM. The subject matter was how language can control political power and certain types of people in the world. They discussed how people talk—doesn't matter if it is left or right wing, it is the power of the language and speech that gets through to people.

I went to jogging with friends. It took a couple of hours, although the weather was not good. It was raining, but we were able to manage it.

Here is some work from my field method with observational skills in café culture:

> To the right-hand side of the café counter, a customer (black man) was also busy drafting his notes, after which he started to use his laptop. He was working on his computer constantly. He looked like a mathematic student from college or university because he was also using a calculator while he was writing. On the left-hand side of the counter, four customers were having a drink, and they looked like non-English speakers, but their body language and facial expressions were very happy. They all looked middle-age, and everyone was obviously enjoying themselves. Their facial expressions and body language were very happy and excited. Most of the tables had two or three customers, and only one table had four men around it. The researcher noticed that when they came out from the café, they were talking in their own language, which was not English. They talked loudly, gesturing with their hands as they came out from the café and walked on the street. They spent a longer time in the café compared to other customers. Two of the men had long beards and two

were shaven, and they were all dressed in casual jeans and tops, for examples, white, blue, and brown T-shirts. It was easy to notice that many people spent a shorter time inside the café while they had coffee.

These social skills are modified by the researcher by the age, class, gender, ethnicity, language, and cultural background. The researcher was seeking to enhance ethnographic skills to interpret the social scene in front of the researcher. The ethnic minority group, on the other hand, showed a greater degree of bonding and sharing and feelings compared with other customers. As it had not been possible for them to meet in their individual environments during the pandemic, the researcher noted that they found the café environment a place where they could share their feelings openly. These ideas are relating to the researcher (Poland, Aneta and Piekut (2013) who have found cultural assurance and public comfortable in the café culture.

My research is a very interesting subject to me. We are seeking more knowledge on all of the ethnic groups' interaction within this culture.

The death toll from Covid-19 rose by 61 today, less than the previous day, bringing thte total to 45,784.

Time: 1.09 a.m. I have finished late, so good morning, diary!

Sunday, 26 July 2020
126th day of lockdown

> ***In the news***: New coronavirus quarantine rules have come into force in the UK, requiring travellers arriving from Spain to self-isolate for 14 days.

I woke up at 8.30 a.m., and it was a rainy morning. I quickly got up and prepared my uniform, then went to work at the Royal Military Academy Sandhurst.

I drove as fast as I could through the college-town gate. The gate security stopped me for my pass permission. I put my mask on and went to the office, but the staff from the gate did not wear any masks, so I was scared to approach any person. It took a few minutes to update my pass, and then I went to work.

The new government guidance rule requiring compulsory mask wearing started on 24 July 2020, which was a few days ago, but still, many of the staff are still not using any masks.

I was very busy at work due to the social distancing, and we tried to stay 1 meter away from one another, but due to this, the workload is increasing to take these measures into account. I tried as much as I could, because I'm still scared to come close to staff and other people.

Once I had finished work and returned home, my husband and eldest daughter were preparing authentic field cooking. It was very interesting to learn about things before technology took over our lives. My husband pointed out that he learnt how to do this without an electric oven. It is something the army does on safari, and it can be done in a hole in the ground. This means she cooked dinner without an electric oven.

I helped to cook a vegetarian option for my youngest daughter, whilst my husband and eldest daughter were busy field cooking BBQ pork curry, pork steak, rice curry, pickle, salad, and fruit and drinks. My eldest daughter took a video for her channel. Before this, she filmed Korean Mukbang with Korean chicken wing, pork, BBQ rice curry, and so on. You can watch it here: https://www.youtube.com/watch?v=YEUFNOMoI4Q.

I spent few minutes doing research work about my observational project:

> A young couple arrived with two buggies. The mother was pushing a new little baby girl and the father was pushing a girl toddler over 1 year. They did not have to wait in the queue at this time because the café was quieter than 40 minutes earlier, and they did not use the hand sanitiser from the café. Nearest to the counter was a young couple (black boy and white girl) having a drink. The boy was working on his iPad computer and writing notes with a pen. The boy looked very busy, and the girl was

just watching him while having coffee. They looked like girlfriend and boyfriend according to their body language and facial expressions.

For many, the café is an important meeting place that can be established as part of a routine. Greeting friends and family in normal everyday life as well as being able to have a short rest from life for an urban human being.

I have learnt so much about many cultures throughout my observational research—how they speak to one another and how they interact through their body language.

The death toll from Covid-19 rose by only 14 today, much less than the previous day, bringing the total to 45,798. This drop in the death rate has filled me with hope once again. It is less than 15 and has come down dramatically from the previous day.

Time: 12:05 a.m.

Monday, 27 July 2020
127th day of lockdown

> ***In the news***: The UK has updated its advice against all non-essential travel to Spain to include the Balearic and Canary Islands following a rise in coronavirus cases. The Foreign Office guidance was changed on Monday to include both mainland Spain and islands such as Ibiza and Tenerife. This is in addition to the self-isolation policy that began on Sunday.

I woke up at 7.30 a.m., checked my mobile, and read a few news articles about Nepal. The weather was rainy, and the sky was dark. Although the weather was like this, I went out for jog for around 30 minutes.

On the way for a jog, I saw beautiful squirrels and birds looking for food. I imagined to myself that these creatures had no worry about coronavirus.

I did not meet that many people today in the morning, but I saw a lady walking with her dog. I quickly changed direction to go on the opposite side of her path and ran very quickly away, whilst she walked hastily in the other direction.

I came back home quickly and had a shower, and then I washed my and my husband's clothes by hand. I had a glass of warm water and fed the cat.

I studied a journal article which was sent to me by the university lecturer and found that

> the ethnic diversity of the clientele of the chain cafés we studied did appear to contrast with other cafés in our field sites, and often in ways that sit uneasily with the critique developed by Ritzer and others in their call for resistance to the McDonaldization.
>
> While our research did not intend to be comparative of the distinctions between the corporate café spaces and local, independent café spaces, it became apparent both from our participant observation and also in our interviews with participants. While we asked about places, we did not ask about café use specifically in our interviews but participants did, nevertheless, talk about the role of cafés as social spaces in their localities.

At 6 p.m., my son had a private lesson, so I decide to go out jogging with six ladies. I always use a mask when I go out jogging when with a group. I try to maintain social distancing every time I am jogging for a couple of hours.

I tried to come home as soon as possible have dinner with my family. I cooked dinner before going out for a walk. I had dinner after I came back home.

I watched a movie which was about a matchmaking agency for Indian families from an upper-class member.

Today I undertook a lot of exercise. Throughout the pandemic, I have taken part in yoga, jogging, and walking, with both friends and family. I have enjoyed the time I have spent with my family whilst remaining healthy through exercise.

The death toll from Covid-19 rose by 7 today, much less than the previous day, bringing the total to 45,805. Another low-death-rate day in the UK. This continues to fill me with so much hope for the future.

Time: 11.25 p.m.

🖉 Tuesday, 28 July 2020
128th day of lockdown

> ➤ *In the news*: The boss of Heathrow has called for airports to be allowed to test for coronavirus to avoid the "cliff edge" of quarantine.

I woke up at 7 p.m. and joined in with yoga exercise on Zoom, which was organised by the GRNC.

I spent a long time doing my assignment. My online class finished at 6 p.m., and then I went out for a jog with friends. It took around two hours. We normally do around 10k.

My son had a private lesson online at 7 p.m. I came back home from jogging, made some fruit, strawberry-flavoured smoothie drink, and salads, and we had dinner with all the family members. While we had dinner, we watched *Memory King*, a film about a young boy called Bijay Shahi from Nepal. I tried to check the BBC News, although I was tired.

The death toll from Covid-19 rose by 119 today, a lot more than the previous day, bringing the total to 45,924. This doesn't fill me with a lot of hope. The death rate is rising, and this makes me so worried for the future.

Time: 11.00 p.m.

🖉 Wednesday, 29 July 2020
129th day of lockdown

> ➤ *In the news*: The length of time people with coronavirus symptoms have to self-isolate for is set to be increased to 10 days.

I woke late morning; the birds and doves were chirping in the field. The cars were leaving. It was a nice, bright, warm morning, and it made me feel happy.

I set an alarm clock for every two hours to study my course module for my assignment, and I spent enough time to find important information from the link from the Surrey University Library. I checked my dissertation feedback from my supervisor and worked on this for around an hour. Then I wrote up a few data analysis sections. I attended my online class for the new 2500 University assignment.

Later in the evening, I attended the Rushmoor Heathy Living quarterly meeting, which was on Zoom due to coronavirus. This was a great way to connect with everyone. It only took a couple of hours; the meeting discussed very important agendas; and we admitted new trustee members after we had interviewed them and their CVs were checked by the chief officer.

My youngest daughter cooked a very tasty pasta dish for dinner, and we sat down and ate it as a whole family. I decided to have a few moments of fresh air and went with my husband to go out for a walk locally, due to how late it was. After coming back from the walk, we watched BBC news UK, then noted it into my diary.

The death toll from Covid-19 rose by 83 today, less than the previous day, bringing the total to 46,007. Even though the increase is less than yesterday, it is still higher than the previous weeks.

Time: 11.00 p.m.

Thursday, 30 July 2020
130th day of lockdown

> ***In the news***: Self-isolation period to be extended to 10 days.

I started the day as usual. I decided to set up an alarm clock for an hour to look through the Surrey University log-in. I searched the university library to find out some new information for my dissertation. I spent enough time to find the important information link from the library.

I started to do the field observation assignment for a couple of hours, and I wanted to complete my 2,500 words today. Later in the afternoon, I focused on my dissertation and the introduction section that was commented on by my supervisor.

I felt very tired and sleepy after all the work I had done, so I decided to stay at home and work more on my assignment rather than go jogging. I informed my friends that I was not going for a walk today.

My husband had the day off, so he cooked dinner, and we had it with all the family. We watched a documentary of a border plate between North and South America:

> The Cocos Plate is a young oceanic tectonic plate beneath the Pacific Ocean off the west coast of Central America, named for Cocos Island, which rides upon it. The Cocos Plate was created approximately 23 million years ago when the Farallon Plate broke into two pieces, which also created the Nazca Plate. The Cocos Plate also broke into two pieces, creating the small Rivera Plate.[2] The Cocos Plate is bounded by several different plates. To the northeast it is bounded by the North American Plate and the Caribbean Plate.

I found this very interesting, and it was nice change from the BBC News.

The death toll from Covid-19 rose by 38 today, much less than the previous day, bringing the total to 46,045.

Time: 11.07 p.m.

Friday, 31 July 2020
131st day of lockdown

> ***In the news***: Boris Johnson postpones lockdown easing in England. The further easing of lockdown restrictions in England—due to come in this weekend—has been postponed for at least two weeks, after an increase in coronavirus cases.

I woke up at 7.30 a.m. The trees were moving slowly and gently due to the warm air that was blowing, and the birds were chirping very nicely in the field. The weather was very nice and sunny, and it put me in a very good mood.

I spoke to my parents and sibling in Nepal. It was nice to catch up with people.

I set up an alarm clock for every two hours to look at the Surrey University log-in. I searched the university library to find out new information for my dissertation. I spent enough time to find the important information from the link from the library.

I typed constantly all day and searched through the library, so much so that my right arm started to ache. I felt very tired, and my neck was sore. I decided to stay home and do some yoga.

The temperature was very high, and I was scared to go out. My husband had the day off, and therefore, he managed to do all the housework, and he also cooked lunch and dinner.

I had some free time to focus on me today. We ate dinner as a family. We watched a documentary on Raute tribe people, who are nearly disappearing. They are a small Nepali tribe that would like to be isolated and keep to themselves and keep their own lives and traditions away from the outside world. They have no modern education or medication and still hunt and kill their food. They don't do any farming and rely on hunting as their main food source.

We are trying to get so many communities to work together within the rest of Nepal to help them survive within their tribe. The Raute tribe has very few members left, and we are working hard to keep these long traditions alive and leave them to their lives and culture.

The death toll from Covid-19 rose by 120 today, more deaths than the previous day, bringing the total to 46,165. Throughout this week, the death toll has been fluctuating from the low hundreds to the high teens. There is a graphical war going on with the data, and this is due to the summer infection rates, with people being allowed out.

Time: 11.07 p.m.

August 2020

✎ Saturday, 1 August 2020
132nd day of lockdown

> ➢ ***In the news***: Pubs "may need to shut" to allow schools to reopen. Pubs or "other activities" in England may need to close to allow schools to reopen next month, a scientist advising the government has said.

I woke up early to a cool morning. I awoke less hot than the previous morning. My neighbour was being very loud, and I could hear her language.

I had a shower, brushed my teeth, then undertook my worship for God as usual on Saturday. There was a loud noise of aeroplanes in the sky while I was worshiping.

I talked to my parents and sibling in Nepal. Then I focused on my literature review, as I had received feedback from my supervisor. I worked on this for a couple of hours.

My husband prepared lunch, and we all ate together as a family. I joined the global network conference online. An advocate and lawyer were giving great presentations. They discussed the International Labour Organization and the 169. The ILO was created in 1919. It is a standard-setting specialized agency of the United Nations which aims to improve living and working conditions for working people all over the world, without discrimination as to race, gender, or social origin. The ILO, which was created in 1919, believes that poverty anywhere is a danger to prosperity everywhere.

After I finished the conference, the family and I went out for a jog. My youngest daughter stayed at home, because she wanted to cook dinner. The weather was hot, and although we had fun jogging, it took around 90 minutes. We crossed three different lakes and a beautiful field. We saw so many people fishing, and some people were having picnics at the lakes. We tried to avoid people who came near us. We went an alternate way when we saw a new group of people due to the coronavirus. We had dinner and took a shower and checked the BBC News.

The death toll from Covid-19 rose by 74 today, less than the previous day, bringing the total to 46,239. Again, the death toll has fluctuated and dropped from the previous day. Let's see what tomorrow brings.

Time: 11.07 p.m.

✏️ Sunday, 2 August 2020
133rd day of lockdown

> **In the news**: A major incident has been declared by authorities in Greater Manchester following recent rises in coronavirus infection rates.

I woke up early this morning. The warm air was blowing through the window. It was very quiet, and I could hear the birds chirping in the field and the wind coming through the leaves in the trees.

I prepared my uniform, went to the car park, and started my car, but it wouldn't start, so I had to call out my husband to come and get another key to either my husband's or daughter's car.

My husband went and got me a key to my daughters' car, and I had to drive so quickly to get to work on time. I had to take my daughter's car because it was allowed on site at work.

Everyone at work was really busy, and so was I. We tried to maintain social distancing as much as we could, but a few staff members forgot about it, even though all the information is there at work for everyone to read.

I came back home, got changed, then contacted my parents because I saw a new picture had been uploaded onto my father's Facebook. His health is getting better than last time, and we talked with my mum, cousin, and nieces.

I did not go out for a jog today. Instead, I sat down to do research for my literature reviews. My husband made dinner, and we ate it all together. We watched a Nepali film (*Gham pani*), and the story was based on social changes according to equality and democracy.

The death toll from Covid-19 rose by only 8 today, much less than the previous day, bringing the total to 46,247. This amount of only 8 people dying makes me feel so hopeful. It seems that we are finally beating this horrible virus and that life can get back to normal.

Monday, 3 August 2020
134th day of lockdown

I woke up as usual, and a friend of mine came over with some fresh vegetables from her garden for me. I had made a cup of tea for my friend and my husband. We all tried to make sure that we stayed apart from one another, but it is really hard to do in our own home.

My plan was to stay on the computer all day today because I had to work so much on my introduction and literature section. I did not go jogging because I had to search certain topics of information. I found the new subheading topic in the following:

> Southall Black Sisters (2018) was established in 1979 for an advice, advocacy and campaigning centre for BME women in the UK. Southall Black Sisters and the other 30 organisations have welcomed the report of the Domestic Violence Bill, which suggested to the UK government to make sure there is equal support for immigrant women who experienced domestic violence—that if "the Domestic Violence Bill" did not include all women regardless of their immigration status, it will have failed. They seriously focused on the idea that the forthcoming bill should support all women regardless of immigration status who were victims of domestic violence. This bill must address immigrant and Black ethnic minority women who were affected by cuts in funding.

This established group is a fantastic asset to have. Many women don't know about the help that is there. But it is there for them.

I tried to avoid cooking dinner, so we decided to order a Chinese takeaway. Everyone was happy with the curry that we chose. I stopped and checked the news on my mobile phone.

The death toll from Covid-19 rose by just 9 today, more than the previous day but not a great deal, bringing the total to 46,256.

This continues to fill me with hope. It is only one more death than yesterday, and it is helping me see a happy and healthy future.

Time: 11.50 p.m.

🖉 Tuesday, 4 August 2020
135th day of lockdown

> ➤ ***In the news***: A large blast in the Lebanese capital, Beirut, has killed at least 70 people and injured more than 2,700 others. Videos show smoke billowing from a fire, then a mushroom cloud following the blast at the city's port.

We watched this whilst having dinner, and we were so shocked by the scenes that we were seeing, especially within this pandemic time.

I was having a very nice dream. I was happily laughing and smiling at my birthplace, Oyam (Yangwarak), Panchthar. Actually, I was looking for the toilet, but there was no toilet used when I was child. It was bright and must have been about 11 a.m., and I saw my auntie was carrying a load of grass for the cows and buffalos.

My actual birth house was the same as before they destroyed it, and the place was also looking exactly the same as before all the infrastructure development began, such as new roads and housing. It is not possible to notice now how it was before due to development.

I woke up at 6.30 a.m. I was not at the same place as I was in the dream. I was in my bed in the UK and stayed silent for a few minutes and reflected on my dream—the floods of memories of my past or my childhood days. Even I cannot imagine how it looked before in reality. But in the dream, I can visualise exactly the same place where I was born, and that was my first house.

We moved to our second house after my parents had it built, and then we moved to a third house quite far away from these two houses, which was the last one that my parents moved into. It has a lot of land.

I had a shower, cleaned the toilets and bathroom, made a cup of coffee for myself, and sat down at the computer. That was my plan for today.

My plan was to stay on the computer and work again on the introduction for my literature review. Due to this, I couldn't go out jogging. I wanted to concentrate on my work and a topic that interests me. I found something very interesting when I was doing research on my topic. It was about the language problem and interpreters in domestic violence against Black minority ethnic (BME) women:

> The language difficulties created problems for victim, perpetrator, interpreter, and Criminal Justice System in the case of domestic violence against BME women. Williams and Yarnell (2013) conducted the research in Northern Ireland to see how language interpreters were supporting victims who could not speak in English. This study was carried out between many state bodies, for example, Criminal Justice system, the Police Service, Health and Social Care Services Trust, Housing service, and social security interpreters offered without discrimination based on race and ethnicity in Northern Ireland. This research found that there was a lack of language interpreters for the public services and they found that the interpreters translated into inappropriate meaning owing to a lack of proper training for interpreters who are working in the social services. An event was revealed by an NGO worker that the language interpreter had not translated correctly. The video recorder showed that the interpreter did not explained accurately the case of DV.
>
> An untrained interpreter may be unaware of BME women's customary values and norms. The Health and Social Services Trusts trained 80 out of 300 interpreters to specialise in domestic abuse cases. Victim of domestic violence had been receiving regular support from Health and Social Services, but many organisations demonstrated that this service was unavailable to BME domestic violence victims owing to language problems and lack of available interpreters for these women.

The policing and the Criminal Justice system discovered that the cases of domestic violence among BME women had not raised due to lack of interpreters. It was suggested that the government should fund budgets to train interpreters to access BME victim services available from authorities and organisations.

Due to the lack of training in translation and interpretation, a lot can go wrong, and women and children are suffering because of it. More training is needed to interpret different languages in order to help people in need.

I decided to go out jogging, although it was 9 p.m. I needed a break after working at my computer all day. I went for an hour and then came back and checked the BBC News UK.

The death toll from Covid-19 rose by 89 today, much higher than the previous days' totals of 8 and 9. The total as of today is 46,345, and still the UK has the third highest number of recorded coronavirus deaths in the world. I am worried, with the steady rise in cases and deaths, that a second wave is coming, but we can only hope that it doesn't happen.

Time: 11.27 p.m.

Wednesday, 5 August 2020
136th day of lockdown

> *In the news*: UK government "ready to go" with £5m aid to Lebanon. There was a huge explosion in Lebanon yesterday. The UK is ready to send medical experts and humanitarian aid to Lebanon following the deadly explosion in Beirut. Foreign Secretary Dominic Raab has said the UK would "stand by the Lebanese people in their time of need" and promised a £5m aid package.

I woke up as usual and decided to clean the toilets and bathroom. I made myself a cup of coffee and sat down at the computer.

At 10 a.m., the AA came to collect my car (Jaguar SE model) due to it still not starting. They checked the car and noticed that there were not any engine faults, but it needed to be filled with air fluid. It had not been stocked since it was bought. A staff of the AA team drove it to the MOT service garage and promised to call me back after it had finished the MOT test.

I stayed on the computer all day today, because I had to work so much on my introduction and literature section again.

After spending so long on the computer, I went jogging with friends for two hours to help me rest. Friends decided to go to their vegetable gardens in Church Crookham Fleet Hampshire.

The death toll from Covid-19 rose by 59 today, less than previous day, bringing the total to 46,404. The death rate keeps going up and down throughout the past few days, and we hope that it continues to stay under 100.

Time: 12.02 a.m.

Thursday, 6 August 2020
137th day of lockdown

> *In the news*: A man has said it was "upsetting" to see the Duke and Duchess of Cambridge visit a care home where his father lives before his family was allowed to. The Royal couple visited Shire Hall Care Home in Cardiff on Wednesday.

It seems unfair that the royal family can go and visit strangers in a care home, but their own families can't. It was done for publicity, and that was it.

It was a cold day, not like the previous warm and sunny days. I woke early at 7:30 a.m. I brushed my teeth and washed the floor mat. I had a glass of warm water and then began to type my work on the computer.

I spent a long day managing my thesis introduction, literature review, subheadings, and data management. These were the rules from the university:

> As interviews will be taken remotely, data will not be transported or moved. Data will be stored during the

research and will be managed according to university policy and procedures. Raw data will be kept in a locked cabinet and once transcribed will be stored in a locked cabinet until the study is completed and then will be destroyed. Sharing of data will be according to the policies and procedures of the university, and this will be done with the participant's consent.

I stayed on the computer all day today because I had so much work to do on my introduction and literature section. I typed nearly 25,000 words. This made me feel tired and sore in my right hand and shoulder, due to all the typing that I had done.

My family ordered Domino's pizza, and someone cooked some chips, then we had dinner. I felt stressed because of spending all day looking at the computer, and I was happy that I didn't have to cook dinner.

I went jogging at 9.30 p.m. for one hour. I saw a few people with their dogs walking in the street, and I tried to stay far away from the other people because of the global pandemic, the coronavirus. I came home and had a shower. Then I started to record my diary.

The death toll from Covid-19 rose by 49 today, less than the previous day, bringing the total to 46,453. The number of daily deaths is still around the same number that it has been through the past couple of days, but it is still not like previous days, when it was 8 or 9.

Time: 12.02 a.m.

✎ Friday, 7 August 2020
138th day of lockdown

> ***In the news***: The UK has seen its hottest day in August for 17 years, as temperatures reached more than 36C (96.8F) in southeast England. Crowds headed to the coast to enjoy the weather, but people have been urged to adhere to social distancing. Exceptionally hot weather is set to continue in parts of the UK throughout the weekend, the Met Office said.

This weather reminded me of when I was in Brunei in 1999. People cannot survive without air-conditioning inside the house in Brunei, and I also felt too hot, although I used the fan inside the house.

I woke up at 7 a.m. and I peeped out from the window. The warm wind was blowing slowly, and the weather was hot and sunny. It looked liked a midday morning. I talked with my mum and dad for a little while. I had a glass of warm water and then began to type my work on the computer.

My eldest daughter cooked a special lunch and dinner, and my husband cooked vegetables, and we all ate together.

I started to read and manage my work on the computer, and I had to take a shower three times today whilst I was typing due to it being the hottest day in over seventeen years.

I spent a long time on the computer to complete the first step of my thesis from abstract, introduction, literature review, to limitation. I felt so tired, but I managed my thesis introduction, literature review, subheadings, and data management. Below is some of my research of my literature review:

> The study of Black South Asian minority ethnic women (BSAME) in the UK found new data from the respondent. There has been a new issue revealed by a few participants that middle-aged women suffer more violence because they think about their children's futures and don't want their child to grow up in a single-mother environment, which in turn may lead to shame.
>
> Furthermore, lack of education and literacy means that few elderly BSAME women can even type 999, so these women in particular suffer financial abuse and fall through the system and services, and they are more at risk for domestic violence. This data has surprised the researcher as well, because this issue has not existed in the previous studies in the literature review. This statement suggested that there should be a basic literacy class for

middle-aged BSAME women to enable them to make a 999 call.

It is horrible to find out that middle-aged and older women struggle to get help from domestic violence due to their lack of English education. The fact that they can't phone 999 due to not knowing English literacy or numeracy is both saddening and shocking. Everyone needs to know how to get help in any language, and this needs to be accessible for all.

The death toll from Covid-19 rose by 98 today, more than the previous day, bringing the total to 46,551. Deaths are slowly on the rise, and this is very worrying.

Time: 12.12 a.m.

Saturday, 8 August 2020
139th day of lockdown

I woke up at 7 a.m. It was a hot and bright morning. I fed the cat whilst doing some yoga exercises, which I did for around one hour.

I had to shower after I worshipped (*pooja*), and then did I did worship for my own tribe culture religion (*pegram*). I had a cold glass of milk and some warm water, and then I began to check my new assignment question.

I spent a couple of hours on my work and later joined the Zoom meeting for the global network channel, which was hosted by Dr Marohang from the United States. There was a great presentation from the Asham Limbu Mahasang community, which is part of the India community established in 2008 to unite and protect the cultural identities of Limbu (Nepali).

I missed going jogging with friends due to the global conference. Therefore, I went with my husband for a long walk to Twesle Down Horse Riding Field. We have never been to this area before and noticed that it was a big field for a walk.

The death toll from Covid-19 rose by 55 today, less than the previous day, bringing the total to 46,606. The death rate has fallen again today and is staying low, even though people have been outside enjoying the sunshine. We will soon find out if this is going to impact us.

Time: 11.45 p.m.

✎ Sunday, 9 August 2020
140ᵗʰ day of lockdown

> ➢ **In the news**: International Day of the World's Indigenous.

I woke up very early due to the weather being so hot. When the alarm went off, I got up quickly so that I could go outside to get some fresh air. My cat was waiting for me near the outside of the door, and he wanted to eat, so I fed him, and then he had a cup of tea and went to work.

Everyone was busy at work. I was concentrating on work continuously and had no time to talk with my work friends. I drove really fast to join the virtual meeting for the celebration of the International Day of the World's Indigenous People on 9 August 2020.

There is a range of great people from around the world who are committed to the indigenous people of Nepal. The chief guest was from the London Nepal ambassador and barrister. It was a great day, although it was a virtual meeting. It took five hours; it was a long meeting. Here is some information about it:

> The International Day of the World's Indigenous People is celebrated on 9 August each year to recognize the first UN Working Group on Indigenous Populations meeting in Geneva in 1982. On December 23, 1994, the UN General Assembly decided that the International Day of the World's Indigenous People should be observed on 9 August annually during the International Decade of the World's Indigenous People.
>
> In 2004, the assembly proclaimed the Second International Decade of the World's Indigenous People (2005–2014). The assembly also decided to continue observing the International Day of Indigenous People annually during the second decade. The decade's goal was to further strengthen international cooperation for solving problems faced by indigenous peoples in areas such as culture,

education, health, human rights, the environment, and social and economic development.

We had some very sad news today about the death of my niece, the daughter of my youngest sister-in-law from Nepal. She was very young, only 23 years old. My husband and I contacted my sister-in-law's husband's youngest sister to update us about the dead girl, who left a 7-year-old daughter behind. She was in her in-laws' house, and her husband was working in another country. It was said that she committed suicide, but nobody knows how she was killed. It was a mysterious death.

The death toll from Covid-19 rose by 8 today, a lot less than the previous day, bringing the total to 46,614 people. This is a lot better than the previous days, and it fills me with hope.

Time: 11.45 p.m.

Monday, 10 August 2020
141st day of lockdown

> **In the news**: There is "anxiety" over exam grades, the prime minister has said, as pupils prepare to receive estimated results this week for tests cancelled during lockdown. Visiting a school in London, Boris Johnson said he was also "very keen that exams should go ahead as normal." A-level results in England, Wales and Northern Ireland are due on Thursday.

I woke up at 7.00 a.m. but could not sleep nicely due to the very hot weather and bright morning. I peered out from the window, and my cat was sleeping on the floor. The birds were raising awareness with the other birds because they did not like the cat. I brushed my teeth and had a glass of water.

It was a very intense day because I had two assignments due within ten days. I set up an alarm clock for each hour for the time that I was sitting down to type my work.

When my alarm clock beeped, I got up really quickly and went out for some fresh air. My cat was waiting for me just outside the door. He wanted to eat, so I fed him, and then I had a cup of tea and got back to doing my work.

I was able to manage to type 2,500 words today, which makes me feel happy at the end of the day. I have found the definition of domestic violence provided by the United Nations, Declaration on the Elimination of Violence against Women Article 1,1993, cited in Thiara and Gill, 2010: "Any act of gender-based violence that results in, or is likely to result in, physical or psychological harm or suffering to women, including threats of such acts, coercion, or arbitrary deprivation of liberty, whether occurring in public or private life."

The United Nations looks after everyone under the domestic violence bracket. They do not discriminate against anyone, and they are trying to work towards everyone having equal rights, especially in areas such as domestic violence.

Even though organizations such as the UN strive towards equality for everyone, this doesn't happen. As part of my literature review, I have come across the following information, provided by Gangoli et al. (2005) and Batsleer et al. (2002) and Shaheen et al., (2000), who have conducted a study to investigate the experience of domestic violence among Black minority ethnic (BME) women in the UK:

> They have found that domestic abuse is unnoticed in ethnic community women owing to the effect of class, race, gender, and culture systems in BME society in the UK. Many factors are highlighted to keep women in abusive relationships because of the cultural dynamic, for instance, shame and honor, which play an important role to control these women. In addition, BME women experience more domestic violence than other communities of women because they face a number of difficulties; for example, language and culture differences and economic dependency causes difficulties in accessing support from many social services.

This shouldn't be happening in the UK, but it does happen. BME women suffer discrimination due to language and culture and therefore can't access the help they need. The UN is trying to help them overcome it.

We postponed our son's 13th birthday celebration due to the sad news from my family about my niece. My son's birthday is today, and we had made plans to celebrate with family and visitors, but unfortunately, we could not celebrate because we had lost a young girl, my niece, who was the daughter of my husband's youngest sister in Nepal. She was born in her mum's birth house, which is the same as my husband's home. Myself and my husband explained to the children that we cannot celebrate or show happiness when someone has died, a sibling in the family. We decided to celebrate his birthday after her funeral had taken place in Nepal.

As a family, we all (brother-in-law, sisters-in-law, cousins, nieces) talked on Facebook Messenger. My husband's eldest brother and sister-in-law are near to us, so we discussed this sad situation and tried to console my youngest sister-in-law on the death of her child. My husband and his brother tried to cheer her up and make some jokes.

I remembered back to the date and time of my son's birth in 2007. My parents and many family members came to see and welcome a new baby at Frimley Park Hospital. His two sisters tried to hold him on four hands when we were discharged from hospital the second day after the baby was born.

Today, we had no energy to cook, as we were all very sad about what had happened in Nepal. We are so speechless. So we ordered a vegetarian pizza and some chips.

I went jogging with husband for one hour after we had dinner. I read the BBC News UK and noticed that, understandably, there is concern over exam grades.

The death toll from Covid-19 rose by 21 today, more than the previous day, bringing the total to 46,635.

Time: 11.45 p.m.

Tuesday, 11 August 2020
142nd day of lockdown

> ***In the news***: US Senator Kamala Harris was chosen by Joe Biden as his Democratic vice-presidential candidate. She is known as a prominent black politician. But she has also embraced her Indian roots. Her introduction is given here: "My name is pronounced

> "Comma-la", like the punctuation mark," Kamala Harris writes in her 2018 autobiography, *The Truths We Hold*. The California senator, daughter of an Indian-born mother and Jamaican-born father, then explains the meaning of her Indian name. "It means 'lotus flower", which is a symbol of significance in Indian culture. A lotus grows underwater, its flowers rising above the surface while the roots are planted firmly in the river bottom."

With Kamala Harris being elected into the White House in American, it is time for social change in the world. This has made me so happy that social change is happening and is becoming a predominant feature in the media.

I woke as usual. It was a very hot day, and I needed some fresh air before I got washed and dressed. I contacted my parents and cousin in Nepal. Then, later, I contacted my sister-in-law. She confirmed when her daughter's funeral was and when she was coming back home.

I explained to the children about our cultural ritual system and how it works. We have to eat just plain food without salt, ginger, garlic, and meat to respect the dead. We have some times to pray and some times to mourn, which is one night in the UK.

I remembered when my niece was born as a new baby at home, and she has left us at such a young age. She was such a beautiful person, and it makes me sad that this has happened and that we are far away.

I started to read a book for a new assignment for corporate crime and corporate social responsible. I read two books and selected important chapters to refer back to with my new assignment. The weather was very hot, and I had to have a shower three times today to cool me down. Even the fan was spinning hot air.

The death toll from Covid-19 rose by 69 today, more than the previous day, bringing the total to 46,704.

Time: 11.45 p.m.

✎ Wednesday, 12 August 2020
143rd day of lockdown

> ➢ ***In the news***: England's death-count review reduces UK toll by 5,000; it comes down from 46,706 to 41,329, a reduction of 12

per cent. The recalculation is based on a new definition of who has died from Covid-19. Previously, people in England who died at any point following a positive test, regardless of cause, were counted in the figures.

I had to get up very early because I had a very busy day. I had to get my assignment done. I set my alarm clock for each hour in order to keep on track and to complete my assignment for the interview project. It took nearly three hours to complete.

My parents called to update me about my late niece in Nepal. I later contacted my sister-in-law, and the family was ready to do the final cultural and ritual. The weather was very hot, and I changed study rooms due to the very hot temperature.

I felt very tired. My right arm was aching and my eyes were tired. I went out with my husband for a jog after dinner and came back home. Immediately, I took a shower, then read the news and recorded my diary.

The death toll from Covid-19 rose by just 20 today, so much less than the previous day. The total dropped 5,000 according to the methodology, and stands at 41,329. With the drop in deaths counted, the total is so much better than it has been in a long time. This is a hopeful time, and it looks like it's going to be a positive future.

Time: 11.45 p.m.

Thursday, 13 August 2020
144th day of lockdown

> ***In the news***: There is anger among schools, colleges, and students after nearly 40 percent of A-level grades awarded on Thursday were lower than teachers' predictions. In England, 36 percent of entries had a lower grade than teachers predicted and 3 percent were down two grades, in results after exams were cancelled by the pandemic.

> Dule, from the Dalit community, formerly known as "untouchables" and considered at the bottom of India's caste hierarchy, says he has

finally found his calling in rap music. But he is not interested in Bollywood and wants to write about the daily struggles of India's poor.

I woke up at 8.00 a.m. It was a hot and beautiful morning; I was having a beautiful dream. I was walking up towards my previous school in Nepal. One of the staff members from my previous school was going down, and he was telling me to start teaching once a week, as a teaching job in Nepal. My dream reminded me of my past days. I was very happy, and the sun was shining on the eastern side of my birth house. I was walking to school and at the same time viewing my house from up on the hill. It was a very nice dream.

I brushed my teeth, had a glass of water, and started to work intensely on my assignments. I set my alarm clock for each hour to read and type my assignment for the Corporate Crime module on this new topic.

My youngest daughter also woke up earlier than the other day so she could check her result, and she achieved good grades and reserved her place at the Queen Mary University of London, doing mathematics and economics. It was a happy moment for me and the family due to the success of her results today. We have been very sad recently due to our niece in Nepal, and this was some good news to be celebrated.

I watched the BBC News and found that 46 percent students had been degraded from the moderator this year due to the situation of Covid-19. This means only 60 percent will be going to higher education at this time of year because of coronavirus, and it is not fair.

My daughter's results reminded me of my student life, because my parents celebrated with a big party when I and my brother passed in the same year from different colleges. We had gone far away from home at that time. There were not many colleges like they have now in Nepal in those days.

Time flies by very fast. Seven years ago today, on 13 August 2013, I met UK Prime Minister David Cameron at the Royal Military Academic Sandhurst. I was serving the pre-drinks for our guest on sovereign parade. The prime minister also took a glass of drink from my tray, but he was so busy talking with other officers that he did not say anything.

I had a chance to serve Queen Elizabeth on 09 January 2006 at same place, but the Queen said nicely "Thank you" after she picked up a glass of water from my tray. She was very polite.

The weather was very hot, but it was raining during the day. That made feel cool, because it has been hot for the last week. I set up an alarm clock for every hour as I read books and noted a few important pieces of information. As part of my assignment, I found that

> corporate crime emerged in early Roman times (Geis, 1988). This was introduced to generate legal entities which control churches, universities, and organisations. The first legal entity recognised as a corporation, the East India Company, was established in 1602 and known as the first world-wide corporation which distributed shares and stocks (Mason, 1968). The East India Company has developed as corporation and been recognised as a body chartered by the government. It had the right to hold property for a common; it had the right to sue and be sued in a common name. The company had a legal identity which extended beyond the life of the members of corporations.

I felt so very tired, so I went for a jog with my husband and son for around 80 minutes, and this helped wake me up. It was nice and cool because of the rain. We saw many people out for a jog, but they were scared to approach us, and we also planned to change direction when we saw them along the walk.

After I came back home, I started to cook mushroom curry for dinner. A few items of curry were cooked by my daughters, and everyone has their own choice of curry for dinner. I prepared dinner on a plate for all the family, and then we ate it. I was tired, so I went to take a shower after dinner. My right arm was aching, and my eyes were tired.

The death toll from Covid-19 rose by 18 today, less than the previous day, bringing the total to 41,347.

Time: 11.45 p.m.

📝 Friday, 14 August 2020
145th day of lockdown

> ***In the news***: Free exam appeals for schools in England

I woke up at around 8 p.m. It was a very different day from the previous day. It was hotter and sunnier yesterday; today the weather was very dull and rainy.

I keep seeing my vegetables growing in the garden from the window. My neighbour on the opposite side of the road was shouting to her children, and I could hear loud music from the car. My next-door neighbour talked to her friends in her own language, but I did not understand. Everyone was at home due to Covid-19.

I quickly brushed my teeth and had a cup of tea and warm water. Then I started to read books to collect information for my assignment. At midday, I cooked lunch for myself and my son. Then I went back to searching for reading articles again.

My sister-in-law contacted me, and we talked for quite a long time about our family and relatives who were affected by coronavirus. Some were tested, some were not. We decide not to meet until the virus had cleared in the UK. The children were complaining that they wanted to go their uncle and auntie's house, but I suggested to them that we would meet with family and relatives soon.

I did not go out for a jog due to the bad weather. I concentrated on my subject again for few more hours. I read the following:

> In 1844, the nature of corporations had changed into the UK Joint Stock Companies. A corporation was allowed to define itself, and investors were allowed to collect funds for the good purposes of corporations. During this time, control over corporations moved from government power to the legal stage of court.
>
> In 1858, limited liability had been given to stakeholders. That meant shareholders were liable for the companies' debt only to the value of the money they invested in the

company. The case of Santa Clara Country Southern Pasco. (118 U.S.394[1886]) agreed on corporate personhood that corporations now could enjoy, with a variety of rights and responsibilities as individuals, including signing of binding contracts, payment of taxes, and ownership of property. Corporation crime law explained corporations legally as a person, and that was included in the constitution of the United States in the 14th Amendment. However, corporations were not liked very much by people who were living in the colonies.

I found this very interesting, due to it being about the starting of corporations and liability, and this was put into a contract. Both parts were liable for many things.

I have never heard of a bad result of students in the UK since I came here, but today there were a lot of bad results for A levels and GCSEs due to the structure and delivering of results. The government will cover the cost of schools in England appealing against A-level and GCSE grades. This made me incredibly sad. I put myself into these students' shoes and can't really comprehend how they are feeling. Education is such a big part of everyone's life; everyone works so hard to get the grades they want. They were unfortunately let down, and we had many tears in our house due to my daughter's results, and we saw many more on the news.

The death toll from Covid-19 rose by just 11 today, less than the previous day, bringing the total to 41,358. The number of deaths has stayed under 20 for the past few days.

People are dying from coronavirus more and more every day, and the fear and stress is everywhere. But the daily figures are a lot lower recently, and this is beginning to fill me with a lot of hope.

Time: 11.45 p.m.

Saturday, 15 August 2020
146th day of lockdown

> ***In the news***: UK commemorates 75th anniversary of VJ Day, when World War II came to an official end. The Prince of Wales

led a two-minute silence at the National Memorial Arboretum in Staffordshire as part of a service of remembrance. Later, in a TV address, his elder son Prince William urged the public "to learn the lessons of the past". And a message from the Queen thanked those "who fought so valiantly".

I woke up at 7.00 a.m. The weather was cold and rainy in the morning. I took a quick shower and then cleaned the kitchen and toilets. Following this, I began to worship.

I had a cup of tea as well as some warm water. I was dressed already in my uniform for work, but I decided to set up an alarm to read and highlight passages from a book before work. When my alarm went off, I had to stop and drive to work.

A lot more cars were on the road today compared to the last time. It is still lockdown, but a lot more cars and people were out. It makes me feel that the second wave of coronavirus will increase soon.

All the staff have brought a variety of delicious foods for their lunch. There were many different tastes and many different kinds of food. We had lunch at 12:30 p.m. Everyone was happy and excited and busy with their food.

I joined a virtual meeting with the Global Network Conference of people from around the world. Nepali people had joined to be a part of it. We discussed an educational subject, which was how to open up a new university, and how it will offer equal opportunity and education in Nepal, which is very much needed. Providing education anywhere is always a positive thing.

The death toll from Covid-19 rose by only 3 today. The virus has only taken 3 people today, the lowest amount since this pandemic began. It fills us with such hope that maybe we have been able to win the fight against the pandemic of coronavirus. The total as of today is 41,361.

Time: 11.45 p.m.

✎ Sunday, 16 August 2020
147ʰ day of lockdown

> ***In the news***: A-level results "huge mess" as exams appeal guidance withdrawn

I had another dream last night. I was in my birthplace in Oyam, Nepal, again. I was inside the demolished house, which is not there anymore. My brother was lying down on the bed, and my parents were walking around the house.

The sun was rising on the eastern side of the house. It was around 7 a.m., and there was nice early-morning sunshine that illuminated the sky beautifully. I was feeling so happy and relaxed at that time.

I did not realise that I was in my bed in the UK. When I woke up, I felt upset for waking up, as I miss my birth home so so much.

I realised that the birthplace and navel are so attached, like a nail and skin. I thank my dream world; it reminds me of opportunities and who I am, and that I am grateful to have all these experiences.

I joined the Zoom yoga class. I have had to miss this class for a long time due to work and my assignments. Luckily, I was able to attend today.

I quickly took a shower, cleaned the kitchen and toilets, and then had a clove water because I was experiencing pain in my upper left jaw. The clove can help to control pain. This is something I have learnt from a dental nursing course.

It is still lockdown, but my next-door neighbours' children are playing and crying on the opposite side of the neighbourhood, and they are playing loud music. I have never seen students talking on the street regarding degraded GCSE and A-level mock exams in the UK.

I was so worried about the 46 per cent of students that have been put behind a year due to Covid-19 and the new marking system. Many people didn't get the results they wanted due to the government's decision on the algorithm for the A-levels, which shattered a lot of teenagers' dreams of going to university.

The exams regulator is reviewing its guidance on how to appeal against A-level and GCSE grades using mock exam results, hours after publishing it. On Saturday, Ofqual set out what constituted a "valid" mock exam for students appealing A-level results in England.

A friend of my daughter's came around our house, but I'm still doubtful about the virus and social distancing, and I was very nervous.

The death toll from Covid-19 rose by only 5 today, two more than the previous day. It is still a lot less than the previous week. The total as of today is 41,366.

Time: 11.45 p.m.

Monday, 17 August 2020
148th day of lockdown

> ***In the news***: A-level and GCSE students in England will be given grades estimated by their teachers, rather than by an algorithm, after a government U-turn.

I woke up early to a nice warm and bright day. I looked out my window and saw my cat lying on the ground asleep in the garden. The birds were chirping and having their food from the cage. It was a lovely start to the day.

I quickly brushed my teeth and had a cup of tea and a glass of water. I set an hour alarm and typed some information for my assignment.

Today is a special day for me and for Nepal. It is the month of 1st Bhadra (fifth month of the Nepali calendar). I remembered when I was back home and my childhood days, when we used to go to the field market to meet friends and relatives.

There was no telephone and internet back then, so we used to meet in a certain place and in a certain fixed field market. It was very festive and a tradition back then. We only saw some people once a year and didn't speak to people due to lack of communication. Today, everything is in the palm of your hand. You can talk to anyone in the world and arrange to meet up and celebrate due to mobile phones and advances in technology. Back in my childhood, we couldn't do that, and this was one of the highlights of the year.

At 10 a.m., I attended a Zoom meeting with my tutor about the corporate module. After tutoring, I started to search information relating to my question:

> In the 17th and 18th centuries, corporation crime was involved in several egregious acts, including slave trading and destroying the culture of Native Americans (Sale, 1990). The Industrial Revolution was expanded as an economic activity in an early 19th century to produce very rich capitalist corporations. Capitalist culture evaded regulation and control systems, and corporations have engaged in as price-gouging, fraud, work exploitation, operation of stocks, and unsafety for workers (Myers, 1907; Clinard and Yeager, 1980). Critiques of the capitalist system and the way that middle classes or bourgeoise can be involved in crime suggest that capitalism is based on greed and preservation of the self, inevitably producing crime (Bonger, 1900). Hence, corporate crime emerged with capitalism.

I found this interesting because it shows that corporate capitalism has been built on throughout the centuries. It is one on the main reasons for the slave trade.

My son made me a sandwich for lunch because I was very busy with my class and assignment. I took a short break but spent my time cleaning the kitchen and toilet, and then I went for a breath of fresh air.

My daughters had gone out with one of their friends, who had come back from Bath, which is quiet far away. I knew she had been tested for the virus, and I was very wary and scared to talk near her due to this. I really tried to maintain my social distancing.

At 5 p.m., I joined my regular virtual class for language and then had dinner with the family. I checked the news and the records of death toll and A-level and GCSE results.

The death toll from Covid-19 rose by 3 today, bringing the total to 41,369. It makes me believe that the virus is so close to being beaten.

Time: 12.10 a.m.

✏️ Tuesday, 18 August 2020
149th day of lockdown

> ➤ ***In the news***: Twice as many adults in Britain are reporting symptoms of depression now compared with this time last year. One in five people appeared to have depressive symptoms compared with one in ten before the pandemic.

I woke up at 7 a.m. The weather had changed, and it was really cold. It was funny how the weather changes so quickly from the previous week, when it was 36 degrees.

For a couple of hours, I continued to work on my assignment, then I attended a lesson at midday. I ate lunch and had some fresh air for around 30 minutes.

At 4 p.m., I again joined my language class with my university tutor. After that, I continued with my dissertation and had to tidy up and have dinner. I felt so tired because of the number of lessons I had today, and I had to stop and go out for a walk to clear my head, as I had been sitting in front of a computer all day.

I tried to open the BBC News UK and record the news about depression.

The death rate from Covid-19 rose by 12 today. It is slowly getting higher. The total as of today is 41,381.

✏️ Wednesday, 19 August 2020
150th day of lockdown

I woke up at 8 a.m. The weather was awful compared to the previous day. The weather changed so quickly. It was 36 degrees four or five days before. There were no birds outside, and it was very quiet due to this. I quickly brushed my teeth and had a cup of tea and a glass of water.

I was concentrating on the dream I had. I was in my school, which was named Gupte Shawor High Secondary School. I used to go to school with my father, from nursery to GCSE, and he was a head teacher of that school. It was market day, which comes every year. People used to meet and were dating in that market and the festival and got married. In those days before technology, it was more important than now. Meeting people in public was important due to there not being any technology to help with communication and getting to know people.

My father and youngest daughter were walking in the middle of the market, early in the morning, in my dream. I woke up and suddenly realised that today was Nepali Father's Day, so I quickly contacted my father and mother, and we talked for a few minutes and I wished him happy Father's Day. We are not allowed to meet due to the outbreak of coronavirus this year. Mum was talking about her worship for all the family and her vegetable garden.

A picture of my dear father Bhim Kumar Seling uploaded on Father's Day

I tried to focused on my work again, because my deadline was very near. I was concentrating on Corporate Crime, which is invisible to the public and difficult to prosecute because corporations play a powerful role in society. Corporate crime emerges through organisations which are complex and affected by the relationship between authority and power—for example, individual, social, and wider groups, including many operating corporate crimes.

I was able to complete the first draft for this essay. I emailed my university lecturers for the sublimit folder. I emailed Basingstoke Technology College regarding a math class for adults.

I looked at a lot information on Google regarding my assignments. In the evening, I joined on the RHL monthly meeting again and discussed many things on the agenda. I spent the rest of the evening on my dissertation analysing data. I tried to balance my study of each topic. Due to this, I had dinner late.

The death toll from Covid-19 rose by 16 today, more than the previous day, bringing the total to 41,397. The UK continues to have the third highest number of recorded coronavirus deaths in the world.

Time: 12.06 a.m.

Thursday, 20 August 2020
151st day of lockdown

> ***In the nwes***: The coronavirus crisis has dramatically compounded domestic violence against women, new research has revealed. Two-thirds of women in abusive relationships have suffered more violence from their partners during the pandemic, according to an investigation by the BBC's Panorama. Three-quarters of victims also say the lockdown has made it harder for them to escape their abusers.

It is upsetting that people who were suffering from domestic violence had to stay with their abusers due to the lockdown restriction and feared they had nowhere to go. I hope that this will change.

I woke up at 7.30 a.m. The weather was brighter than the previous day, but still cold. I got up and continued to work on my assignments. I decided to stay at home all day and to focus on my assignments. Therefore, I did not check any messages or calls on my phone.

I worked all morning and then attended the online class for Corporate Crime. I discussed my questions with my teacher.

Early in the afternoon, I joined my Zoom class for English and did not have much time to have some lunch and drink. Here is a few bits of information from my assignment:

> It was possible to prosecute white collar crime in 2017, when the UK was successful in the prosecution and sentencing of the Swett Group PLC for failing to stop bribery by its workers in a foreign country. A later case involved Rolls Royce, which had engaged in systematic corruption between 1989–2013 in many countries. Many instances of money laundering and corruption were involved during this time. However, they were unable to

prosecute (SFO v Rolls Royce, 2017) to prevent the impact because of the out-of-date system of corporate criminal liability in England and Wales, despite a willingness to do so. Up until then, the normal enforcement response to corporate corruption had been one of accommodation and non-prosecution. From this time on, white-collar crime was identified as a corporate crime in the UK and successfully prosecuted in 2017, in spite of it taking a long time to be generally accepted in the UK. Rolls-Royce was subsequently prosecuted, but prosecution was deferred. Nevertheless, the company paid out £497,252,645 for corruption and profits of £258,170,000, (Govt.UK, 2017). Thus, white collar crime led to corporate crime through the use abusive power to gain business profit, and it was charged as corporate criminal liability rather than individual criminal liability.

At 9 p.m., after a busy day of studying, I went out for some fresh air with my husband after dinner. I needed the break.

The death toll from Covid-19 rose by 6 today, considerably less than the previous day, bringing the total to 41,403.

Time: 11.30 p.m.

Friday, 21 August 2020
152nd day of lockdown

I woke up at 7.00 a.m., and my target for today was to complete two assignments and upload them. Therefore, I focused on typing my final project.

I worked hard on my assignments until 3 p.m. Then I went out for some fresh air and spent 20 minutes in the back garden, picking beans and vegetables because they were ready to pick.

I broke my day up and spent the morning concentrating on doing my corporate crime essay. I want to include a few words of my subject:

According to Boger (1900), "Capitalism was based on greed and preservation of the self-producer of crime. Competition markets exists within capitalist corporations, but as people are desperate to work due to poverty which leads individuals to commit corporate crimes; and that in turn leads corporations into creating corrupt systems to facilitate the crimes of their employees, shareholders and owners."

I was struggling to sort out my assignment problems, so I emailed the university and my module teacher to make sure it was correctly uploaded on the Surrey University learning page. One of teachers was on holiday, so I kept sending emails to my supervisor, the assessment team, and my subject teacher. I felt stressed due to the uncertain situation.

At 4 p.m., I uploaded my two assignments, as my lecturer suggested, but according to the system, it didn't look like they had uploaded in a different place, so I made sure that I emailed my tutor to make sure. He replied to me straight away that my submission was seen on his log-in. Therefore, I was relieved to submit my assignment.

My eldest daughter cooked us Korean BBQ for dinner, so I had delicious food with my family. Afterwards, we watched a documentary on the mountain life of Nepal, which was nice new knowledge for the children.

I felt happy and relaxed after eating dinner. I went out for a jog with my husband. We met a few joggers and some dog walkers, but everyone was still avoiding each other. My husband and I did the washing up and cleaned the kitchen after we came back from jogging.

The death toll from Covid-19 rose by 2 today, the lowest increase since March and a third of the previous day's amount. This brings the overall total to 41,405, and we have dropped down to being fifth in the world for deaths due to Covid, after Brazil, USA, and India.

Time: 12.25 p.m.

Saturday, 22 August 2020
153rd day of lockdown

> ***In the news***: Coronavirus will be with us forever, a member of the government's Scientific Advisory Group for Emergencies has said. Sir Mark Walport said people would need to be vaccinated at regular intervals. His comments come after the head of the World

Health Organization (WHO) said he hoped the pandemic would be over within two years, as the Spanish flu had taken two years to overcome.

I woke up at 8.00 a.m. The weather was bright, and the wind was blowing slowly and gently in the early morning. I was not able to join the Zoom meditation due to my work, but I was able to do my yoga exercises for an hour. After I took a shower, I played some religious music while I was doing worship. Afterwards, I carried on typing my research findings.

My target was to complete a few paragraphs; therefore, I spent a few hours on this and then made lunch for the family. Some of the data from one interviewee is extracted here:

> What kind of issues do black South Asian minority ethnic women face in the UK. relating to domestic violence?
>
> When analysing the majority of the participants' responses to the above question, they were very similar with the exception of one participant. One of the respondents' quotes is as follows: "I feel that this group faces obstacles before and after they experience domestic violence. These include lack of understanding, cultural barriers, and financial barriers."
>
> According to the above interview data, BSAME women face many difficulties before and after their experience of violence due to language barriers and economic problems in the UK. The researcher found that many BSAME women felt fear and helplessness due to language difficulties. However, they could not leave the house because of financial dependency and their children's futures. This links with the research carried out by Barat (1998) and Ahluwaila and Gupta (1997).

This is very relevant to what is going on in society at the moment, with the rise of domestic violence due to the pandemic. The pandemic has shown that the rate of domestic violence has risen, but it hasn't been documented in the BSAME community. The pandemic has probably made this worse. Afterwards, I spent a couple more hours typing my dissertation.

The death toll from Covid-19 rose by 18 today, a lot more than the previous day, bringing the total to 41,423.

Time: 12.25 a.m.

Sunday, 23 August 2020
154th day of lockdown

> ➢ ***In the news***: It is "vitally important" children go back to school, with the life chances of a generation at stake, Boris Johnson has said in a message to parents. As schools in England, Wales, and Northern Ireland prepare to reopen, the PM said the risk of contracting coronavirus in one was "very small". He said "it is far more damaging for a child's development and their health … to be away from school any longer".

I woke up at 8.30 a.m., and the weather was bright, but there was a slight breeze blowing slowly and gently in the early morning. I was not able to join my Zoom lesson again due to my work. I typed my work all morning, and after a few hours, I took a short break and prepared stuff for dinner. I went to the garden and planted some vegetable seeds for next year.

In the afternoon, for a few hours, I focused on finding sections for my dissertation. I had not done the first draft yet; therefore, I was determined to do it. I was able to explain one of the heading data:

> What can we do to improve the relationship between professionals and the BSAME communities in order to better support Black South Asian minority ethnic women suffering domestic violence, and how can this be achieved?

> The majority of the responses analysed revealed that there was a need for more education, and training for all professionals working in the social services. In addition, there needs to be an increase in the numbers of interpreters

who are properly trained in recognizing the sensitive nature of the wide cultural differences within the BSAME community. This is supported by Respondent 1: "I would say that training, education and knowledge are important for professional improvement to help these women."

Another interviewee, Respondent 4, expressed a similar view: "In my professional experience, it is difficult to divulge individual case histories due to confidentiality. Generally speaking, I would say all agencies and organizations need more training, and more funding needs to be made available in order to give greater support. There are not enough social workers, interpreters, and professionals working in this area. At the same time, there is not enough pay for support workers."

All interviewees suggested that there was insufficient focus on training, education, and knowledge of the subject. At the same time, there was a lack of interpreters due to the poor pay and conditions for these people. In the long term, this impacts on the victims of DV through delays in bringing cases to justice.

This whole area of interpreters and language difficulties was highlighted by Williams and Yarnell (2013) in a literature review which demonstrated how lack of language skills on the part of interpreters led to many misunderstandings in translations. Many other social organisations, including NGO workers in Northern Ireland, reported similar findings in regard to the discrepancies, which in some cases caused conflict between interpreters and victims of DV.

 I submitted my assignment, which was a 2,000-word essay for Corporate Crime and Corporate Responsibility. It is actually due tomorrow, but I felt some relief submitting it earlier than the deadline.

Lockdown has lasted so long for all the children. It has all been the same for them, day in and day out. Hopefully this will all change soon.

The death toll from Covid-19 rose by 6 today, less than the previous day, bringing the total to 41,429. It fills me with such hope that only six people have died. It seems that the virus is almost gone.

Time: 12.15 a.m.

Monday, 24 August 2020
155th day of lockdown

> ➢ *In the news*: More schools ask pupils to wear face coverings in the UK.

I woke up at 8.00 a.m. The weather was nice and bright, and the wind was blowing gently. I brushed my teeth, had a cup of tea and a glass of lemon water, then began to type my work.

I worked all morning and took a short break to prepare ingredients for lunch, as well as clean the floor and toilet in the kitchen. I needed to have a break from my morning of work, and this helped to calm my head.

My plan was to continue working on my thesis. I have not yet completed my first draft due to the deadline for my other assignments.

In the early afternoon, I focused on ending the finding section of my dissertation and presented what I thought was a great thought, which was expressed by one of my interviewees. The question was, "In your experience, do you think the police handle Black South Asian Minority ethnic women (BSAME) and domestic violence cases with cultural sensitivity?" I found it a very interesting idea which supported my thesis aim.

Regarding this question, all five participants held a similar view that the police could not handle domestic violence cases accurately. However, specific differences did emerge. For example, one respondent commented that although the police were sympathetic owing to the nature of the abuse, they were in the main unable to help:

> In my experience, police have little, if any, understanding of the different backgrounds of victims even if they want to help. Furthermore, victims often find it difficult to speak

freely to police officers from totally different backgrounds; therefore, I would say that the police cannot handle 100 per cent of domestic violence cases with cultural sensitivity within the BSAME community.

The above quote illustrates the complex sensitive nature of this issue. Domestic violence and domestic disputes are often highly emotional and, in some cases, traumatic incidents, which are almost impossible to resolve. The differences in cultural backgrounds together with language difficulties mean that domestic violence victims cannot give police officers a full account of the abuse they have suffered. Therefore, until this aspect of the system is addressed, there is unlikely to be any change.

Recent research carried out by the *Independent* (2020) newspaper supports this view. One of the findings revealed by this piece of research commented that BAME females were "left on the scrapheap" and there was a much higher proportion of domestic violence victims from that specific community compared to women in the wider community. It also highlighted a lack of access to services, together with a lack of cultural trust in the police.

According to the research, these women felt that they were not treated fairly by the police. There would appear to be a need for entry to the criminal justice system to be revised in the light of the above findings. There also needs to be greater understanding of diversity, including the cultural differences within the BSAME community, in order to tackle hidden domestic violence.

After a day of continually working on the computer, I felt very dizzy and had to take a rest for an hour.

For dinner, I cooked rice and a special called *quwati curry* made from a dry mix. I had water and fruit at break time, as well as cooking time. I was interested in reading the BBC Mews.

My assignment's actual deadline was today, but I completed and uploaded it yesterday. This stopped me from being stressed, especially if something went wrong.

The death toll from Covid-19 rose by 6 today, same as the previous day, bringing the total to 41,435.

Time: 12.15 a.m.

Tuesday, 25 August 2020
156th day of lockdown

> ***In the news***: Secondary pupils in England will have to wear masks in school corridors in local lockdown areas of England.

I woke up very early. It was cold outside, and the wind was blowing. The rain was on and off all day, but the wind stayed, and it didn't stop for the rest of the day. I did my university work all morning and only had a break for a few minutes. My cat had been sitting waiting for me to feed him and to open the door to let him outside.

All my children are at home, and they are preparing their stuff for university for the girls, and my son is ordering his new uniform for his new school. My plan was to work intensively on my thesis today, and therefore I didn't talk to anyone and didn't do any yoga. I wanted to get my first draft done.

I had to stop working on this at 4 p.m. because I had my usual class for language with my university teacher. After this, I tried to continue writing my thesis, but I had done so much already and felt it was too much for me today. I explained the reveal data form to my participants, and here are some paragraphs from my work:

> The research findings were labelled under the six headings which support this study and give more knowledge about this field.
>
> I interviewed 5 people for this question, "What kind of issues do Black South Asian minority ethnic women face in the UK relating to domestic violence?" The majority of the participants' responses to the above question were very similar, with the exception of one participant, who said, "I feel that this group faces obstacles before and after they experience domestic violence. These include lack of understanding, cultural barriers, and financial barriers."

According to the above interview data, BSAME women face many difficulties before and after their experience of violence due to language barriers and economic problems in the UK. The researcher found that many BSAME women felt fear and helplessness due to language difficulties. However, they could not leave the house because of financial dependency and their children's futures.

Another thought from the respondent: "I think the issues are many and wide ranging. ... economic, social cultural, financial, emotional, physical, coupled with issues such as housing and immigration. ... if a UK citizen marries a BSAME woman and brings his wife back to the UK, he could threaten her with divorce and deportation back to her homeland. For that reason, the woman can't or won't speak up."

The above interviewee presented more experience with DV issues compared to the other participants. This could be because of her language skills and greater experience in the field of DV. Some of the underlying factors involved in domestic violence cases are largely hidden, but they include issues such as housing and immigration status.

This study gave me knowledge to understand domestic violence issues and BSAME women. I never thought that this could happen in society. I do not have personal experience with this. I am very lucky to have a good, hard-working, and loving husband. To me, this is something that I have uncovered whilst doing my research. In some cultures, this is still happening. Men still feel that they are the head of the house and the most important person or "boss mentality".

The death toll from Covid-19 rose by 16 today, the most it has increased for the past couple of weeks. This is a bit worrying, as we haven't had an increase like this for some time. The death toll as of today is 41,451, and the UK is still fifth in the world for the highest number of recorded coronavirus deaths.

Time: 11.24 a.m.

✎ Wednesday, 26 August 2020
157th day of lockdown

I could hear the low voice of a bird chirping outside the house, and it woke me up. Once I woke up, my husband and I had a conversation about the latest crime and corruption issues that were going on in Nepal. He made a cup of tea for me, and I watched the news about the goings-on in a women's shelter in Nepal and how they were improving women's lives after domestic violence.

I joined my lecture and really enjoyed it. It was only for an hour, but I found it so interesting. After class, I cooked lunch for my family, and I decided to stop studying for today.

We had a special plan to celebrate multiple occasions today, such as my son's 13th birthday, my youngest daughter's A-level achievements, and her place at the University at Queen Mary, as well as our 28th wedding anniversary. We only celebrated at home with family due to the coronavirus.

After we had cut the cake, we went to Camberley Mimosa for dinner. There was a long queue out the restaurant, and we had to wait to be seated. We spent a long time at the restaurant, and the food wasn't as good as before, but the food was set out differently.

I wasn't able to contact my parents and relatives and also did not do any exercise or yoga for myself due to intense work and a special day.

I had to relearn how to study from scratch in the UK due to the education system not recognising the level of work that I was able to achieve in Nepal.

My study corner in our house in Fleet UK

I worked on the discussion part of a key area of my findings on immigration status and shame (*sharam*) and honour (*izzat*), domestic violence, and BSAME women in the UK for my thesis. One key area of this research was that many BSAME women suffered domestic violence due to their fear of deportation because of their temporary immigration status:

> As the law stands, if a UK citizen marries a BSAME woman and subsequently threatens her with divorce, she is afraid to speak out. Gupta (2003) studied the Two-Year Rule and how women experienced DV in Black and South Asian-led associations and suggested that the rule forced women to stay with abusive husbands due to a spousal visa.
>
> The Two-Year Rule and the Five-Year Rule both trap BSAME women in a DV environment. The issue of domestic violence should be investigated broadly from the social, economic, and political standpoint to break through this inequality.
>
> Anita (2010), Dasgupta (2000), Narayan (1995), and Raj and Silverman (2002), cited in Anita (2011)— previous researchers' who worked with immigration-status women—suggested that the immigration policies

contributed to a build-up of racism, class bias, and gender oppression, which resulted in a culture of domestic violence and abuse of BSAME women. Thus, the findings were supported by a literature review and by these researchers' studies.

Moreover, a respondent highlighted the displacement issues due to cultural shame (*sharam*) and honor (*izzat*). Shame is very high on the list as a reason for DV in BSAME communities. Culture and gender background displacement also happens if the daughter or wife requests help from social services or agencies.

This view is linked with past studies from Gangoli et al. (2006) and Batsleer et al. (2002). Because of *sharam* (shame) and *izzat* (honour), women were forced to stay in abusive relationships.

If victims asked for help, they had to leave their home, which is against their human rights. Shame (*sharam*) and honour (*izzat*) is an unwritten code but a very powerful tool within the BSAME community. For example, Shafilea Ahmed was murdered (BBCUK, 2012) by her Pakistani parents because her disobedience brought her family and society shame in the UK.

Fortunately, this study has not revealed any murder case due to culture, but this may be because it is a small sample, and for this reason, it could not capture all kinds of issues and cases relating to this topic. Shame and honour are socially constructed within the BSAME community (Gill, 2014).

The fact that this is still going on is very heartbreaking. Women face a lot of pressures to get married and create happy homes and bring up little families. Yet they face hardship when trying to escape domestic violence.

They need a place to go and people to understand them. We are working towards it.

The death toll from Covid-19 rose by 16 today, the same number as the previous day, bringing the total to 41,467.

Time: 11.13 p.m.

✏️ Thursday, 27 August 2020
158th day of lockdown

Nineteen years ago today, my eldest daughter and I landed in the Falkland Islands for our holiday after an eighteen-hour flight. We had a short break on Ascension Island, where my husband's regiment had moved six months earlier. I was travelling with 2-year-old, and was I was twenty-one weeks pregnant with my other daughter. Yet I wasn't tired at all.

The Falkland Islands War, also called the Falklands War, Malvinas War, or South Atlantic War, was a brief undeclared war fought between Argentina and Great Britain in 1982 over control of the Falkland Islands (Islas Malvinas) and associated island dependencies. The Falklands brings back emotional memories for me. Many people died. Many Gurkha soldiers fought alongside British soldiers, yet only one died.

It was an emotional and hard time for everyone involved. It is hard for me, due to being a mother of two children whose father is fighting, who might not being coming back that day. The memories are sad due to so many young men not being able to go home and continue with their life.

I woke up at 8.30 a.m., and I still felt sleepy because I went to bed late (1:30 a.m.). I went out for some fresh air to help wake me up because I felt so sleepy, and I started to prepare for my Zoom class, which was starting at 9 a.m. The class was over very quickly.

I spent the majority of the day after class typing the conclusion section of my thesis. It took a long time to complete my draft conclusion. I worked constantly to finish this section and then created the first page of my dissertation, acknowledgement of abstract, and contents. I read the whole dissertation before emailing it to my supervisor later in the evening.

My family was waiting to have dinner with me, but I was too busy stressing about completing this work and sending it to the university for the first draft check. I told my family that I couldn't have dinner with them today due to my intensive work schedule, so I had to eat after 9 p.m. I felt stress-free for a few days, as it was finished. This was until the further comments were emailed to me.

The death toll from Covid-19 rose by 12 today, less than the previous day but still a lot higher than the previous week. It seems that we are beginning to see an increase in the virus, and this is worrying. The total as of today is 41,479.

Time: 11.00 p.m.

Friday, 28 August 2020
159th day of lockdown

I woke up at 7 a.m., and I felt really sleepy, although I went to bed before midnight compared to earlier in the week. I watched the news about Nepal on my mobile.

I looked around the kitchen for dried peaches and put them in hot water to make them soft. I went into my study room, and I could hear many cars driving around. There were many doves singing a lovely "Kur doo, Kur doo" song. I looked out the window, and the dark fog was disappearing to show a bright day.

I booked a seat for my son's school bus. He is going to the new private school from year 9 in September.

I have completed my self-assessment for GCSE Maths for September 2020. I passed Math Numeracy Level-2 many years ago, which helped me to pass my post-graduation (master's in science), but I'm interested in it for future study.

I went jogging with friends after many days off today. I stopped jogging because of my assignment deadline, and I'm very tired of doing assignments.

I watched the news about the protest in the eastern part of Jhapa Nepal. It was showing an innocent man killed by an inspector, and the issues were raised of killing an ox.

As a Hindu (in religion), we believe that the cow is a symbol of wealth. There are multiple cultures, languages, and ethnicities in Nepal, but not only one religious believer's idea is written in the constitution by the government. Therefore, the police killed a man because he killed an ox.

The death toll from Covid-19 rose by 9 today, less than the day before, bringing the total to 41,488.

Time: 11.00 p.m.

Saturday, 29 August 2020
160th day of lockdown

> **In the news**: Head teachers and teachers have criticised the government for "last-minute" guidance on what to do during virus outbreaks and local lockdowns. The guidance for England was published on Friday evening, just days before many schools begin term.

I woke early to a cold and windy morning, but there was a nice bright sky. I peeped out the window, and all the branches of the trees were waving slowly and gently in the breeze.

I watched the news about the Nepal inequality of human rights and the policy-making from the government of Nepal. I listened to Beth Hoven's music when I was typing this diary.

I cleaned the kitchen and took a shower, then worshipped for a few minutes. After I made a cup of tea for myself and my husband, I sat down at the computer to check my emails and applications.

I completed the BAME infrastructure funding application on behalf of the Greater Rushmoor Nepali Community, and I was elected as secretary of this community. I was so pleased about this, but I know there is a lot of hard work to come. I decided to fry a chaumin and pasta for lunch today. It was very yummy.

I went jogging with my husband after dinner for over 30 minutes for fresh air. There was a small amount of rain.

I am currently feeling very sorry for the women who are suffering from domestic violence issues, because I wasn't aware of these problems before I started to research this topic as part of my post-graduate degree. I am very lucky that I am not in an environment like this.

The death toll from Covid-19 rose by only 12 today, three more than the previous day, but it is rising. The total as of today is 41,500.

The first death from Covid-19 came on 5 March 2020. This is the fiftieth day of eased lockdown. Bars, pubs, and shops are open, but still people are dying from coronavirus more and more each and every day, and the fear and stress is everywhere. It's difficult to manage social distancing; however, all schools are opening next week. Let's hope this goes well, and we hope that the numbers don't rise too much.

Time: 11.00 p.m.

Sunday, 30 August 2020
161st day of lockdown

> ***In the news***: Universities in the UK are being urged to scrap plans for face-to-face teaching until Christmas in order to prevent a second wave of coronavirus. Academics' union UCU said more than a million students moving around the country was "a recipe for disaster". It comes as daily recorded cases of coronavirus in the UK reached 1,715 in 24 hours, the highest since early June.

I woke up to a cold foggy morning. There was more news from Nepal about the constitution of Nepal, which was written by the first prime minister, Janga Bahadur Rana, in B.C. 1910. It was full of inequality of human rights, and many policies and constitutions (*Muluki ain*) are not fair for everyone and can come across as discriminatory. The constitution hadn't been changed since 1910 but was changed two years ago, especially where women's rights are concerned. There is a long way to go, but this is a great start.

My sister contacted me and talked about the extended lockdown that was happening for another week in Nepal. She was telling me that many people that I knew, such as my old next-door neighbour and a few friends, had caught Covid—and unfortunately, some had died. It is an emotional situation. Nobody knows about what tomorrow will bring.

My husband and I went to visit a relative's house for lunch, and we talked about our community and social construct and how it is running according to our norms and values in the UK.

I went jogging with my friends for the first time in a long time. I could not go with them due to my assignment deadlines. We walked for 10 kilometres, which took around 1.45 hour.

The death toll from Covid-19 rose by 1 today. It is the first time this has happened since the beginning of the pandemic. This has filled me with such optimism and hope for the future. If only one person can die a day, as sad as that is for that family, we can all get back to some normality for the rest of us. The total as of today is 41,501.

Time: 11.00 p.m.

Monday, 31 August 2020
162nd day of lockdown

> ***In the news***: Ninety-second day of eased lockdown.

Today I learned of the death of the uncle of my grandfather, Purna Bahadur Seling (Fedang Saila). I woke up early to check my messages on my mobile. I was aware that my uncle grandpa was in the final serious stage of life. Outside, it was dark. I realised this when I opened the window.

It was confirmed that he had unfortunately had died. I contacted my dad and cousin, and my dad was so upset. This man who had unfortunately died had been his friend since early childhood.

I tried to get back to sleep again, but I could not sleep anymore. I got out of bed at 8 a.m., cleaned the kitchen, and mopped the floor, upstairs and downstairs.

It was a quiet morning, and the sky was a little brighter than when I first woke up. I also felt very emotional due to this loss.

His daughter was two years older than me, but we used to be friends since my childhood days. I used to go to the market, and we worked together on the weekend, but she did not go to school for formal education. My late uncle grandpa used to make a nice chicken curry, and I liked it very much in those days. This is a memory I will cherish.

I wish I could go and see his body, and attend his funeral, to give my respects, and think about all these lovely memories. I'm geographically too far away from Nepal, and due to the outbreak of Covid-19 and the lockdown restriction, it is not possible to give him my final respect and say my goodbyes.

I cooked a delicious *chhola* soup made with potatoes and peaches for my family. I made a different dinner for myself, as it is the final ritual food for my late uncle grandpa in Nepal.

Six years ago today, on Sunday 31 August 2014, I organised for the very first time a get-together programme of Kirat Yakthung Chumlung Women Community (Thamengdingma) UK in Aldershot Nirmaya Rodhighar (now Delaunge). I was the founding president of this women's community, which was established on Sunday, 20 January 2013, in Feltham, London, on behalf of the Central Community.

I have established seven women's community branches. Their main aim was to encourage women to come for social contact, individual development, and promoting our cultural language and property with confidence within the UK. *Yathung* means Limbu tribe, which is part of the Nepali who have been living in the eastern part of Nepal.

I feel proud of being able to have these opportunities to promote, highlight, and unite many women within my community. I wanted to highlight issues and empower women to come and speak up about many issues, and make them feel they can do so without repercussions.

I did my yoga exercise for an hour and then went for a walk with a friend of mine. We went to see friend's my vegetable garden (allotment), and she gave me a bag of potatoes and fresh beans. I brought it at home later that evening.

The death toll from Covid-19 rose by 2 today, one more than yesterday, but it is still good that it is only a single number. The total as of today is 41,503.

Time: 11.00 p.m.

September 2020

✏️ Tuesday, 1 September 2020
163rd day of lockdown

> ***In the news***: At least ninety people have been arrested at climate change protests, causing disruption across England. Extinction Rebellion organised action in London and Manchester to urge the government to prepare for a "climate crisis". Campaigners were arrested after they sat in the middle of the road next to Parliament Square to stop traffic.

I am very passionate about environmental issues and have been interested in this for a long time. I am a fan of Extinction Rebellion and what they are achieving with this issue.

I woke up to a bright and nice morning. I could hear the sounds of dogs barking in the background around my area and the aeroplane noise coming up. This reminded me of being back in my homeland, KTM. My house was close to the international airport, and people could hear the loud noises from the time of the plane's landing and flying time and position.

Many cars were making sounds of starting up because today is Tuesday, and a few people are going to work.

I got out of bed and talked with my mummy and daddy for about half an hour. I prepared ingredients to make naan bread for lunch. I asked my son for help to mix it properly. I cooked the naan bread and fried the potatoes and fresh bean curry to eat with bread for dinner.

I joined my class in the evening for my language lesson, then I had dinner. I didn't have a chance to go jogging with friends, so I went out with the neighbours for around forty minutes after dinner. The sky was so clear that we could see the nearly full moon. It was very quiet, and it was a nice calm evening walk.

The death toll from Covid-19 rose by 3 today. It is rising by a person a day, but it is still only in single figures at the moment, which is great. The total as of today is 41,506.

Time: 11.00 p.m.

Wednesday, 2 September 2020
164th day of lockdown

> *In the news*: Greater Manchester lockdown is easing after a U-turn as cases rise. Measures in Bolton and Trafford were due to be eased overnight after a fall in cases earlier in August. But they will "now remain under existing restrictions" following "a significant change in the level of infection rates over the last few days".

I woke up at 7.30 a.m. The weather was a bit cold, and it was a dark morning. I could hear the sound of cars moving out. I have not heard the chirping of birds for a few days, especially after the strong winds over the past few days. I could hear conversations in the background around me from my neighbours.

I went to Brenda's shop for my son's uniform for his new school. We ordered this a week ago online and went to just collect it. It is time to start school after lockdown in the UK due to Covid-19. I am worried about the children going to school.

I had to drive for 30 minutes to get there, and it was very difficult to find a car parking space in Camberley. We had to wait a long time in the queue because of social distancing, and there were many parents and children there for their school uniforms. I do worry about my children who are going back to school after a long time in lockdown. Millions of pupils are returning to school after the historic lockdown.

My son and I collected the uniform, then drove to Firmly Town boots shop. I parked my car in the car park near the previous HSBC bank.

We had to stay in the queue again for a long time, same as the other shop. I bought two pairs of reading glasses, and I asked about the Halifax Bank because I was going to deposit cash, but it had moved out from there, I was told by a member of staff at the boots shop. I decided to go to Aldershot and parked in the town centre. We stood for a long time in the queue outside of Halifax Bank. Many parents and children were walking around town, and some were standing in the queue for the bank.

Unfortunately, I was not able to deposit my cash into my account, because my bank card was left at home. I wasted time and the car park charge for nothing.

After coming back home from Aldershot, I updated my email from the university, then went jogging with friends.

I'm scared to send my children to school, but I have no choice. I think it is too early to send them to school, because the deaths have not stopped yet, and new cases have been increasing.

The death toll from Covid-19 rose by 10 today, the first time we have seen double digits in a while. We had hoped it wouldn't jump up so much, and so quickly. The total as of today is 41,516.

Time: 11.00 p.m.

Thursday, 3 September 2020
165th day of lockdown

> ***In the news***: Bosses in charge of the coronavirus testing system have apologised after it emerged that UK labs were struggling to keep up with demand. Some people are being asked to travel hundreds of miles to get tested.

I woke up at 7.00 a.m., and the weather was cool and bright. I could hear the sound of cars moving out. My husband prepared breakfast for the children. It was my son's induction day at his new school, so I went and dropped him off (Salesian College boys boarding). After I dropped him at school, we went to Aldershot town and Halifax bank. I had to stay in the queue again for putting cash into my account.

I bought a phone call card and came back home, and I contacted relatives of my late uncle grandad in Nepal. I called my childhood friend and was reminded of our childhood days and her late dad. She was crying due to the loss of her dad. I tried to distract her and talk about another subject and cheer her up.

It was time to go back to pick up my son from his induction day. We picked him up from school and bought him back home. I prepared food for dinner. I tried to cook dinner early and then went jogging with friends. There was a light rain, but we still went jogging for more than one hour. The weather was better after 30 minutes.

I watched a talk show where they discussed how the indigenous Dalit (untouchable people) minority are being oppressed in Nepal. I am hoping that with the use of technology and social media, these issues will become public, and people will be made aware and understand what is happening and what change is needed in society, not just in the UK but all over the world. Everyone can learn with technology in the palm of your hand, and people need to know how to do things about it.

The death toll from Covid-19 rose by 13 today, the fifth increase in a row. We thought we were OK and rid of Covid when the numbers were so low, such as 1, 3, and 2. Now it is slowly creeping back up, and this is never a good sign, but I am still optimistic. The total as of today is 41,529.

Time: 12.00 p.m.

Friday, 4 September 2020
166th day of lockdown

> ***In the news***: Coronavirus pandemic—tracking the global outbreak

I woke up at 7.00 a.m, and the weather was cold and cloudy. I could hear the sound of a lot of cars moving, because today was the first time children went back to school after long time of lockdown in the UK.

I quickly brushed my teeth, had a cup of water, and got ready to drop my son to the school. My alarm clock was going to go off at 7.30, but I woke up earlier than expected, although I went to bed at midnight. My husband prepared breakfast for the children and went on duty.

I was worried about my children and the outbreak of coronavirus because it is transferable from person to person. Therefore, I told my son to put sanitiser and a mask on before leaving home. It is the first day of a new school today, and we had to travel for around thirty minutes, so for us as a family it is far away.

After I dropped him off at the school, I came home and tidied up the outside of the front garden, then I continued my cleaning inside.

Quickly, I checked my university account and found that my supervisor had commented on a piece of my work and sent it to me after a week. I noticed that I had a lot to do in the area of corrections according to her suggestions. I decided to leave for a few minutes, and I went out back in the garden and picked all the beans and green vegetable leaves. I planted water crescents for next year and tidied up. It took more than an hour.

I was supposed to pick up my son up from school, but my husband came home earlier than normal and decided to do the pick-up. This gave me time to prepare chicken curry for dinner tonight. My youngest daughter was preparing her stuff for university, because she is going for the first time.

I cooked kasmiri chicken curry, salad, and *paperdam*, and cooked paneer for vegetarian options to have with rice and naan bread.

I went jogging with husband in Long Valley Field for more than an hour. We saw a big reindeer walking in the middle of the path. Many dove voices were echoing in the background of the field, and we left when it started to get dark.

After coming back from jogging, we had dinner, and at the same time my husband and I watched a Nepali film; the title was *Bhauju*. It was a three-hour-long movie. The story of the film was the caste system and how it impacts lower-caste people in hierarchy culture and creates inequality in human society.

I read the BBC News every day. The death toll from Covid-19 rose by 10 today, less than the previous day, bringing the total to 41,539. The UK has the third highest number of recorded coronavirus deaths in the world after the USA and Brazil. To lose 41,539 people within 188 days is very serious life and health matter.

Time: 11.00 p.m.

🖊 Saturday, 5 September 2020
167th day of lockdown

I woke up late morning and decided to have a lie-in due to it being Saturday. When I got up, I talked to my dad and mum, and then my cousin. I was updated by the news about Covid-19 in Nepal. It was increasing very rapidly, with more than 200 deaths.

I was glad that my father's health was improving so much, and he had started to write and read news articles. Mum was busy in the field and garden.

I took a shower, brushed my teeth, then worshiped for few minutes. I boiled a pot of potatoes to make special items for the children, and then I cleaned the kitchen and wiped all the walls. My husband made breakfast, and my two daughters went shopping.

I read in the *Independent* (2020) about the impact of coronavirus and noticed that during the present Covid-19 pandemic, mass school closures were tending to entrench learning gaps between girls and boys, and put many more girls at risk of sexual exploitation, early pregnancy, and early or forced marriage.

With schools closed, children are unable to report abuse to a trusted teacher. With restrictions on home visits by police and health workers, violence shelters being converted into health facilities, and courts being forced to close, many victims may find themselves trapped and feeling abandoned. The devastating impact of this hidden pandemic of domestic violence requires strong and concerted action.

My eldest daughter prepared material for Korean BBQ, with varieties of fried chicken, for her birthday. She cooked potato chup, *pakauri*, vegetable curry, dal, and rice, especially for her birthday.

I could not organise a big party as normal this year due to the lockdown, but a few of her close friends were invited for her birthday. I found her childhood-days album and gave it to her to see her baby picture and up until now. I watched cartoons with my daughters' friends in the TV room.

I thought about her birth. Luckily, we had been able to survive in KB Hospital in Brunei. The doctor told us that if it was two minutes later, mummy and baby both could have died. She was not born on her due date, and I had to stay for six days before she was born. I did not have any knowledge about the baby. The doctor moved me to an operation theatre as soon as possible after they checked my X-ray. We both survived because of the medical facilities.

Once I had the baby by C-section, my husband had eleven days off from his regiment, then he went to the Eastmoor war. I could not imagine how badly a Gurkha wife suffered when the Gurkha soldiers (British

Army) had to go to war, especially when she has a new baby and has just had a C-section delivery.

I had to rely on myself and no one else, I had to cope with my C-section and a new baby. I was totally unable to help myself; I was alone in the married quarter in the barracks at that time.

I had her after arriving in Brunei seven months earlier. I was feeling very homesick, because I had left my birth house and family for the first time. My husband was busy in training for the Eastmoor war during my pregnancy. I had no help from my family when my new baby turned up.

The death toll from Covid-19 rose by 12, only two more deaths than the previous day. The total as of today is 41,551.

Time: 11.19 p.m.

Sunday, 6 September 2020
168th day of lockdown

> ***In the news***: Further 2,988 cases confirmed in UK, government data showed. It is the highest number reported on a single day since 22 May and a rise of 1,175 on Saturday, according to the UK government's coronavirus dashboard. The government was "concerned" about a rise in cases "predominantly among young people".

I woke up early, around 7:30 a.m. I had a cup of tea and toast, then started to change into my uniform for work. A best friend of mine called and began to talk to me about a few issues in our social community which had been going since last month. I started to drive while I was talking to her, but the call was cut off due to the poor network connection.

It was time to welcome the new officer cadets at the barracks. My responsibility is to serve the food for new staff sergeants during my time.

Members of staff were raising issues about PPE again. They were complaining there was not enough PPE since Covid-19 started. I used to take my own PPE sanitiser for myself every time, and I have never taken off my mask because I want to save myself and other people as well.

After I finished work, I came back home and started to check the draft of my thesis, which was commented on by my supervisor. I studied a theory of domestic violence against women in patriarchal culture and how women can be controlled by male power:

> Male power can be used in domestic violence and can be a hidden factor in patriarchal culture and authority.
>
> Many women are controlled and governed at home by domestic violence (Dobash and Dobash, 1979, cited in Heidensohn,1996). Male power can be used in domestic violence and can be a hidden factor in patriarchal culture and authority. The Policy Studies Institute team carried out an investigation into women police officers who were sexually discriminated against. It was found that the police officers did not want to intervene in cases of domestic violence or to make an arrest when the case was one of marital dispute, especially in rape cases. In patriarchal culture, most of the women were controlled and governed by their husbands and or male power.

Women are hugely restricted and limited from their choices and freedom.

Six years ago, today, 6 September 2014, I was elected vice president of Kirat Yakthung Chumlung UK. The general convention was held in Feltham London UK, with many people attending. This is community work for and on behalf of their members in the UK. We are trying to promote and preserve our language and culture for the next generation, as part of the indigenous/Limbu tribe. We have newly got the right to do this, and it is something that we need to do.

The death toll from Covid-19 rose by 2 today, which is very low compared to the previous days and weeks. The total as of today is 41,553.

Time: 11.07 p.m.

Monday, 7 September 2020
169th day of lockdown

> ***In the news***: The second wave of coronavirus has begun in the UK, and the latest "big change" in coronavirus infections across the UK is of "great concern", England's deputy chief medical officer has warned.

I woke early, and the weather was a bit cloudy compared to the rest of the week. My husband made me and my son breakfast and dropped him off at school. I had a glass of warm water and decided to check the format of my dissertation. I visited the University of Surrey to find out the new updates on my thesis.

I corrected my introduction of thesis data of official sources, including the City of London: "A recent survey on British South Asian women's primary health care revealed that 56 per cent experienced domestic abuse: 46% from their husbands and 10% from their mothers-in-law, 76% of the victims were unaware of helpline services while 83% found language inability to be a barrier to seeking help" (Government Office for London, 2009).

The above statistics demonstrate how deep-rooted and serious the problems are for SAME women in the UK. More recent research undertaken by Harrison (2015, cited in the *Guardian*) over a two-year period revealed an alarmingly high level of domestic violence. In some cases of historic sexual abuse, the family put shame (*sharam*) and honour (*izzat*) before their children's welfare. In some instances, the abusers were never brought to justice.

Lack of knowledge of British law meant that, in certain cases, many women were not even aware that marital rape was a domestic violence crime. Some male extended family members were also protected because of the cultural issues within the SAME communities. These women in some instances had been abused as children.

This is important for all people to know. It doesn't matter if you're white or from a BAME background; it happens to everyone. This is shocking statistic amongst the BAME community, and we should try to bring these statistics down.

I attended an online Zoom meeting from NEFIN UK because we

had to discuss issues which were on going on between the EC team and the local branch.

The death toll from Covid-19 rose by 3 today, only one more death than the previous day, bringing the total to 41,556.

Time: 12.20 a.m.

Tuesday, 8 September 2020
170th day of lockdown

> ➤ ***In the news***: A director of the government's test and trace programme in England has issued a "heartfelt" apology for problems with the coronavirus testing system. In a tweet, Sarah-Jane Marsh explained it was the laboratories, not the testing sites themselves, that were the "critical pinch-point". This comes as scientists have sounded the alarm about rising coronavirus cases. A new Lighthouse lab is due to open in Loughborough in about a fortnight.

The testing system in this country should have been a lot more advanced than what it was. We should have looked at countries such as South Korea and China and seen how testing was done and applied it here. The Loughborough test centre never materialised.

The weather was so cold, and it was very cloudy. My son was about to leave on the school bus, and I told him to make sure that he uses sanitiser and mask. My heart jumps, and I do not feel as relaxed as before when I think about the oncoming second wave of Covid-19. The cases are increasing in young people, and that makes me worry so much.

I had a glass of warm water and decided to check the format from the University of Surrey. I searched many articles to support my thesis. I spent a couple of hours changing and adapting my work. I found the following:

> The two-year rule stopped BSAME women from fearing deportation. The exploration of literature revealed that while the two-year rule stopped BSAME women from fearing deportation, it did not stop the fear of destitution or being trapped in a violent home.

The reason for this was that the Immigration and Asylum Act 1999 stated that these women had to be sponsored by their spouses or be self-supporting, placing them in a vulnerable position. The restriction of public funds reinforced the dependency of abused women on their spouses and prevented them from escaping. However, the 2003 consultation paper from Safety and Justice acknowledged that benefits and access to housing are important requirements for victims of abuse and provide a safety net, allowing them to leave. (cited in Southall Black Sisters 2007).

The application time for benefits should not be linked to a specific time frame for victims of DV. The researcher highlighted that the Domestic Violence, Crime, and Victims Act (2004) needs to be extended to all victims and that the most important area that needs to be given priority is welfare and housing benefits. The decision period on applications under the domestic violence rule should be given a clear time limit, and the same benefits should be made available for those applications which have been sent to appeal. Therefore, DV victims could access support on time (Gov.uk, 2004).

The rate at which applications are processed is too slow. We need to shorten this process in order to help more victims of domestic violence.

The death toll from Covid-19 rose by 32, which is a jump in the number of deaths from the previous day. The total as of today is 41,588. The increase in deaths shows that the possibility of a second wave happening is almost imminent.

I am very interested in keeping track of the Covid-19 numbers throughout the UK in my diary. It is a good measure of time and a reminder in the future of how good and bad things became.

Time: 12.20 a.m.

✏️ Wednesday, 9 September 2020
171st day of lockdown

> ➤ *In the news*: We must act to prevent second lockdown, says PM.

It was 6.40 a.m., and a very quiet morning. There was no noise of birds chirping as before. Everything was still.

I made breakfast very quickly because my son was leaving at 7.30 a.m. for his school, and he had to catch the school bus. My heart was not feeling relaxed as before when they used to go to school. I kept thinking about the second wave of Covid-19. The cases are increasing in young people, and that is making me worry so much.

I sat and retyped my dissertation for three hours, and it took a long to time to do and to follow the format that the supervisors suggested. I took advice from the comments provided. I joined a meeting with my supervisor at 2 p.m., and she gave me very important points and feedback to support my work.

I did have another class and meeting today, but I was very tired from doing all that work on my dissertation.

The death toll from Covid-19 rose by 8, less than the previous day, bringing the total to 41,596.

Time:12:20 a.m.

✏️ Thursday, 10 September 2020
172nd day of lockdown

I woke up at 7.00 a.m. and prepared breakfast. The weather was nice and cool. The sky was clear. I sat down at my computer to work for a few minutes, and then I went to an interview. I cooked dinner and again joined a lesson for an hour with my tutor. I corrected work as below:

> Another important finding which emerged out from the interviewees' responses to questions revealed that the police could not handle all of the DV cases within the BSAME community. This was mainly due to the complex

sensitive nature of this issue. The language barrier is a real obstacle to reporting DV crime.

Recent research by the *Independent* (2020) demonstrated that DV victims from the BAME women were unable to access help from the police because of a lack of trust in the police forces. The present system of access to police services should be studied in order to provide a more easily accessible route.

In addition, according to Dobash and Dobash (1979, cited in Heidensohn, 1996), research undertaken among female police officers illustrated that they did not want to be involved in cases of domestic violence. There was a general reluctance to intervene in marital disputes because of the highly emotive issues involved.

This reluctance applies to all marital disputes, but in particular, the cultural sensitivities in the BSAME community make it even more difficult. Consequently, BSAME women were more prone to suffer domestic violence and had difficulty seeking justice due to a lack of trust between the police and victims. This means that many women in the BSAME community who suffer DV are disadvantaged and suffer more than women in the wider community to seek help to bring cases to court due to these hidden factors.

The lack of access to support through certain avenues is one issue, but when they get some help, the helpers are ill-equipped to handle these cases. We are hoping that the education of people such as police officers will improve, and the help will be better.

The Covid-19 death toll rose by 814, a dramatic 81 per cent more than the day before. It is a staggering increase in deaths. This shows that the second wave is beginning in the UK, and we will see what will happen in order to control it. The total as of today is 42,410.

✏️ Friday, 11 September 2020
173rd day of lockdown

I woke up at 7.00 a.m. and prepared breakfast. The weather was nice and cool, and the sky was clear. My son had breakfast, and I had glass of water and sat down at computer for the rest of the day because of deadlines that were coming up within the next two weeks.

I typed out a lot of words today, including "created coding for analyse interview data selected highlighted all for analyse and discussion. The coding is a good method to engage with the respondent's data because it helps to analysis the data. It emphasized coding when fitted in line by line the interview data and this exercise enabled the researcher to check and make sure data to forward for analysis" (Charmaz, 1983).

I was reminded of 9/11, which was nineteen years ago today. I was back in the UK five days before that from the Falkland Islands holiday with my eldest daughter, and I was expecting my youngest daughter about twenty-one weeks at that time.

My husband was deported to the Falkland Islands for six months' exercise from his barrack (1st Royal Irish Regiment). I was watching the TV news at the moment the Pentagon was being ruined by fire and the aeroplane was targeting the building.

Almost 3,000 innocent people perished on that horrific day 19 years ago, including 343 New York City firefighters and 72 law-enforcement officers from the NYPD and the Port Authority Police Department, along with 55 military personnel.

Hundreds more have died in the nineteen years since from what are commonly called 9/11-related causes. There are still over 1,100 persons who perished that day whose remains have not been identified despite the advances in DNA technology and testing procedures.

It feels like the tragic events that happened on 9/11 only happened yesterday. Documenting this is in my diary has shown the importance of writing down that day's events and feelings, especially during this pandemic time. I will come to a point in the future where I will look back on this day and remember my thoughts and feelings thanks to my diary.

The death toll from Covid-19 rose by 6 today, bringing the total to 41,416. Time: 1.00 a.m.

✎ Saturday, 12 September 2020
174th day of lockdown

Twenty-seven years ago today, I qualified as a teacher and started to teach. A few years later, I was appointed as head teacher.

Today, my youngest daughter went to university for the first time. It is the first time that she has her left parents and family.

I awoke early, had a shower, and cleaned the house. The weather was very much like yesterday. I had glass of water and started to cook lunch special for vegetarians and meat for non-vegetarians.

My youngest daughter was preparing her stuff to go to university. What a coincidence the day was for me, that twenty-seven years previous was the first day I started to teach in Siddeshowari Primary School Oyam-Warebung Panchthar Nepal. The school was established by my father, Bhim Kumar Seling. He kept telling us there was no facility for pen and paper and candles. They had to burn wood bamboo to make bright light for study in the night-time.

It is hard to imagine now, a school like that. Students in the UK are very fortunate to not have these worries when turning up to school every day.

When my youngest moved to university, I still remembered that my father transferred money into my bank account whilst he left me at college for higher education. It was very far away from home, and I felt homesick back in those days.

My husband went to drop my eldest daughter off and help her at university. She was blessed by a video call from her grandparents before she went to university. But my heart is worried due to the coronavirus.

I sat down at the computer all day because of an upcoming deadline in the next two weeks. I worked on a recommendation section of my thesis:

> ... in order to explore how in particular, the older generation of women can have more support in order to help their understanding of their rights in the UK.
>
> For this purpose, we need specially trained support workers able to organise local women's groups. These groups could

meet on a weekly basis for general discussion of relevant topics in their language.

There could also be a designated support worker within this group or, alternatively, the women themselves could act as a spokesperson on a rotational basis. Self-help groups give a lot of support because they are local so there is more trust. This would help them to gain confidence to express their views in an empathetic environment. At the moment these women have no voice at all.

We need to be able to give the older generation of domestic violence victims a chance to have a voice and to gain the help that others are getting. Self-help groups help to make information and advice easily accessible and hopefully give them confidence to leave and find help.

The death toll from Covid-19 rose by 9 today, bringing the total to 41,623.
Time: 12.28 a.m.

Sunday, 13 September 2020
175th day of lockdown

> ***In the news***: A student who was fined £10,000 for an illegal house party of more than fifty people has apologised. The 19-year-old was issued with the fixed penalty notice after ignoring warnings to shut down the party at his Nottingham home on Friday night. In a letter sent to his neighbours, he said the "foolish gathering" was a "major lapse of judgement".

I do think these students have a lack of resources, especially where money is concerned. How is he going to pay this fine? It is a very big life lesson for him.

I started my day as I usually do. I got up and went to work, and met the many staff I usually do, and had some delicious food. It was hard to maintain social distancing due to Covid-19. I'm still scared to approach friends and colleagues, but a few friends did not care about the social distancing 1 meter suggested to them. I did not want them to come near me.

After I came back from work, I joined on a Zoom lesson regarding data analysis for a couple of hours. I tried to concentrate on my class, but I was very tired from work.

The death toll from Covid-19 rose by 5 today, staying low again. It is very good that the death toll is staying low. The total as of today is 41,628.

Monday, 14 September 2020
176th day of lockdown

I woke early, went out into the garden, and enjoyed the warm weather and fresh air, but I kept thinking of my dissertation draft. I went inside and sat down at my computer. I started to type, and I was able to complete a few sections of the dissertation headings by 2 p.m.

I had an hour break, so I went out into the garden, picked up vegetables leaves, and did yoga for thirty minutes, but weather was very hot compared to the previous days.

I heard the beautiful song of many birds as well as the chirping of baby birds. The adult birds were flying around the house and in the trees in my garden. I noticed this easily because I had not heard them for many days.

I decided not to go out jogging with friends due to my project. I cooked curry dal (gravy lentils, and rice) for dinner during break time. My husband and daughter left, and my son went to school. I joined a Zoom lesson regarding data analysis for two hours. I tried to concentrate on class, although I was tired of typing. I found this research on my topic:

> It was noticed that some of the underlying factors involved in domestic violence cases are largely hidden, but they include issues such as housing and immigration status. It is true that the immigration policy restricted marriage to a non-UK citizen, whereby applicants had to prove that the marriage was legitimate and not for settlement in the UK.

This puts BSAME women in a vulnerable position if their marriage breaks down because of domestic abuse. This is supported by the research carried out by the Southall Black Sisters (2007). Participant's revealed data and the existing literature review are both linked to this research topic. This research recommended that BSAME women who had been subject to DV should be supported regardless of their immigration status. Data suggested that language and cultural barriers raised issues and caused displacement for victims and survivors. The interview data revealed comparable points from three participants about displacement caused by issues around shame and honor.

Language and cultural barriers are becoming a main concern for victims reporting crimes. With the vulnerability for BAME women when a marriage breaks down, they need to have the full support needed, but sometimes this is hindered by professionals not being able to speak the language or understand the culture. These women shouldn't be scared about their immigration status either. Each should be considered on a case-by-case basis.

The death toll from Covid-19 rose by 9 today, still very low but a rise from yesterday's daily deaths. Only a small rise, but still a rise. The total as of today is 41,637.

Tuesday, 15 September 2020
177th day of lockdown

Results are out on two subjects in my module field method (observational and interview project).

I woke early, got ready, and went outside into the sunshine. The birds were in the trees, and I could hear them around the house. The preschool near my house was busy, and I could hear the children screaming in the background.

I was so intent on getting work done on my project that I began to read and didn't stop for three hours, 9 a.m. to 12 p.m. But there always seemed to be something wrong.

I went out back in the garden, had some fresh air, and poured water for the vegetables when I was on a short break. I kept thinking of my dissertation draft whilst I was on my break.

I had tutor from 1 to 2 p.m. I made lunch at the second break but did not have time to cook dinner today. I just took another short break, then went on Zoom for my language class from 4 to 6 p.m.

I wanted to include a few lines from my studies on how cultural concepts are socially constructed as South Asian Minority Ethnic (SAME) women face domestic violence in the UK:

> Evidence gathered from this study found that South Asian women experienced more domestic violence than white women in the wider community in the UK. This was due to many factors, including culture, language, financial factors, dependency, and immigration status. Hague et al. (2006) conducted a case study on women from India, Bangladesh, and Pakistan who had married UK citizens and faced domestic violence due to immigration issues and forced marriages.
>
> This research was particularly of interest, as it was based on SAME women and related to the topic of immigration status, which can be a hidden factor commonly used in perpetrating domestic violence. In addition, this study interviewed a range of South Asian women using many languages. These were Hindi, Panjabi, Urdu, and English, which gave a first-hand account of the victim group's experiences. Further revelations emerged as a result of the study which found that some victims' relatives were not in the UK. They were living with their husband and his extended family members, thereby creating highly vulnerable situations and, as a result, they are completely cut off from their family support and homeland.

The United Kingdom is very relaxed regarding marriage, and therefore, this concept of forced marriages and this level of domestic violence that is specifically targeted to this ethnic group is alien to British citizens. Even though British citizens do experience certain levels of domestic violence, SAME women are forced into married life by their own families and then alienated and trapped with their other half's family.

I missed going jogging with friends due to the work on my project. I cooked curry dal (gravy lentils and rice) for dinner during break time. I had dinner at 7 p.m. and had a few minutes rest, then I began to type and correct project work until 9 p.m.

I checked the Surrey University log-in after I had finished. It showed that my results were out on two subjects in the module field method (observational and interview project), the last module of this master's degree, which made me feel relieved, at least for a while.

Thursday, 17 September 2020
179th day of lockdown

I woke up at 8 a.m. with my right arm aching from typing my draft. The weather was hot, and the sun was shining. I went out to the garden and buried garlic seeds for next year.

I did an oil treatment for my hair for an hour and then began to do yoga for an hour. I decided to clean the kitchen, toilets, and bathroom, and then I took a shower.

I checked my email from the university and colleges and viewed many jobs online for a few minutes, and then I began to cook dinner. I did this because my husband had to go on night duty at his barrack.

After I finished cooking, I went to pick up my son from school, and I took him to buy colours and paints for his project in the town centre.

I went jogging with friends at Long Valley Field for 90 minutes. It was getting darker and darker, and for that reason, we tried to walk fast. We discussed about the second wave and the rising cases and how we were worried about school and the university children.

From reading the news, they have been discussing the following:

If most people with a cough or fever request a coronavirus test this winter, there won't be enough tests every day for five months, a study estimates. Based on normal levels of coughs and fever alone—which are common symptoms of flu and cold—demand will peak in December. The researchers say current UK testing capacity should be "immediately scaled up to meet this high predicted demand".

It is worrying that they believe that this could happen, and we just have to hope that there are enough tests for everyone over the winter.

The total Covid-19 death toll as of today is 41,705, and still the UK has the fifth highest number of recorded coronavirus deaths in the world.

Friday, 18 August 2020
180th day of lockdown

There was a slight breeze this morning when I woke. I could see the trees waving back and forth gently. I went out into the garden for fresh air and to enjoy listening to the sweet voices of a pair of doves. It was nice to listen to their voices.

I went back into the house, into my room, and sat down at the computer to begin checking my work from the previous days and emails from the university and school. I filled out an application form for part-time evening work and carried on with my day.

The death toll from Covid-19 rose by 21 today, bringing the total to 41,726. Still, people are dying from coronavirus every day, and I fear and am very stressed about the situation. It is everywhere.

It is so difficult to manage social distancing. However, all the schools are opening as of next week. The low death rate is good news, but I am worried by the fact that there are still cases every day.

🖉 Saturday, 19 September 2020
181st day of lockdown

> ***In the news***: It is the 3rd Nepal Constitutional Day, but subgroups are opposing.

I woke up later than normal due to it being the weekend. The weather was bright, and the sun was shining, but there was a slight breeze, and the tree leaves were waving backward and forward gently. There was no chirping of birds today, just the strange noise of a bird that I had never heard before. Due to the lovely hot weather, I spent an hour outside.

I did some yoga exercises for 30 minutes, put an oil treatment on my hair, and took a shower. I worshiped for 5 minutes as a religious perspective, which made me feel happy all day. I cleaned the house and made food for lunch.

I watched a virtual programme on anti-constitutional day in Nepal. Many scholars, intellectuals, and political spokespersons were expressing that this constitution did not include diversity and multicultural equal rights due to controlled hegemonic power in Nepal.

This day is very controversial throughout Nepal. The constitution hasn't changed and is a very outdated, patriarchal document. It is still implemented in part. The documents haven't moved with the times. Women are still viewed as second-class citizens, making them still unequal. It discriminates against Nepalese women and tribal minorities as well as many other groups. Rape and killing of young women and children is an ongoing issue. The rapist isn't being held accountable for his crime, and these young women aren't getting the justice they deserve. This is just one example of the impact of this constitution.

In this modern world, it is strange that this is still happening. The constitution in Nepal hasn't moved with the rest of the world and is an outdated document that is used as a form of control.

I went back into my room, sat down at the computer, and checked my work and emails from university and school again. I then went jogging with a friend at Long Eushot Park Farm, Redfield Gardens, and the Fleet Area Valley Field for around 90 minutes. We constantly went in the opposite direction of other people on the field when out walking.

My youngest child, my son, had the flu and was constantly coughing and sneezing. I gave him some vitamin C and Lemship to reduce the flu symptoms.

I read in the BBC news that the prime minister is considering new restrictions amid a second coronavirus wave. Boris Johnson is spending the weekend considering whether to tighten Covid-19 measures in England, after saying the UK was "now seeing a second wave". The government is understood to be looking at a ban on households mixing, and reducing opening hours for pubs. At least 13.5 million people, roughly one in five of the UK population, are already facing local restrictions. I am worried about the second wave and what it will bring.

The death toll from Covid-19 rose by 27 today, slightly higher than yesterday, which shows that cases are rising; even though it is only a few, it is a rise. The total as of today is 41,753.

✎ Sunday, 20 September 2020
182nd day of lockdown

I woke early and joined in the yoga class organised by the Greater Rushmoor Nepali Community team. I had missed it, as I hadn't been able to take part for ages due to my work.

I met my next-door neighbour and talked about Sunday worship, which is with six people, due to social distancing and government guidelines.

I made breakfast and made sure that everyone ate. I ironed my son's uniform for school and mine for work.

I then sat down at the computer and checked my work and emails from university and school again.

I went to work and met all the staff members. I was very busy and worried at work because it was difficult to manage social distancing. None of the staff members put masks on, so I never took mine off. My friends kept teasing me. I convinced them about the second wave cases, which are increasing every day.

The Covid-19 death toll rose by 18 today, less than the previous day. The total as of today is 41,771, and still the UK has the fifth highest number of recorded coronavirus deaths in the world after the USA and

Brazil, with the loss of 41,771 people in 199 days. Although only a few people are dying each day, it is a very serious matter of life and health.

Monday, 21 September 2020
183rd day of lockdown

> ***In the news***: The UK's coronavirus alert level is being upgraded from 3 to 4, meaning transmission is "high or rising exponentially", according to the chief medical officer. It comes after the government's scientific adviser warned there could be 50,000 new coronavirus cases a day by mid-October without further action.

The weather was bright and sunny this morning when I woke up. I could hear the birds chirping around the house, and I could hear the children going to school.

I went out for some fresh air and had a cup of tea. I normally have plenty of warm water, which I have as much as possible, but I also love a cup of tea as well.

I checked my emails to see if I had any feedback from my university supervisor, but there was nothing. I was looking forward to hearing from my supervisor and awaiting a response. I prepared lunch and made sure that I had a full tummy. I checked my emails regularly regarding my dissertation feedback, and I finally found it. There were so many corrections in the different sections that I decided to leave it and come back to it later, as it was quite stressful.

I decided to cook dinner for the family and then went to walk for 70 minutes in the local park. It was a beautiful hot day. I walked behind two horse riders for about 30 minutes. I usually meet many evening walkers and dog walkers too. It was a lovely evening. I needed the experience of normality and tranquillity after the stressful email from the university.

Everyone practised social distancing. So many people changed their direction once they saw me, and I also did the same in order to respect other people's space.

I went back home and had dinner with my family and watched TV. We discussed the latest news and talked about the second wave of coronavirus. This made me feel very worried and nervous about the future.

The death toll from Covid-19 rose by 11 today, less than the previous day, bringing the total to 41,782. This figure covers the period of 200 days since the first case of Covid-19 was identified in the UK on 5 March 2020.

It's hard to think that we have been living with this situation for 200 days. In the beginning, we thought all the measures that we had put in place would save lives and that we could then go back to a "normal life". This version of near normal life is different than the life we knew before, and we have learnt lessons along the way about what is important to us and what isn't.

Tuesday, 22 September 2020
184th day of lockdown

> ***In the news***: Covid restrictions could last another six months, according to PM Boris Johnson. The UK has now reached "a turning point", so it has been necessary to implement a raft of new coronavirus restrictions for England which could last for up to six months. Shop workers will now have to wear face masks, and weddings will be limited to a maximum of fifteen people under the new rules. Fines for breaking the new laws on gatherings and not wearing a mask will increase to £200 for a first offence. The PM also warned "significantly greater" restrictions could become if necessary.

I woke up early, and the weather was as beautiful as the day before. I searched the university site to find out extra information for my research project. I focused on my dissertation feedback, which had stressed me out the day before. I read it through again carefully and found that I had so many corrections to make that I could feel the stress coming back.

During my lesson, a phone call came in from my son's school. So I stopped the lesson and called the school back. The receptionist asked me why my son was not in class. I was speechless. What had happened to him? I told her to please contact me when they knew where my son was.

When I got off the phone, I was so worried, not only because of the global pandemic but in case he was in an accident or lost. But I was mainly wondering where he was.

I called the school again to get an update on the whereabouts of my son. I found out that he had been at school the whole time, and he arrived on time. The teacher forgot to record his entry. I felt a wave of relief after the phone call. It took me a few minutes to regain my composure before I could rejoin my class.

I was very busy all day, so my husband cooked dinner, and we had it on time.

The death rate from Covid-19 rose by 37 today, more than triple the amount from the day before, bringing the total to 41,819.

Time: 12.00 midnight

Wednesday, 23 September 2020
185th day of lockdown

I tried to read the BBC News and record the daily death rate, although I was so tired of working on the computer. I found out that the supermarket Asda is set to enforce rules on face coverings more strictly across its shops amid the pandemic. This is the first time I had seen this. It is good this is happening, and I hope that other people follow what Asda is doing.

I woke up at 7.30 a.m. The weather was not as nice as the day before. The sky was partially cloudy, and it wasn't as sunny. The birds decided not to play their song today.

I am intent on getting my final draft of the thesis done today, so I therefore spent the first few hours from 9 a.m. to noon getting it all done. I took break for 30 minutes, went out for fresh air, and had a cup of coffee.

I searched for some information on the university log-in to check the correct deadline for my thesis and focused on it. A few elements of the information part of the abstract of my dissertation are given here:

> This project explored and evaluated the hidden factors relating to domestic violence (DV) against Black and South Asian ethnic minority (BSAME) women in the UK. This group of women are more at risk of DV owing to language, education, financial dependency, patriarchal culture, and immigration status, alongside honour-based violence and hidden factors unique to the community.

> Class structures together with patriarchal practices, such as honour-based forced marriages and female genital mutilation (FGM) practices within the BSAME community, make the situation worse. This project has enabled further exploration of the topic. It also analysed and supports current findings and research. The researcher explored ways in which BSAME women can access support despite facing barriers.

I am finding throughout my research that the class and cultural system within the BSAME restricts and harms so many people. Practices such as FGM should not be happening, and it is something that is only done to females, and to control females. It is normalised and is seen as a rite of passage. But men do not go through anything like this. It has been normalised and is used as a form of control, but in any form, FGM is domestic violence and should be seen as such.

I could not join the meeting for Rushmoor Healthy Living due to my work and online classes.

I prepared food, put the cooker on, and joined my language class from 6 to 8 p.m. I told the children to turn off the dinner after thirty minutes, but they forgot to turn off the gas. So, the smell of burning gas came through kitchen to the bedrooms and study room. Finally, my youngest child noticed the smell of food burning, and he turned it off. I did not say anything because I did not have time to shout at them, I was so busy. I could smell it burning but could do nothing about it.

I really missed doing my exercise—yoga and jogging—because I spent all day doing this work. I felt my arms and right hand ache so much, but I had no choice, so I had to keep going.

Today the death toll from Covid-19 rose by 37, the same number of deaths as the previous day, bringing the total to 41,856. This is the second wave of coronavirus.

It is good that all the schools opened last week. It is good news for children who go to school. They will have some normality. But I am worried, because the cases are rising every day.

Time 12.29 a.m. Good morning, diary!

✎ Thursday, 24 September 2020
186th day of lockdown

I woke up at 7 a.m. The sky was a beautiful shade of blue and very clear. It's rare to see a clear blue sky in the United Kingdom.

I spent another day intent on getting the final draft of my thesis complete, so I spent the morning getting it done. I only took a break for 30 minutes, went out for fresh air, and had a cup of coffee, something I don't usually have. I normally stick to my warm water. But today, I needed the caffeine to get my thesis complete.

A bit of information on the topic of Black South Asian minority ethnic women (BSAME) who have experienced more domestic violence (DV) than the wider community of women, and evidence is given here:

> Thiara (2005, 2006, cited Thiara and Gill, 2010) carried out a study which revealed that South Asian and BME women experienced more severe domestic abuse over a longer period than women in the wider community in the UK.

> However, very few researchers explored the different backgrounds of these women. Gill (2004), Razack (1998), and Stark(1995) found that in a number of domestic violence cases, BSAME women emphasised their perceived experience of racial discrimination when reporting this violence. Examples include reports made to agencies, housing authorities, social services, and the police.

It is unfortunate that women have to experience this when reporting something that is a horrible life event. These services should be there to help, not to add to the problem.

I joined my online class from 3.30 to 5 p.m., then took a short break. I cooked dinner during the break time.

After I finished cooking, I joined another class from 7.30 to 9 p.m. I told my family to have dinner, and I would have dinner after my class ends. I really missed exercise yoga and jogging again today, but I needed to get my work done and attend my classes.

The UK has recorded 6,634 new coronavirus cases, the government has announced, the highest daily figure since mass testing began. This makes me worry every time, because life is very uncertain at this critical time.

The death toll from Covid-19 rose by 40 today, more than the previous day, bringing the total to 41,896. With all the schools being opened from last week, it is good for children and their lives, but I am worried about the rising cases.

Time 12.10 a.m.

October 2020

🖉 Tuesday, 20 October 2020
212th day of lockdown

> I lost four weeks of my diary.

I woke early to another nice clear sunny day. I spent time in bed for a while due to it being my day off from work.

I had to handle many calls, and I had an appointment with the bank about the house mortgage. It took a long time to complete all the programme.

I accidentally lost four weeks of my diary records by deleting what I thought was an old document and saving the wrong document on my computer. This shows my lack of computer knowledge and the fact that I am not confident or, in some respects, competent with it. The younger generation are so used to technology, as it is something they were born into and learned from a young age. Whereas I have had to learn this as an adult and, therefore, mistakes will happen. I am very upset that I lost my regular diary. It was something I worked on every day and put a lot of time and effort into. I will try to put it back together from memory, but it will not be the same.

The findings of part of my dissertation, I have included as a paragraph under the title of "The handling of Domestic Violence cases by the police services and the lack of cultural sensitivity":

> Regarding the above point, all five participants held similar views that the police could not handle domestic violence (DV) cases adequately; however, specific differences did emerge. For example, one respondent commented that although the police were sympathetic, owing to the nature of the abuse, they were in the main, unable to help.

Despite their best efforts, because of cuts in public services and the sensitive nature of the DV cases, the police sometimes fall short when providing adequate support for women from the BSAME community. This can sometimes include finding suitable accommodation from the local authorities in particular areas.

Respondent 1 confirmed the view that the police were in the main unable to deal with the complex nature of DV cases in the BSAME community. Here is evidence of interview data given below. R. (1) "In my experience, I would say that the police do not have the right training and knowledge to handle domestic violence in a sensitive way overall, and especially when it concerns minority groups. This is because they deal with the incident(s) and adhere to legalities, rather than being empathetic and sensitive".

Respondents agreed with the researcher that the police dealt with the incidents according to the narrow limits of the legal system as it exists, rather than in a patient or compassionate way. In addition, they were restricted by the length of time they could spend on individual cases. Furthermore, owing to the very different cultural backgrounds, there was little hope of any change in the future until professionally trained officers were assigned to work with these communities.

The fact that the police (who are supposed to be able to help us) generally, overall, are not sensitive or do not have the correct training and knowledge to handle domestic violence cases, especially within the minority group of the BSAME community. This may be due to cultural or language differences or having the relevant training within this subject. This is something that very much needs to change. The police need to look internally into the way that these cases are treated and make sure that the people allocated to these cases have the relevant compassion and training.

I feel like the pandemic has created antisocial behaviour, and people are becoming depressed, because people have lost trust with everyone in this situation. The death rate is rising day after day due to the second wave of coronavirus. The number of deaths has risen rapidly due to the second wave, and the Covid-19 death toll rose by 241 today, so much more than the previous day. It shows that many of the measures aren't working.

The total as of today is 43,967, and still the UK has the fifth highest number of recorded coronavirus deaths in the world, after the USA and Brazil.

Time: 12.00 a.m.

Wednesday, 21 October 2020
213th day of lockdown

The morning was dark due to it being early. The time was 6 a.m. I quickly got ready for work. It was raining, and I wore a thick jacket to get to the car and drive to work.

At work, one of the people had had a really bad fall. He had fallen from his bed after pressing the wrong button on the bed control that helps to raise and lower the bed. Another member of staff and I opened the door. He was shouting loudly "Help, help!" because he was lying flat on the floor.

I immediately got hold of both his legs, and the other person held the other side. We managed to get him onto the bed, made breakfast, and gave him a cup of tea. He wanted to stay in bed and needed more painkillers. He was single and had no next of kin and no one around him to help him or to keep him company. I felt so sorry to leave him alone in the house. I was very worried about him being alone.

This is a very strange situation for me, someone having no friends or family around him. I come from a family that is socially bonded to other people, and we therefore look after each other. People don't have to be married or have children; we make sure that we look after one another. So, this person being on his own is very worrying for me.

I came back home after finishing work and later went to the bank for my appointment. I revised for a few hours for my Maths class. We had homework, so I made sure that it was done.

I cooked dinner and had it with the family. I watched the TV panorama programme on Princess Diana and the BBC Panorama interview that changed everything. Why was it so controversial?

According to the news, Queen Elizabeth II has long been said to adopt the mantra "never complain, never explain" in a bid to keep family matters behind closed doors; to not become embroiled in media reports or speculation; and to maintain the much-distinguished line between royalty and public. Largely this approach has worked, with the family circling the wagons at the hint of danger or scandal. Watching this interview reminded me of the time I met both Diana's sons (Prince William and Prince Harry) when they joined as officer cadets at RMA Sandhurst. They both spoke a few Nepali words because of the more than 200-year-old historic link between Gurkha soldiers and the British Army.

The death toll from Covid-19 rose by 191 today, less than the day before but so much more than the previous week, bringing the total to 44,158. The death rate has risen rapidly due to the second wave, and still the UK has the fifth highest number of recorded coronavirus deaths in the world.

🖉 Thursday, 22 October 2020
214th day of lockdown

At 6 a.m., it was quite dark. I quickly brushed my teeth and dressed for work. The weather was dry and bright. I used full PPE. I maintained social distancing with people and customers.

After I finished work, I returned home and went to the bank with my husband to discuss our mortgage repayments. It took a long time to work out an agreed plan to cover our repayments during the next two years. I did some revision for my Maths for an hour. I then went to class from 5 to 9 p.m. Class was very interesting and busy because the teacher covered many topics.

Deaths are increasing rapidly due to the second wave. The death toll from Covid-19 rose by 189 today to 44,347, and the UK still has the fifth highest number of recorded coronavirus deaths in the world.

I'm still able to type up my short diary entries, although I'm very busy.

Everyone is affected by the pandemic, and it is very difficult to maintain social distancing. Most schools are still functioning, but there is a great deal of fear and anxiety, which even affects the younger children.

Friday, 23 October 2020
215th day of lockdown

I woke up at 6 a.m. It was quite dark outside. I quickly brushed my teeth and dressed for work. I was told that I was going to work with the same staff as the previous day, so I waited for a staff member to pick me up from the same agreed location.

This person used to pick me up from the office during my training time. My mobile kept ringing whilst I was waiting for his car. I called back immediately after parking my car, and a man told me that I should have been in a different location today.

I was shocked and told him that I had been instructed to wait at the same place as on previous days. I also told him that as I was not fully trained yet, how was I supposed to work in another place without supervision?

He came to the office, and I followed him and went to work with one of the senior staff. I had to drive one of non-drivers to work in the field.

At work, one of the residents we visited happened to see my Jaguar car and asked me if I was in the right job and whether I liked it. I replied that I loved it. I used my PPE all the time, but other staff members are not so diligent, and one of residents even asked where her mask was.

The death rate is rising day every day due to the second wave of the coronavirus. The death toll from Covid-19 rose by 224 today, a massive increase from the previous day, for a total of 44,571. The second wave is very serious to life and our health. The second restrictions were put in place, and people are still dying from the coronavirus, more every day. I fear and have stress due to it being difficult to socially distance everywhere.

✎ Saturday, 24 October 2020
216th day of lockdown

I awoke at 8 a.m. this morning, with the weather being foggy and windy with a few bits of rain. I was peeping out through the curtains at the trees outside. The trees had just a few leaves left. The leaves had all dropped off due to winter coming.

I could hear many noises of aeroplanes and cars outside. I exercised for an hour, took a shower, and finally cleaned the house.

I contacted my parents and family in Nepal, who were gathered to celebrate the Nepali festival of Dashain. This festival reminded me of something from my childhood days back in my homeland. I used to play with my friend's siblings when they visited their relatives' house. We used to have a lot of fun in those days. I lost a few friends who were so close to me. I wished to meet them again in my homeland, but I was not able to meet them before they died due to me being in the UK.

I felt very sorry to leave all the residents and family, but I had to get to work on time. I also had to drop a staff member off at her home after we had finished our shifts.

From 12 to 2.30 p.m., I attended a meeting on Zoom. It was with the Global Network Conference, and the subject was national statistic issues for the next year. The presentation was national statistical data in this census in Nepal. We were trying to discuss the possibility of opening up the census data to include languages and religions from different minorities within the Nepali community.

I read my dissertation and tried to add a few points from my research findings:

> Some of the key theme of this study revealed that Black South Asian minority ethnic (BSAME) women experienced DV because of cultural displacement and gender backgrounds. Many women lived in extended family units, so often there were hidden pressures from their family members which prevented victims seeking help from outside agencies. An important factor which affected these communities in particular was patriarchal

culture. Most decision-making in the home was done by the male head of the household. In general, these women were financially dependent on the family and the husband, and therefore, their security was fragile. This left them in a very vulnerable position, and even the more educated women, who were aware of their rights, felt that the family honour came first, even though they were suffering constant abuse.

In BSAME cultures, men are still the head of a household, and it is still a male-dominated culture. Many aspects of the women's life are controlled, especially financial. They become financially dependent on the man of the house, so when fleeing a DV situation, they feel trapped due to this one issue of having no money. They will stay within the abuse. This is across the board for both uneducated and educated women.

The death rate from Covid-19 rose by 174 today, less than the previous day, for a total of 44,745.

Sunday, 25 October 2020
217th day of lockdown

Due to the clocks changing, I woke earlier than usual at 7 a.m. The weather was foggy and a bit windy, but it brightened up through the day. I did yoga for about 30 minutes and went to work and met all the staff members. One member of staff had just recently lost her mum, and we sympathised with her situation. We sent a card via a friend due to us not being able to visit her.

All army officers had to put masks on as well as staff within a work environment. It was very busy due to trying to maintain some form of social distancing. We had lunch before closing down the hot area (food serving place).

I came back home after I finished work, and I took a short break. It is Nepali festival time, so I cooked a special cultural food with pork, chicken curry, and paneer, with vegetables for my youngest daughter.

I received many calls from relatives and friends with well wishes for Dashain. Unfortunately, we could not meet up with each other.

This situation made me so sad, frustrated, and upset, especially after this year.

A member of staff from work told me a story about her friend's situation. Her friend had suffered from family abuse for many years, but she was not able to express herself due to cultural shame (*sharam*) and honour (*izzat*). This was the same as my research findings from my dissertation, which was linked with past studies from Gangoli et al. (2006) and Batsleer et al. (2002). Shame (*sharam*) and honour (*izzat*) is an unwritten code but a very powerful tool used within the BSAME community. Shame and honour are socially constructed (Gill, 2014) as part of their traditional culture and is included in their family values. These practices are commonly used as controlling mechanisms to keep women in abusive relationships.

The death toll from Covid-19 rose by 151 today, less than the previous day, bringing the total to 44,896.

Monday, 26 October 2020
218th day of lockdown

I woke up at 6 a.m. I did prime and factors work for a few minutes in bed because it was dark outside. I went back to sleep after a short time, and I dreamed about my birthplace house.

I was having a sweet memory of my childhood days, especially about the environment and the festival time. At the same time, today is Dashain, especial Bijaya Dashami for the Hindu religion in Nepal. Before democracy, this used to be celebrated by all Nepalese people, but this festival is an ongoing debate, because it is complained about by non-Hindu religious ethnicities at the moment.

I had a day off from work to celebrate with my husband and children. In general, we used to celebrate with many relatives, such as cousins, nieces, siblings, uncles, aunties, grandpa, and grandma, but due to Covid -19, we are locked down in a house for this year.

our Korean meal

My eldest daughter cooked special Korean-flavoured food for the festival, although she had to attend class and then go to work. My husband and I contacted my sisters-in-law and their families, my brothers-in-law and their families, and my parents, siblings, and other relatives with my children via video chat. We all shared our best wishes with each other internationally and demographically. The food was ready, decorated on the table, and all the family had a delicious meal.

We had delicious food to celebrate Dashai with the children, and then my daughter and husband went on duty. Due to us being an ethnic minority, we had no choice to have a holiday unless it is an English national holiday such as Christmas. We had to take time off work, and the children still had to go to school. Therefore, we had to delay celebrations, which is hard, as this is our culture.

Sometimes it is very difficult to celebrate with family because of there being no public holiday for us. I'm very happy to see all the children at the same time on this occasion at this festival.

The death toll from Covid-19 rose by 102 today, less than the previous day, bringing the total to 44,998.

✎ Tuesday, 27 October 2020
219th day of lockdown

> ➢ ***In the news***: Two adults and two children have died after a boat carrying migrants sank off the coast of northern France. A large search-and-rescue operation began earlier, after the vessel was seen in difficulty near Dunkirk.

During this pandemic time, people are still desperate to get into this country, and we forget that people are still fleeing from war and conflict. It is heartbreaking to think that this is happening, but some people have no choice.

I woke up at 7 a.m. this morning. The weather was cold, and it was windy and rainy all day. I watched some videos of the indigenous and Dalit (untouchable) women in violation in Nepal. The video explained that these women were exploited in 6,000 restaurants as cheap labour, and there were many violations in the main cities. This made me feel so bad that they could be still facing this situation in the 21st century. Nepal has its first woman president, and 33 per cent women are secured MPs in parliament, as well as in many other countries.

I had planned to do a lot of my exercises for mathematics on my day off from work. I searched on YouTube for a video to explain to me exactly what I was looking for. My youngest daughter was doing a test after her lecture had finished, and then I asked her a few questions before she left home for university. My youngest daughter did prime and factors work for a few minutes in bed because it was dark outside.

It was the second day of the festival, so others could still go and visit relatives, if it was not for the lockdown in the UK. I cooked food, meat and vegetables, and packed takeaway food for my youngest daughter.

A picture of my family - my three children, Siliya, Silija Phurup, and, at the back, my husband and myself

My eldest daughter and my husband had dinner and took a takeaway for when on duty. Outside, it was so dark, but it was only 5.36 p.m. I was feeling stressed due to the dark and foggy winter weather.

The death toll from Covid-19 rose by 367 today, double the number of deaths of the previous day, bringing the total to 45,365.

✏️ Wednesday, 28 October 2020
220th day of lockdown

> ➢ ***In the news***: The second wave of coronavirus restrictions had started.

I woke up early and did everything very quickly in order to get out the door early. This was my third week of training as a community support worker. But I kept being distracted, as my main focus recently has been on my math GCSE and my upper intermediate English lesson in the evening.

I have been feeling recently that I really missed my teaching and head teacher's job in Nepal. Also, I have missed working in dental nursing due to my part-time courses. I chose this new job because it suits my time.

I'm interested in learning new experiences with a new job, but I miss my previous job. I searched on YouTube for a video of how to do pie charts for my Maths. I watched this for a while, then I did my yoga exercise for an hour.

I made dinner. My family had ordered pizza, but I wanted to typical herbs and spicy curry and rice.

The weather was dry and bright in the early morning, but it changed in the afternoon, and it became cold and very windy, with some heavy rain.

I watched a video of Rushmoor Healthy Living before I start the monthly meeting today. I sit on the Board of Trustees and am a director of the RHL. I joined the meeting from 6 to 8 p.m., and we discussed many agendas and decided what we were doing for future projects.

The meeting made me think of the discussion part of my thesis, and I have included a few paragraphs of my findings:

> The sixth theme that emerged from this study was how the police handled domestic violence (DV) cases in the BSAME community women. This was mainly due to the complex sensitive nature of this issue.

> The language barrier was a real obstacle to reporting DV crimes. Recent research by the *Independent* (2020) demonstrated that DV victims from the BSAME women were unable to access help from the police because of a lack of trust in the police forces. According to research carried out by Dobash and Dobash (1979), female police officers in particular indicated that they did not want to be involved in cases of domestic violence, and there was a general reluctance to intervene in marital disputes because of the highly emotional issues involved. This reluctance applies to all marital disputes but in particular the cultural sensitivities in the BSAME community made it even more difficult (Dobash and Dobash, 1979, cited in Heidensohn, 1996).

Consequently, BSAME women were more prone to suffer domestic violence and had difficulty in seeking justice due to a lack of trust between the police and victims. This meant that many women in the BSAME community who suffer DV are disadvantaged and suffer more than women in the wider community to bring cases to court due to these hidden factors. Respondent four highlighted the "taboo" subject of FGM and forced marriages. Although this is an area of study in its own right, it is also one of the hidden factors in the BSAME community.

Language and culture shouldn't hold back an individual from seeking help in any situation, especially a DV situation. Just because people have a different language or come from a different culture doesn't mean they should be ignored. This is happening all to often within society and links back to the immigrants who risked their lives yesterday due to conflict. It is the same. Doesn't matter who we are, we all deserve the same amount of help.

In addition to this, I read on the BBC News and that "Two black men were stopped and searched by Met Police officers on suspicion of exchanging drugs because they had bumped fists, a watchdog has found. The Metropolitan Police officers are four times more likely to use force against black people compared with the white population, new figures have suggested. Restraint techniques are also more likely to be used on black people, according to force records."

This links back to what I was saying above. Just because you look different, whether that is due to colour of the skin or the way you are dressed, doesn't mean you should be discriminated against.

The death toll from Covid-19 rose by 310 today to 45,675.

Thursday, 29 October 2020
221st day of lockdown

Last night, I had a dream, and it made me smile with such happiness. I was in my birth town of Oyam Panchthar in Nepal. I was near an area of the primary school where I used to teach and was head teacher before I came to the UK.

I felt I was on top of the world when I dreamt of my birthplace, and it always makes me feel pleasure. I believe that my dreams are showing that I am missing home a lot. Due to the pandemic, I have been unable to go back to Nepal and see my family. At the moment, I have to rely on my dreams to comfort me whilst I'm missing home.

I woke up at 6.40 a.m., quickly had a cup of warm water, brushed my teeth, and dressed for work. This was my third week of training as a community support worker. I got to work with one of the senior staff for the morning, and I got to finish early due to this.

I joined a Zoom meeting for North East Hampshire constituency for the Labour Party meeting. It was nice to do so after such a long time. I had missed many meetings due to post-graduate classes.

Every day we have more deaths, and today is no different. The death toll from Covid-19 rose by 280 today. Even though that is fewer deaths than the previous day, it is still very high compared to the summer. The UK is still a place with one of the highest death rates in the world. The total as of today is 45,955.

Friday 30 October 2020
222nd day of lockdown

An alarm clock was beeping at 5.30 a.m. It woke me up. The weather was horrible and dark. It is a rainy morning.

A staff member and I went to work as community support workers. We had to feed a client from her tummy by syringe. It is called a PEG feeding and is only used when people have problems with swallowing and can't get enough food or drink due to normal means.

I had never met this female client before. She was very young and very friendly, and she coped with the PEG feeding very well. She was very helpful to me, and it is very nice to have a client like this, especially when you have a long day on duty.

I dropped off one of my colleagues at her home after finishing work. I came home a bit later than expected and prepared for class at 4 p.m.

After I had finished having dinner, I went jogging with my husband because he was off from work. There was still a light rain, and the weather was miserable, although I forced him to go out. It took more than an hour for a jog.

The death rate from Covid-19 rose by 274 today, less than the previous day, bringing the total to 46,229.

Saturday, 31 October 2020
223rd day of lockdown

> ***In the news***: Prime Minister Boris Johnson has announced a second national lockdown for England to prevent a "medical and moral disaster" for the NHS. He said Christmas may be "very different", but he hoped taking action now would mean families could gather. Non-essential shops and hospitality will have to close for four weeks from Thursday, he said. But unlike the restrictions in the spring, schools, colleges, and universities can stay open.

I woke up early in the morning at 5.30 p.m. and tried to get back sleep again but could not. The weather was dark, dry, and lightly windy.

My mind had had been elsewhere recently; this was due to my concerns about the second wave and how it would affect me and my family and the whole of the UK.

I massaged oil in my hair and left it for an hour to moisturise, and then I took a shower. I decided to do a revision of stem and leaf diagrams in Maths for an hour.

I joined the Global Network Zoom conference. We discussed the common identity of religion of the indigenous people in Nepal. The presentation that was given was good and informative.

Today is Halloween. It is a quieter affair than normal, with many of the usual parties and celebrations not going ahead and no one coming door to door. After centuries of this tradition, it is strange for it not to happen. I hope next year, Halloween will continue and everything returns to normal, and the children will go trick-or-treating again, something that they all very much look forward to.

The death rate is starting to rapidly increase, and we are now firmly cemented in the second wave of the pandemic. The death toll from Covid-19 rose by 326 today, higher than the previous day, bringing the total to 46,555. This is making me nervous and unhappy.

November 2022

✎ Sunday, 1 November 2020
224th day of lockdown

I woke up early in the morning, at 6 a.m., and tried to fall asleep again, but I could not. I wrote some information for a book being published in our town of Oyam, my birthplace in Nepal. It was written by my cousin's brother. I wished him good luck before going to work. The weather was dry, but there was a light wind when I went out.

At work, everyone was busy serving the officer cadets in the military college. It was really tough at lunchtime. I came home from work and had a rest for an hour, and then I began to cook dinner for my family.

I went jogging with my husband for an hour after dinner, even though there was a little bit of rain.

I watched the BBC News and was informed that the second lockdown will be starting from this Thursday, so I contacted my youngest daughter at her university and told her come back home before lockdown began.

The death toll from Covid-19 rose by 162 today, less than the previous day, bringing the total to 46,717.

The second-wave restrictions have been put into place, and people are dying from coronavirus more every day. There is fear and stress everywhere, and it is difficult to manage social distancing. All school were open, and young children are now affected due to them shutting. The amount of death from the second wave of coronavirus is making me extra-worried.

✎ Monday, 2 November 2020
225th day of lockdown

> ***In the news***: England's lockdown will be "longer and more damaging than it needed to be" due to government "inaction", Labour's leader has said about catastrophic way that the first easing of lockdown has been handled by the prime minster and country.

People feel that this second lockdown shouldn't be happening, especially when so many people have been following the rules.

I woke up early in the morning, at 6.45 a.m. The weather was dry and windy. I prepared breakfast for my children, and my son had breakfast and then went to school. The school is eight miles away from home. He has to walk to the bus stop to catch his school bus.

I clearly could see many leafless trees waving to each other when the strong wind was blowing. It created a noise when they were pressing on the house window as well as some slight banging.

I spent my time doing Maths revision for two hours. I called my youngest daughter and told her to come home before all the restrictions started, but she preferred to stay in the university accommodation due to it being her first year.

I went shopping in my local area of Fleet town. There were so many people who were queuing in every place, such as the salon, haircut, Boots, post office. I also went to the mobile shop, Boots, Clarkes, and Sainsbury for shopping after a long time.

It was 5 p.m. when I came back home and started to do yoga for forty-five minutes. One of my friends called me, and we communicated for quite a long time. I cooked dinner whilst I was talking with my friend.

The Covid-19 death rate rose by 136 today, less than the previous day, bringing the total to 46,853. The loss of 46,853 people over the past 240 days has become a very serious life and health matter. The first death from Covid-19 was on 5 March 2020, and we are still battling with the virus now.

The second wave of restrictions have now been put into place, and more than ever, fear and stress are everywhere.

Tuesday, 3 November 2020
226th day of lockdown

I woke up earlier than usual, and it was still dark outside. When I checked, it was 5.20 a.m. The weather was very windy, and it was horrible and dark in the morning due to it being winter. I quickly got up, got ready, and left the house to go pick up my fellow staff member on my way to work.

The staff member and I went to the first client and service user, and we performed a PEG feeding at 6.30 a.m. for this lady at her house. She has a really good network of help, either from friends or from neighbours. Sometimes her neighbour gives her support to get her changed and dressed if her daughters and support workers are not there.

The death rate has not been updated since yesterday.

Wednesday, 4 November 2020
227th day of lockdown

I woke up at 7 a.m. The weather was cold, and I could clearly see the frost on the roof of the house and on the cars. People are scraping the ice off their cars to go to work. The ice was shiny like silver with the morning sunrise reflected off it.

I have done revision in mathematics for a few hours on a range of topics.

Today, the death toll from Covid-19 rose by 492, bringing the total to 47,742. Who knows how long the second wave will last, but we know that it will get worse before it gets better. The UK is still one of the hardest-hit countries in the world. I am very scared and worried for the future.

I have been writing this diary since 17 March 2020 and didn't know how the whole pandemic would unfold. Like many, I have been able to spend time with my family, spend time on my studies, and generally keep myself busy. This diary has helped me get through the pandemic and record everything that has happened and how events have developed.

References within the Diary

Gurkhas
Over 1 million Gurkhas were enlisted, and over 150,00 Gurkhas have died for Britain, including during the First and Second World Wars, as well as modern wars such as Iraq and Iran.

Joanna Lumley brought the campaign to the forefront of the media in the early 2000s regarding the Gurkhas not being able to become British citizens, and they can't claim equal pension. The Gurkha soldiers in the British Army experienced prejudice and segregation from day one. They were compensated 1,800 to 2,000 per cent less in pay and pension compared to any British soldier

Since the enlistment of the Gurkhas in the British Army, the British government has decorated the Gurkha soldier with various battle honours such as the Victoria Cross, the highest. But Britain has a shameful secret which is hidden from the British public and the wider world.

Many friends and staff members from work and the community have asked me about my ethnicity. I have explained to them about the Gurkhas (Nepali) and that I am part of it. They are concerned about the Gurkhas Lives Matter movement, and they ask themselves, *Why did we not have an opportunity to study history about the Gurkhas at school?* It has gone on for more than 200 years. It is stupid.

Gurkha Wives
When we talk about Gurkha wives, I talk about myself and many others who have been military wives within the British Army. But this is more specific to my situation and wives whose husbands were part of the Gurkhas and what they had to go through. There is a deep history with this.

BSAME
Black, South Asian, and minority ethnic: This is a section of people discussed throughout my diary. It is an area that was part of my research

for my dissertation for my master's degree at university. I speak about the struggles of this sector of women, who experience underlying and hidden domestic violence.

I was interested and focused on this subject due to being part of the BSAME community in the UK myself.

My Tribe: Limbu Nepali

Limbu Nepali (British) is a small section of Nepal. Limbus are considered indigenous.Untouchables/*Dalit*. Dalits are discriminated against on the basis of caste and "untouchability". They are not only discriminated against by the so-called higher-caste people in the Hindu system but also by people within the same caste. Dalit women suffer much more than Dalit men.

Dalits, formerly known as untouchables, are at the bottom of the ancient caste hierarchy linked to the Hindu faith and form more than 13 per cent of Nepal's population.

Nepal passed a law against caste-based discrimination and untouchability in 2011, yet Dalits face routine segregation and abuse, and ancient biases against lower-caste groups make it harder for them to access education, jobs, and homes. They are frequently barred from public places, including temples and water wells used by higher-caste Hindus. They are restricted to work that is considered dirty or dangerous, such as manual scavenging and disposing of animal carcasses.

There have been thirty-three cases of discrimination or violence against Dalits in 2020 according to Nepal Monitor, a Kathmandu-based human rights organization. Last year (2019–2020), the organization recorded 84 such incidents.

Woman's Rights in Nepal

Between 1996 and 2006, Nepal was embroiled in a civil war in which thousands of human-rights violations and war crimes were committed. As with most conflicts around the world, women were uniquely impacted during and after the war. From rising violence against women to an increase in single women and widows in a society that values the family unit, the consequences of the war for women were far-reaching.

A new constitution

In 2015, a new constitution was enacted that strived to ensure the greater inclusion of women in all levels of government. It guarantees that all political parties run a quota of women candidates for elections, as well as Dalit, indigenous tribes, Madhesi, and other marginalised groups. These changes, pushed forward by the women's movement, have provided more opportunity for women's rights organisations to push for the full inclusion of women's participation and leadership.

Intersecting discrimination

Despite some progress made towards women's political involvement, discrimination against different groups of women is still common. In Nepal, caste-based discrimination is prominent, with Dalit women experiencing more violence and discrimination than women of different castes. Indigenous women, widows, along with lesbian, bisexual, and trans (LBT+) people also face high levels of discrimination.

References

Aisha, K. G. and Karen H. (2018*) I Am Talking About It Because I Want to Stop It': Child Sexual Abuse and Sexual Violence Against Women in British South Asian Communities.* The British Journal of Criminology, Volume 59, Issue 3, May 2019, Pages 511–529, https://doi.org/10.1093/bjc/azy059

Claire W.(2012) *Responding to Violence Against South Asian Movement in The British Domestic Violence Movement.* [online] Gjss.org. Available at: <http://www.gjss.org/sites/default/files/issues/chapters/papers/Journal-09-03--04-Wiper.pdf> [Accessed: 30 January 2022].

Hague, G., Gangoli, G., Joseph, H., & Alphonse, M. (2006). *Domestic Violence, Marriage and Immigration: If you are immigrating into the UK to marry, what you might need to know.* British Academy UK. Available: https://research-information.bris.ac.uk/en/publications/domestic-violence-marriage-and-immigration-if-you-are-immigrating[Accessed:15August 2020]. [30January2022]

Independent (2020) Left on the scrapheap' Higher proportions of black and minority ethnic women suffer domestic abuse but 'face racism from public agencies' Available:https://www.independent.co.uk/news/uk/home-news/domestic-abuse-bame-women-services-a9586111.html[Accessed:30 January2022]

McWilliams, M. & Yarnell, P. (2013) *The Protection and Rights of Black and Minority Ethnic Women Experiencing Domestic Violence in Northern Ireland.* Northern Ireland Council for Ethnic Minorities.

ONS (2018) Domestic violence on South Asian women. Available: https://www.ons.gov.uk/ [Accessed:30 January2022]

Siddiqui H., (2018) *Counting the cost: BME women and gender-based violence in the UK*. Available: https://onlinelibrary.wiley.com/doi/pdf/10.1111/newe.12076. [Accessed:30January 2022]

Grenfell Tower Inquiry (2017) Report of the Public Inquiry into the Fire at Grenfell Tower. Available :https://www.grenfelltowerinquiry.org.uk/phase-1-report [Accessed:30January2022]

The Guardian (2017) Grenfell council 'may have committed corporate manslaughter' Met police. Available:https://www.theguardian.com/uk-news/2017/jul/27/met-says-grenfell-council-may-have-committed-corporate-manslaughter [Accessed:30January2022]

Roper, V. (2018) 'The Corporate Manslaughter and Corporate Homicide Act 2007—A 10-Year Review', *The Journal of Criminal Law*, 82(1), pp. 48–75. doi: 10.1177/0022018317752937

Grenfell Tower Inquiry (2017) Report of the Public Inquiry into the Fire at Grenfell Tower. Available: https://www.grenfelltowerinquiry.org.uk/phase-1-report [Accessed:30January2022

REFERENCES

Aisha, K. G. and Karen H. (2018) *I Am Talking About It Because I Want to Stop It': Child Sexual Abuse and Sexual Violence Against Women in British South Asian Communities.* The British Journal of Criminology, Volume 59, Issue 3, May 2019, Pages 511–529, https://doi.org/10.1093/bjc/azy059

Claire W.(2012) *Responding to Violence Against South Asian Movement in The British Domestic Violence Movement.* [online] Gjss.org. Available at: <http://www.gjss.org/sites/default/files/issues/chapters/papers/Journal-09-03--04-Wiper.pdf> [Accessed: 30 January 2022].

Hague, G., Gangoli, G., Joseph, H., & Alphonse, M. (2006). *Domestic Violence, Marriage and Immigration: If you are immigrating into the UK to marry, what you might need to know.* British Academy UK. Available: https://research-information.bris.ac.uk/en/publications/domestic-violence-marriage-and-immigration-if-you-are-immigrating[Accessed:15August 2020]. [30January2022]

Independent (2020) Left on the scrapheap' Higher proportions of black and minority ethnic women suffer domestic abuse but 'face racism from public agencies' Available:https://www.independent.co.uk/news/uk/home-news/domestic-abuse-bame-women-services-a9586111.html[Accessed:30 January2022]

McWilliams, M. & Yarnell, P. (2013) *The Protection and Rights of Black and Minority Ethnic Women Experiencing Domestic Violence in Northern Ireland.* Northern Ireland Council for Ethnic Minorities.

ONS (2018) Domestic violence on South Asian women. Available: https://www.ons.gov.uk/ [Accessed:30 January2022]

Siddiqui H., (2018) *Counting the cost: BME women and gender-based violence in the UK*. Available: https://onlinelibrary.wiley.com/doi/pdf/10.1111/newe.12076. [Accessed:30January 2022]

Grenfell Tower Inquiry (2017) Report of the Public Inquiry into the Fire at Grenfell Tower. Available :https://www.grenfelltowerinquiry.org.uk/phase-1-report [Accessed:30January2022]

The Guardian (2017) Grenfell council 'may have committed corporate manslaughter' Met police. Available:https://www.theguardian.com/uk-news/2017/jul/27/met-says-grenfell-council-may-have-committed-corporate-manslaughter [Accessed:30January2022]

Roper, V. (2018) 'The Corporate Manslaughter and Corporate Homicide Act 2007—A 10-Year Review', *The Journal of Criminal Law*, 82(1), pp. 48–75. doi: 10.1177/0022018317752937

Grenfell Tower Inquiry (2017) Report of the Public Inquiry into the Fire at Grenfell Tower. Available: https://www.grenfelltowerinquiry.org.uk/phase-1-report [Accessed:30January2022